T0391787

AUTOCHTHONOMIES

THE NEW BLACK STUDIES SERIES

Edited by Darlene Clark Hine and Dwight A. McBride

A list of books in the series appears at the end of this book.

AUTOCHTHONOMIES

*Transnationalism, Testimony,
and Transmission
in the African Diaspora*

MYRIAM J. A. CHANCY

UNIVERSITY OF
ILLINOIS PRESS
Urbana, Chicago, and Springfield

Publication of this book was supported in part by funding from Scripps College.

Library of Congress Cataloging-in-Publication Data
Names: Chancy, Myriam J. A., 1970– author.
Title: Autochthonomies: transnationalism, testimony, and
    transmission in the African Diaspora / Myriam J. A.
    Chancy.
Other titles: Transnationalism, testimony, and transmission in
    the African Diaspora
Description: Urbana: University of Illinois Press, 2020. | Series:
    The new Black studies series | Includes bibliographical
    references and index. |
Identifiers: LCCN 2019040182 (print) | LCCN 2019040183
    (ebook) | ISBN 9780252043048 (cloth) | ISBN 9780252084911
    (paperback) | ISBN 9780252051906 (ebook)
Subjects: LCSH: African diaspora—History. | Blacks—History.
    | Africa—Civilization. | African diaspora in literature. |
    African diaspora in art.
Classification: LCC DT16.5 .C47 2020 (print) | LCC DT16.5
    (ebook) | DDC 909/.0496—dc23
LC record available at https://lccn.loc.gov/2019040182
LC ebook record available at https://lccn.loc.gov/2019040183

Contents

Acknowledgments

Begun as a germ of an idea while I was a fellow of the Black Studies Center at the University of California, Santa Barbara, over the 2006–2007 academic year, this project has taken shape over several years, in several stages. Its themes were primarily developed through the kind invitations of several colleagues to speak from the project-in-progress at organized symposia and as a keynote for conferences from 2007 to 2016 at the following institutions and professional gatherings: Dartmouth College (2016); University of Pittsburgh (2015); Boston College (2015); Institute of Caribbean Studies and the West Indian Literature Conference (Puerto Rico, 2015); Brandon University (Canada, 2014); Trinidad Philosophical Association (Trinidad, 2014); Wake Forest University (2012); Vanderbilt and Fisk Universities (2012); University of Kentucky (2012); University of Oregon (2011); University of Maryland (2010); Florida Atlantic University (2010); College Language Association, Brooklyn (2010); Furman University (2010); Purdue University (2008); Penn State University (2008); and the University of Cincinnati (2008).

I am also indebted to the editors of the following journals and anthologies in which outtakes of the manuscript appeared in earlier form: "On the Edge of Silence: *L'(in)imaginable* and Gendered Representations of the Rwandan Genocide from Photography to Raoul Peck's *Sometimes in April*," in *Raoul Peck: Power, Politics, and the Political Imagination*, Eds. Pressley-Sanon and Saint-Just, Lanham: Lexington-Rowman and Littlefield, 2016; "Subjectivity in Motion: Caribbean Women's (Dis)Articulations of Being from Fanon/Capécia to the Wonderful Adventures of Mary Seacole in Many Lands," *Hypatia: Journal of Feminist Philosophy*, Spring 2015; "'Harvesting' Port-au-Prince, Haiti: Zora Neale Hurston's Literary (Dis)Articulation of Being," in *Dialogues across Diasporas*, Eds. Marion Rohrleitner et al., Lanham: Lexington Books, 2013; "Floating Islands: Spectatorship and the Body Politic in the Traveling Subjectivities of John Edgar Wideman and Edwidge Danticat," *Small Axe* 36 (November 2011); "Desecrated Bodies/Phantom Limbs: Post-Traumatic Reconstructions of Corporeality in Haiti/Rwanda," *Atlantic Studies* 8:1 (Routledge) (March 2011): 109–123; "Border Crossings: Zora Neale Hurston and Claude McKay's Diasporic Travels," *The Harlem Renaissance Revisited: Politics, Arts, and Letters, an Anthology*, Ed. Jeffrey Ogbar, John Hopkins University Press: 2010; and "'Race' Travels in a Post-Genocidal Age: Witnessing and (Re)Counting Rwanda, *Cincinnati Romance Review* 27 (2008): 1–15.

Most importantly, I owe thanks to the John S. Guggenheim Memorial Foundation, which awarded me a mid-career Guggenheim Fellowship in 2014 and supported the project with a full-year fellowship for the 2014–2015 academic year. The University of Cincinnati provided release time during that academic year so that I could proceed with the project, as did Scripps College with a sabbatical in the fall of 2015. I owe special thanks to a number of student research assistants through the years, but most of all to Leah McCormack (now a professor in her own right) who surpassed them all in insight and efficiency in the three years she worked with me as my graduate research assistant at the University of Cincinnati.

To all of the above, named and unnamed, my deep thanks and gratitude.

AUTOCHTHONOMIES

Introduction

Autochthonomies is an intellectual project that engages readers in an interpretive journey: it engages and describes a *process* by which readers of texts created by artists and actors of African descent might engage such texts as legible within the context of discursive practices within African and African Diasporic histories and cultures. As such, I argue that there is a cultural and philosophical gain to understanding these texts not as products of, or responses only to, Western hegemonic dynamics (even if they may be that as well) or simply as products of discrete ethnic or national identities. By invoking a transnational African/Diasporic interpretive lens, I argue that those features of the texts that underscore African/Diasporic sensibilities are, indeed, legible, and offer a potential not only for richer readings of the texts at hand, but also offer the possibility of rupturing the Manichean binary dynamics through which African Diasporic texts have commonly been read to produce an enriching interpretive capacity often deemed either nonexistent or nonlegible by virtue of the sheer constructionism of racial categories. I emphasize the transnationalism of connections between subjects of African descent as the central pole for this study, but doing so is fraught, as I will explain further.

More recently, in his *The Darker Side of Western Modernity*, Latin Americanist and historian Walter Mignolo has argued that "postcoloniality" and "decoloniality" engage different genealogies of thought and spatial historical mappings; the postcolonial continues the trafficking of Western European (ideological) expansion while the decolonial seeks to disrupt it. The postcolonial emerges from British colonial expansion while the decolonial emerges primarily from the French experience of colonization,[1] "emerging long before

French poststructuralism and postmodernism that made the idea of post-colonialism and postcoloniality possible" (xxvi). "The first decolonial step," argues Mignolo, "is delinking from coloniality and not looking for alternative modernities but for alternatives to modernity." In this sense, we could argue that this requires rethinking our received sense of linear, continuous history. That, while the "West" develops its notions of modernity, postmodernity, and so forth, cultures situated outside of these notions develop their own genealogies and reckonings with history. In literary history, then, of the twentieth century, for example, especially in the British/Anglophone tradition, there is a sweeping over of the post–World War II period, a leap from the modern to the postmodern, and from structuralism to poststructuralism; it leaves a gap of twenty or so years in the canon, a period otherwise filled, in the parallel tradition of decoloniality with works Barbara Harlow once termed "resistance literature," that are then retroactively absorbed into the post-'80s reframing of non-British, Anglophone literature as postmodern, poststructuralist, even postcolonial (if the colonial is admitted in the first place). In more recent work, Catherine Walsh (along with Walter Mignolo) has refined the term "decoloniality" further, as denoting "ways of thinking, knowing, being, and doing that began with, but also precede, the colonial enterprise and invasion . . . it is indicative of the ongoing nature of struggles, constructions, and creations that continue to work within coloniality's margins and fissures to affirm that which coloniality has attempted to negate." Furthermore, it "seeks to make visible, open up and advance radically distinct perspectives and positionalities that displace Western rationality as the only framework and possibility of existence, analysis, and thought." Mignolo, in his earlier work, removes himself from the impasse of competing epistemological structures by suggesting that each of these ways of conceiving of history are "options," not alternatives, because options function side by side, vertically, rather than horizontally. This leaves open what Walsh terms "the possibilities of an otherwise" (17). My project, then, comes to rest on this vertical plane, in this "otherwise," when I suggest, for instance, that we explore "modernity" not as situated within the eighteenth-century Age of Enlightenment and advent of industrialization, but (following Gilroy after Morrison) in the dislocation of Africans from the African continent as early as the 1500s; or when I focus on what Mignolo would term "decolonial texts" emerging from the revolutions of formerly subjugated peoples as having an integrity proper to their own cultures rather than that of the dominating. In short, the process embarked upon insists on following the roads of *interpretive options* that have been persistently foreclosed.[2]

A (post)modern, indeed, transnational perspective is thus critical to expanding the scope of what we understand as constituting the texts and discourses of the African Diaspora(s), understanding that there are diasporas within the continent as well as beyond its horizons. I am also suggesting that in order to move beyond the limits of a discourse that confines the discussion of African cultural production to a hegemonic tethering to Europe, what Paul Gilroy has described as "the struggle to have blacks perceived as agents, as people with cognitive capacities and even with an intellectual history—attributes denied by modern racism," which he admits is the "primary reason" for the genesis of *Black Atlantic* (6), we must broaden the grounds for discussion. I propose that an African Diasporic cultural model that focuses not on the European-African relationship but on African *intra*-cultural (and hence, often by nature, diasporic) exchanges will produce another form of dialogue, which will shift the focus onto shared points of convergence intra-culturally, as well as shed light, when warranted, on the trace effects of the European-African legacy.[3] While not denying that in some geopolitical spaces, people of African descent continue to suffer from the long shadow of colonial history, this project posits that it is possible to enter into a reading practice of African-derived texts as being produced from a culturally defined space that is not, in itself, perceived by those who participate within it as a minority space defined only by resistance to dominant cultures.

Through the use of the neologism, *autochthonomy*, I argue that, despite colonial interruptions, we should resist in persisting to conceive of people of African descent, as in the Hegelian paradigm, as peoples "out of history," or, via the Middle Passage, irrevocably divorced from their roots such that our lot is only to conceive of ourselves as "out of time," without kin, or without reliable connections with one another. This concept combines the word "autochthone," commonly used in French and French Studies,[4] to describe "native" peoples, but also used in Anglophone Caribbean studies with reference to populations of African descent in the latter field, literally meaning, "of the earth, ground, or soil" or "of or pertaining to indigenous peoples, or land occupied by them" or "natural, innate, native." I combine the first term with a second, "autonomy," one often used to signify freedom but which literally refers to, "the right or condition of self-government" or "a self-governing country or region."[5] In most countries of the world, indigenous peoples, robbed of their lands through colonialism, seek the right of self-governance that, very few, if any, have been granted since colonialism.[6] By definition, then (and this remains the legal definition of the UN[7]) we might surmise that native peoples are those who have lost access to their lands and who, as such, continue to seek both this access and self-governance; since self-governance without land ownership is difficult to come by, most indigenous peoples continue to struggle for the acknowledgment of their right to sovereignty. Consequently, it has been an increasing practice not to define Africans as "indigenous" except in the case of ethnic groups continuing to live in the manner of their traditional ancestors, to assume that the "modernization," through colonialism, of African peoples has invalidated their identifications as "native" or "indigenous" even as they continue to live on the land of their ancestors or reconstitute their cultures in other than their "native" lands, and therefore to assume that their right to sovereignty is in question. In response to the UN Declaration on Indigenous Rights of 2007, the African Commission on Human and Peoples' Rights (ACHPR) argued that "in Africa, the term indigenous populations does not mean 'first peoples' in reference to aboriginality as opposed to non-African communities or those having come from elsewhere . . . any African can legitimately consider him/herself as indigene to the Continent" (Pelican 5).

Pelican provides a useful overview of recent debates in anthropology by which terms such as *indigenous people* have been contested as essentialist, citing Kuper, and analogous to archaic terms such as *primitive*. Those desiring to retain the term, use it, according to Pelican as a "notion of relational identity (similar to 'ethnicity') and as an effective political and legal tool in the struggle against discrimination and dispossession of historically marginalized groups" (53). Key for my purposes here is Pelican's assertion that, in African contexts, the terminology of indigeneity is problematic because, echoing the findings of Kopytoff, "African societies tend to reproduce themselves at their internal frontiers, thus continuously creating and re-creating a dichotomy between original inhabitants and latecomers along which political prerogatives are negotiated. This recurrent process does not allow for a permanent and clear-cut distinction of first nation versus dominant societies, as implied by the universal notion of 'indigenous peoples'" (52–53). In other words, the term *indigenous peoples* is a product of coloniality and has come to be associated globally with a concept of dominance by which the conquered groups correspond to an ethnic, or more to the point, a "racial" other. This is a concept more easily applied to societies in which original groups were decimated and their lands settled by the conquering group in such a way that a sharp distinction could be drawn between "original" and "settler" peoples, between a non-European original "other" and the European settlers. Such is not the case in most African contexts. Thus, Pelican clarifies: "*Autochtone* and its opposite, *allogène*, are also employed in local discourses in francophone Africa and elsewhere to denote similar, yet diverging concepts (Bayart et al. 2001; Ceuppens and Geschiere 2005). They center on ideas of priority in time ("first coming"), emphasize spiritual bonds with the land and political supremacy, and are used by local actors to substantiate claims to land and power" (54). Without, then, denying that the use of the term *autochthone* is also rooted in colonial mechanisms,[8] and currently deployed within African contexts to levy power and political position, I nonetheless borrow from this common usage in the elaboration of my own neologism in order to accentuate the concepts invoked by Pelican of "first coming," "spiritual bonds with the land," and political supremacy (with the latter understood not in the terms of conquest but in terms of political viability in a variety of national contexts, both African and Diasporic,[9] in which the "native" can also be part of a dominant group in power). In other words, this signification refutes the idea that indigeneity is defined solely or primarily through dispossession and subjugation to shift the focus to self-definition and cultural continuity that is relationally and spatially defined (even if reconstituted in a state of displacement, for example, in the Caribbean). I also prefer the root usage of "autochthone" because it necessarily shifts the reader from an over-association of indigeneity with First Nations people in the Americas that simultaneously refutes the decolonization of the term; it allows us to imagine other indigeneities not themselves foreclosed by the history of the term itself.[10]

My use of the neologism *autochthonomy*, then, to describe present-day Africans and African Diasporics means to highlight the relationship of African-descended people to their lands and cultures of origin, even when displaced and reconstituted. It also signals the fact that, in many geopolitical situations, African-descended populations are already self-governing and those without political self-governance have developed ways of being that are otherwise self-regulating in observance of ancestral knowledge, retention, or revival. My use of the term serves to undercut the continued, false notion that people of African descent have no native lands, no origins, and no binding or defining histories beyond colonial ones. Even so, intellectually, there is a divide between what we consider to be the product of "national" African-descended groups and that which we deem the product of "blackness," as if there is no connection between the two.

In trying to work out what is meant by "blackness," contemporary cultural and black studies scholars most often conclude that there is no "natural" connection between cultures of African descent, and that such connections can be drawn only through histories of suffering and displacement. The refusal to discern "natural" affinities results from reading the trajectory of African cultures and development as ancillary to European colonial expansion; most often, it is a refusal of essentialist categorizations of people of African descent as "black" wherein blackness is read as the border zone of the nonhuman.[11] The term "black," as Achille Mbembe points out, thus belongs to the history of European imperialism and the rise of capitalism; it does not mobilize much more than the specter of a long, as yet unfinished, history that serves to diminish the peoples of an entire continent. Mbembe notes: "Beyond ancestral links, there was very little evidence of an automatic unity between the Blacks of the United States, the Caribbean, and Africa." Without denying "the fiction of unity [the term] carries within it" (25), nor the multiplicity and plurality of subject positions, ethnic and national contained within each region, it seems to me that taking up such a rigid position ironically demands a continued confirmation of Manichean binaries such that, unlike Europeans, people of African descent are denied points of commonality solely on the basis that they should be defined only by the tragic consequences of European interference and by their European *un-naming*. The impact of that interference cannot be swept away: it lives on today. However, I believe that we must resist the sweep of Mbembe's phrase—that people of African descent have nothing more in common "beyond ancestral links" as if such links were unimportant—in order to find in these very linkages a potential for another emergent discourse, one through which African/Diasporic cultural producers find affinity, a language or signs of correspondence through which to communicate world views that underscore a sensibility both African and African Diasporic through which to advance claims about the nature of (their/our) being in the world.

Within Caribbean Studies, specifically, the understanding of syncretism (or *creolization*) as a tool of survival, resistance, reinvention *and* persistence, offers a model through which to reassess wider African and Diasporic continuities. As I shall argue, these continuities emerge through variegated understandings of kinship, affiliations formed through cultural tropes and their manifestations (rather than only through genetic ties), and ontological understandings of the human forged *through* postcolonial realities (meaning before, during, and after these historical moments). That people of African descent can understand one another and "read" each other's cultural productions beyond and within postcolonial pasts/presents is often neglected in order to insist on the nonessentializing nature of racialization. What I argue for in this study is not an essentialist basis for African Diasporic connection but for an observance of the cultural manifestations of transnational and transhistorical kinship exhibited in the creative and literary production of artists of African descent who reveal and seek affiliation through a deeply resonant understanding of African-ness not as racialized but as embodied, lived, and as culturally expressed *through* the body via memory, ritual, song, and language and in *ways of seeing* that reveal citizenship not to a nation but to a larger, transnational body similarly expressed. Doing so is not a romantic notion of a "return" to unspoiled origins but an underscoring of the reality that, despite colonial interruptions and excisions, continuities exist. Unearthing these contribute to the effort of affirming and consolidating non–Euro-Western notions of belonging, both to discrete cultural groups and a larger, global, and transnational reality that transcends national boundaries, in favor of kinship connections bound up both with ancestry and geographical spaces of dis/belonging—both those original and those made so by continuous dint of existence working and settling on land through generations. It is consistent with the intellectual perspective developed by sociologists of the Indigenous Knowledge (IK) movements,[12] as articulated by actors such as Boaventura de Sousa Santos, Nunes, and Menesis, who argue in their text, *Another Knowledge Is Possible*, "that there is no global social justice without global cognitive justice," and that the "epistemological diversity of the world" needs to be recognized in order to practice truly "emancipatory practices" (ixx).

In other words, part and parcel of the decolonial project entails recognizing alternative epistemological models rather than simply observing that "others" exist and have a right to exist within postcolonial structures. It is a recognition of an "outside" to the colonial paradigms whose legacies dominate global exchanges (primarily through capitalist modes). De Sousa Santos, Nunes, and Menesis argue that First Nations peoples of the Americas and enslaved Africans not only experienced genocide but "epistemicide" and thus that it is necessary to promote "non-relativistic dialogues among knowledges, granting 'equality of opportunities' to the different kinds of knowledge engaged in every broader epistemological disputes . . . to build a more democratic and just society" (xx). They elaborate:

> Colonialism has come to an end as a political relationship, but not as a social relationship, persisting in the shape of the coloniality of power. In dealing with the relations between North and South, between core and periphery of the world-system, the coloniality of power, is nowadays, more than ever, inextricable from the coloniality of knowledge. . . . This massive attack on the diversity of knowledges in the world promotes an unprecedented impoverishment of social and cultural experience. (I)

My turn to "culture" within this study is thus not a naive, simple, impulse to recover a nostalgic past and "pure" origins but a directive to engage those epistemes that contemporary African authors reveal in works engaged in intradiasporic exchanges and conversation. Like Audra Simpson argues, as an anthropologist working on issues of native indigeneity, I am, like her, "interested in the way that cultural analysis may look when difference is *not* the unit of analysis; when culture is disaggregated into a variety of narratives rather than one comprehensive, official story; when proximity to the territory that one is engaging in is as immediate as the self" (97). This perspective is extremely pertinent in Caribbean and African Diasporic contexts, the conceptual and ideological ground from which I situate my own study, but is even more useful when one situates artists of African descent as deploying "a variety of narratives" from a plurality of geographical points, as I do throughout this study, points which mapping coalesces around a complex and nonreductive understanding of what it means to belong to communities of African descent whose cultures are imbricated even as they are *also* separate and discrete along national and ethnic lines. As such, the work of *autochthonomies* can also be understood as loosely situated in the premise developed by Pan-Africanists in the mid–twentieth century, to bring together the experiences, movements, and knowledge of populations of African descent both in the continent and dispersed throughout Europe and the Americas in order to emphasize transnational interactions between African cultural producers and sites within the Americas, Europe, and central and Southern Africa. It is not, however, situated in any Black Nationalist movements spawned in the wake of Pan-Africanism,[13] nor does it position retentions from places of origin as defining or sufficient evidence of a unified community. I agree with scholars who have argued that "race" is a metonym for culture that is inherently *not* biological, even as the two have become confused through processes of hegemonic, colonial relations,[14] but, rather than abandon this rich terrain in order to avoid charges of essentialism, I follow in Stuart Hall's footsteps in advocating for a spatial imaginary that consolidates a pan- or trans-African cultural reality. As Hall writes:

> These particular coordinates of space and time are especially important for what I would call the "strong" version of cultural identity inscribed by the concept of ethnicity, where social activities, common worlds, and all-encompassing systems of meaning are imagined as taking place in the same real or highly specific landscape, a place fixed *discursively* at another level by shared blood ties of family and kinship, and thus to a certain degree, perhaps, by shared physical features or characteristics. Where a people share not only a language or common customs but an ethnos, their sense of being bound to or belonging to the group is especially strong. . . . Indeed, *ethnicity in this strong sense is a form of cultural identity that, though in fact historically and culturally constructed, is powerfully tied to a sense of place and of group origins that come to be so unified*

on many levels over a long period—across generations, across shared social space,
*and across shared histories—*that it is experienced and imagined by many not as
a discursive construction but as having acquired the durability of nature itself.
(Hall 106–107; emphasis mine)

My aim is not to err on the side of the latter misapprehension of "natural"
connection but to explore and reveal the discursive nature of the ties that
the texts analyzed in this study reveal between and among groups of African
descent and how their authors negotiate spatial distance through cultural
tropes of recognition and affiliation beyond those made manifest through
colonial racialization (which I otherwise term *lakou/yard consciousness*, to
be explained further, later).

What my text describes, then, is not so much what *forms* such cultural
tropes might take, but the *process* by which readers might engage in order to
discern their contours and render these legible, moving from addressing what
does it mean to identify as of African descent beyond performances of race,
to moving through texts that have not been addressed from the perspective
of their intradiasporic legibility and what this ultimately looks like. It is a process by which I demonstrate how to acquire the *competency* to discern these
patterns and render them legible, rather than overlay an all-encompassing
theory onto a series of texts from chapter to chapter. What I offer, then, is
a way of reading that seeks out the discursive dimension of cultural affinity
while bypassing the too-easy shortcut of "racial" similitude, a similarity that
is literally only skin-deep and an unreliable marker of relation.

Autochthonomy: New Indigeneities

Ultimately, I am arguing that we can no longer think of indigeneity solely as a
sort of preserved primitivity, or premodern form of existence within modern
or westernized societies: we must think of indigeneity as having transformed
over time, as have African/African-descended and First Nations societies.
Such societies bridge precolonial and postcolonial societies, transformed in
the process but also retaining salient features of their original indigenous
societies and their geographies. Ethnographer Mark Anderson, for one, in
his study of the Garifuna of Honduras, demonstrates how indigenous people
of African descent in Honduras were able to assert equivalent legal claims to
that of Indigenous/First Nations people in the same locales. As he explains, in
order to do so, the Garifuna had to overcome overdetermined colonial tropes
separating the two groups and disallowing overlap between them: "Whereas
the figure of the Indian signifies deep cultural roots, the figure of the Black

is understood in the opposite terms, as a being torn from native time and space and caught in the netherworld between tradition and modernity" (12). He later elaborates on Garifuna claims as refuting this positioning, redefining indigeneity through the term *autochthonous* to mean "to bear a deep, rooted difference from dominant national culture as well as the West" (13). Additionally, Anderson makes the broader point that "black" subjects have historically been racialized while "Indios" were rendered ethnic subjects such that black subjects could never be conceived of as belonging to land or a continuity of ethnicity; more recently, black people have increasingly been described as belonging to diasporas, but still within the concept of rupture. To this, Anderson counters: "Black subjects are, of course, not simply members of a diaspora but native citizens of particular nations, regions, places, and communities, who belong in place and make claims to place. They have been positioned as out of place subjects by histories of displacement and ongoing processes of racialization and marginalization" (17). To counter this discourse, Garifuna organizers created a new nomenclature, "the label of 'autochthonous ethnic groups'" (118). This allowed a group racialized as "black" to institutionalize collective land rights as an ethnic group (120). Anderson explains further:

> The terminology of "autochthonous ethnic groups" (*grupos étnicosautóctonos*) also reflects, and helps to produce, a form of equivalence between racially differentiated groups. The word "ethnic" alone would serve this purpose, so it is instructive to analyze the adjective "autochthonous." In a general sense, the term refers to the condition of being the native inhabitants of a particular place. As such, it is often used synonymously with indigenous/indígena. However, in the Americas the term "indigenous" also typically functions as a synonym for "Indian" and has racial connotations, in the sense that Indian is not just a cultural category but carries connotations of descent from the pre-Colombian inhabitants of the Americas. The term "autochthonous" did not have that same direct association with Indian; it could thus serve as a racially ambiguous label to denote "native" or "indigenous" status. (123)

Anderson provides a more elaborate taxonomy of how the Garifuna mobilized the category within the context of Honduran laws concerning land rights wherein ethnicity held more sway than racial categorizations. For my purposes, what is instructive in Anderson's summary is the following: 1) the observation that the term *autochthonous* in and of itself, is not synonymous with indigeneity, or the figure of the "Indian" and 2) that divisions of peoples by phenotype or descent ("Black" vs. "*Indio*") are specious categories imposed by colonizing forces.[15] Operating as a signifier of relation to land, continuous inhabitance over generations (if not always as "original" or "first" inhabitants), cultural manifestations related to ethnicity as a product of historical and ritual discursiveness, then the term *autochthone* can be mobilized in productive directions, somewhat similarly to Stuart Hall's concept of "new ethnicities" by which the term *ethnicity* is *decolonized* for a "new politics of representation" (201), "decoupling . . . ethnicity from the violence of the state" and recoupled with "new forms of cultural practice" (202)—within which Hall situates Caribbean creolization or what he otherwise terms *hybridity* as a reflection of such "new forms": "a conception of 'identity' which lives with and through, not despite, difference" (438).[16] In this sense, then, my neologism, *autochthonomy* does not serve as an analogy to indigeneity (an approximation that it cannot simultaneously be) but as a decolonization of the terms by which indigeneity has been made to function within a colonial ethos to delimit only those peoples who were considered *ethnically* native but not *racially* African. When we consider, as Anderson does above, that the term *Indian* also has had a racializing force in the Americas, we can better understand the need to take such uncouplings further, or as Simpson, cited above, argues, to "disaggregate" native identities from signs of difference.

Relatedly, it is important to understand that just as concepts of race, of "blackness" and of "whiteness," are rooted in discourses of hegemonic difference and of othering, concepts of indigeneity and "first" origins are similarly embattled and constructed. Recent explorations in Indigenous studies have made clear that though land-based claims persist and form the cornerstone of much organizing in settler colonies of North America and of Commonwealth nations (such as Australia and New Zealand), being situated on one's land of origin cannot continue to be the sole means by which Indigenous people themselves are identified or, literally, counted. As Audra Simpson has shown in *Mohawk Interruptus*, colonial dictates as to blood quanta, differentiated by gender and marriages between Indigenous women and non-Indigenous men, meant that who is "counted" as Indigenous is not so much a reliable indication of blood kinship (which had been traditionally passed down through women's lines) as is nationality and citizenship, both within bands and settler states, dictated by European forms of patrilineage: it was a means by which to dispossess Indigenous peoples of their lands. The resulting effect has been to disappear surviving Indigenous people while also making group survival inefficient and bound up in imposed systems of belonging contrary to Indigenous traditions.[17] Furthermore, settler states physically removed native peoples from their traditional lands and moved them onto "reserved lands" (aka "reservations") that may or may not have belonged to their "tribe" such that land-claims have become increasingly vexed and fraught between Indigenous groups.

Shari Huhndorf (who is otherwise engaged in land-claim struggles for Native Alaskans) has argued that nationalist approaches, that is, those situated from within the borders of settler states, have exacerbated the notion that indigenous politics should be "rooted in traditions and campaigns for tribal sovereignty" thereby neglecting "the historical forces (such as imperialism) that increasingly draw indigenous communities into global contexts" (3).[18] Without neglecting the importance of continued land claims struggles, both Huhndorf and Simpson argue that Native communities cannot be understood solely as "First Peoples" conflated with lands of origin from which they have been forcibly removed or displaced over time. Huhndorf, in particular, as I do in this project with respect to African Diasporic communities, argues that "concentrating on the connections that tie indigenous communities together rather than on the boundaries that separate them allows me to raise questions about gender, imperialism, class, and the worldwide circulation of culture which have garnered little sustained attention in Native literary studies" (2). Similarly, this study seeks to expose interlocking narratives of African Diasporic consciousness that increasingly focus on modes of being, aesthetics, gender parity, histories of liberation, linguistic forms, and cultural motifs as part and parcel of what it means to be African Diasporic in the world. Huhndorf argues, further, that the very terms used in Native studies are in themselves problematic and compromising (similar to the continued debates over the term "black" and "blackness" alluded to earlier). In a preliminary note on terminology to her text *Mapping the Americas* (with reference to the terms "Native," "indigenous," "aboriginal," "Eskimo," "Inuit," and "First Nations") Huhndorf writes: "All of these terms, of course, are products of colonization that are used to distinguish indigenous peoples from Europeans and, more recently, to denote their common historical and political situations, but they fail to indicate the diversity among them" (xiii). Both she and Simpson invoke discrete tribal names rather than those imposed through colonial processes;[19] for Simpson, part of the objective is to uncover the ways in which settler colonialism renders impossible modes of subjectivity and legibility (23); its objective is "to disappear" Native people. As she writes: "in settler societies such as the United States and Canada, citizenship is key to this process of rationalizing dispossession and the rapid ascent of power for migrants; so, citizenship is also key to Kahnawà:ke's enunciation of self under conditions in which they would have to disappear" (25). In other words, Native populations are forced (or feel that they have no choice but to comply) with demands to correspond to the terms of citizenship of the nation-states under which they are subsumed, while simultaneously limiting who "counts" as Native in order to access limited treaty rights—both of which demand a self-erasure, a continuous, slow disappearance. Huhndorf additionally argues not only that terms of indigeneity have been constructed and imposed by the State, but that the very *language* utilized to describe and examine the cultures they denote are themselves misnomers and already compromised (and compromising). Both, in their particular ways, enjoin us to think beyond the limits of land and borders, treaty rights and settler states, in order to accept that Native peoples can be defined in a variety of culturally specific ways, bound up in memory, history, and kinship, familial and territorial exchanges that are not necessarily essentialist but that are traceable transhistorically and transnationally. Doing so does not mean that the specificities of Native tribes and ethnicities disappear; in fact, quite the opposite effect is made possible, affirming the truism that "political recognition is, in its simplest terms, to be seen by another *as one wants to be seen*" (Simpson 23). Both recognize the ways in which the realities of Native people under settler colonialism intersect with settler colonialisms elsewhere, especially in the African and North American contexts. If Indigenous studies has increasingly borrowed from African American and postcolonial studies related to African tropes in order to articulate a new agenda for itself, I think that we need to go further than thinking of these situations simply as analogous to recognize that the shifting means of identification and expansion of the terrain of (self)recognition into the global, in each field, can inform the other.[20] Bridging Indigenous Studies with anthropology/postcolonial theorizing, James Clifford has more recently suggested that tensions between the use of the terms *indigenous* (signified as "historical" occupants of a territory) and *autochthone* (signified as "natural" or pre–recorded-history occupants) might be resolved by first identifying how the two terms differ and then by applying to them "diasporic" features (note that these definitions are the reverse of those provided by Anderson in his study of the Garifuna). He argues that in recent studies, "diasporist and autochthonist histories, the aspirations of migrants, and natives, do come into direct political antagonism" (*Routes* 253) as each group vies for cultural and geographical sovereignty in the same territories. But Clifford also appears to collapse "indigeneity" with the immigrant/diasporic experience rather than solely with First Nations identity, leading me to believe that this is another indication that "indigeneity" can be reconfigured for other kinds of "first peoples" and their descendants, even when displaced. In fact, in recent work, Clifford has been pointing out that, like for ethnic minorities related to other diasporas, "first-nation" sovereignty is less a result of being "first" but acquired by "dint of continuous occupancy over an extended period," noting that "how long it takes to *become* indigenous is always a political question" (*Routes* 254). So, if this holds true for First Nations peoples who have had to rearticulate indigeneity because of being forced to occupy territories not their own and who have had to cultivate, as well as reinvent, their disrupted cultures, for post-slavery/indentureship occupants of areas like the Caribbean, where unique syncretic cultures have developed over time, giving inhabitants discrete identities particular to place, Clifford's emphasis on the *process* by which indigeneity is achieved speaks both to its inventiveness as a political response to erasure as to its *performative* features, which pertains as much to displaced Africans and their descendants as to First Nations peoples (as I demonstrate in Chapter 1, the first leg of our journey, to arrive at more competent *autochthonomous*, readings of African Diasporic works). In fact, in order to arrive at this conclusion, Clifford liberally borrows from *African Diasporic* studies to formulate his idea in the context of First Nations/Native American studies, and (echoing some of Said's early work) writes: "diasporist discourses reflect the sense of being part of an ongoing transnational network that includes the homeland not as something simply left behind but as a place of attachment in a contrapuntal modernity" (*Routes* 256). Thus, if we refuse the idea of Africans as always already ruptured from history (as in Hegelian thought, restated more recently by Mbembe, as cited earlier), and refute the idea that removal from the African continent into the Americas constitutes not a rupturing from what has gone on before but a violence that then gave birth to rearticulations of what it meant to be African on new ground—not a nonbeing but a hybridization that results in "new ethnicities"—then we can begin to access the terrain of *autochthonomies* for which I advocate.

In *Returns: Becoming Indigenous in the Twenty-First Century*, Clifford's title suggests that North American Indigenous identities are being made— "becoming"—and, as such, that they are intricate performances that cannot be located precisely in space or time. They are "in-process." Although not explicitly stated, Clifford appears to borrow from advances in performance as well as postcolonial theory, to argue (with specific reference to the Hau'ofa of Hawai'i) that: "interdependence and movement are historical realities that indigenous societies inflect, and partly control. They do this through interactive social processes of articulation, performance, and tradition" (44). Throughout *Returns*, Clifford thus argues for the ways in which Indigenous communities in the Americas have refashioned or rearticulated themselves, reinventing themselves through negotiations with history, museums, traditions lost and recovered, linguistic signs and nomenclature, performances of rituals, geographical locations, and community membership. "Being 'Native,'" he says, "is a way of participating, finding fulfillment, in a regulated diversity" (302); it is not an essence or immutable, and is an ever-changing, evolving process of identifications and assertions, of laying claim to identities fractured by violence and power but also predating the latter. Strikingly, Clifford compares his project to that of the *négritude* fathers (Senghor, Aimé and Suzanne Césaire, Damas), arguing for an *indigénitude*—"a vision of liberation and cultural difference that challenges, or at least redirects, the modernizing agendas of nation-states and transnational capitalism" (16). Clifford's *indigénitude* includes "local traditions . . . national agendas and symbols . . . transnational activism" and "is sustained through media-disseminated images, including a shared symbolic repertoire" to "express a transformative renewal of attachments to culture and place" (ibid.). It interests me that Clifford finds recourse to elements of *négritude* to create a compelling model for North American indigenous communities. It compels me to ask why, as explored earlier, African-descended populations have not, in themselves, been considered "indigenous"—in spite of a widely recognized *indigénisme* movement, which took place in Haiti in response to U.S. occupation, and which is widely acknowledged to be the precursor to *négritude* owing to its turn to self-definition, folk traditions embedded in local (even if dis-located) space, and the roots of Africanity itself, that is, indigenous cultures emanating from Africa and transposed onto Caribbean soil.

The creator of the term and movement, anthropologist Jean Price-Mars, argued in *1928* against the devaluation of African beliefs and sensibilities globally and in favor of the valorization of modes of self-actualization arrived at through syncretism by Haitians, modes rooted in African-derived sensibilities, providing the ground for both a national and existential identity that could be mobilized to sustain the people's autonomy from encroaching external forces. Price-Mars defined the former in this way: "we could sum up everything or very nearly so by saying that they are the fundamental beliefs upon which have been grafted or superimposed other more recently acquired beliefs." These beliefs, he opined further, "are engaging in a harsh and heavy struggle to gain control of the mind" (13). For Price-Mars, then, the beliefs that formed the sum of the whole were epistemic and ontological in nature; they, therefore, defined what made up the mind and existence, and defined or delimited one's place in the world. Such beliefs did not remain static, as translator Margaret Shannon observed, describing the whole of the Price-Mars project in the following way: "He had demonstrated that history is a continuous societal process based on the accommodation of folkloric past to changing behavioral patterns, irrespective of color, and that therefore the role of the black man is an integral and consequential part of the history of civilization" (xvii); in many ways, then, Price-Mars's insights appear echoed some decades in the future in the work of Stuart Hall's "new ethnicities." Price-Mars believed folklore to be part of societal/historical processes to which people of African descent actively contributed on the global terrain. It is thus to this sensibility that I turn in order to ground the present student, the notion that we have everything to learn from how artists/writers of African descent signal their beliefs to one another and what these communications/ understandings reveal about an African Diasporic world view. This was the struggle under U.S.-occupied Haiti and it remains the struggle of many people of African descent residing in postcolonial worlds, both on the continent and elsewhere: to be seen and to see themselves, *as they wish to be seen*, in the context of their Africanity, changed, transformed, and syncretized over time.

My claim, then, is, further, that African-derived autochthonomies signify mobile autochthonies defined by the political exigency of a cultural sovereignty unanchored in a particular, local space. It is a claim that, akin to the Native cultures of North America and elsewhere, African cultures have maintained, through their descendants—whether remaining in local space, forcibly dispersed, or willingly relocated—cultural codes and knowledge that bespeak a heritage with indigenous sensibilities *even as they have been reinvented*. These codes and knowledge may be transformed as they traverse geopolitical spaces and time, but they hold resonance for those who can trace some part of their habits, customs, and knowledge to these spaces of beginning. My objective will not be to argue for the evidence of cultural retention beyond colonialism, the slave trade, the Middle Passage, and partition; it will be to show how autochthonomy shows itself or surfaces despite these in primarily contemporary articulations of identity in the works of a number of texts by individuals of African descent situated in a plurality of locales within and beyond the African continent. Further, it will be to show that this *autochthonomy* is marked primarily in what I term, "intradiasporic" texts, that is, texts whose creators seek to address more than those who share their own, discreet culture or nationality but address others of African descent who may be of different ethnic or national origin. As such, these texts perform a symbolic "crossing of cultures" while also insisting upon an implicit continuity between cultures, making them "intra-" rather than "inter"-cultural. It serves to reason, then, that texts not only perform crossings but mirror these through the trope of travel. The texts I have chosen for this study to explore this ground of exchange and *autochthonomy* thus focus primarily on travel, or mobility, or are in themselves travel narratives. This also allows me to test how mobility comes to form an integral component of transnational African-descended identities, thus suggesting as well that notions of the "nation-state" and appurtenance to the, or "a," nation remain significant loci of investigation.

As I demonstrate later, if anything, "nationality" constitutes a major stumbling block for the constitution of discernible transnational African-descended identities; it may be that "the nation," as understood in the European sense, following Benedict Anderson's erudition on the rise and constitution of European nation-states, will remain a pivot of negotiation among people of African descent, as it remains for us all, since what constitutes national identity is, as Anderson has so well argued, a sort of suspension of rationality in deference to a loose idea of the "common good" for the maintenance of national order and borders. But what emerges concretely through these imaginative texts of intradiasporic exchange is a fundamental understanding and *recognition* of the "other" here, the African (diasporic) other, as a subject in itself. That subjectivity is then maintained through the possibility of *autonomy*, that is, through an apprehension and expression of one and the other's liberty, of culture, of knowledge, of communication, of aesthetics, of subjectivity, and of agency in the process of such engagement. This project is an attempt to illuminate the African subjectivity via a claim of autochthonomy such as I have defined it earlier, and as separate from the racial encoding brought about through colonialism. Doing so also requires redefining what we mean by terms such as "emancipation," "freedom," and "autonomy."

Lakou/Yard Consciousness

If *autochthonomy* is the practice of intra-subjective exchanges girded by mobile, local practices, cultural expressions, or beliefs that form the intradiasporic bridge between cultures of African descent, then what I call "lakou" or "yard consciousness" is the virtual space in which such exchanges take place. Virtual because located in no single geographical space, this imagined locus is composed of autochthonous beliefs and practices, preserved, reformulated or syncretized over time, and often in differing geopolitical spaces, which nonetheless form the basis for communication because of their a priori importance to the identities of those peoples who have continued to practice them—however modified—to subsist, and to persist. Largely speaking, then, I am also arguing that beyond the deformations and reconstitutions of "raced" identities, I am taking for granted that, like Europeans, Africans have their own gnosis and epistemes, their own understanding of "being," and that these understandings of the "nature of man" are transmitted through discursive means that have been preserved through time, culturally.

As pointed out earlier, I call this ground of transmission, *"lakou"* or "yard" consciousness (referred to as *lakou*/yard hereafter) after a concept taken from my own geographical region and area of study, the Caribbean, the perspective that largely informs the current study,[21] as I have come to believe that an energetic, imaginative exchange takes places intradiasporically in such a way that demonstrates the commonalities of perspective that makes such exchange possible. It is true that enslaved Africans were separated from their biological kin and *legally* stripped of any remaining or subsequently created kinship ties, but the reality is also that many forms of cultural expression for the enslaved, as for those remaining in the sites from which the enslaved were stripped, as practices of Vodun demonstrate, *exceeded* colonial laws and maps of power; this is why such cultural replications or manifestations of retentions from source cultures proved, over time, to be strong forms of sustenance and models for resistance. Such pieces of cultural retention, even if refashioned, or syncretized with imposed forms (of artistic, spiritual or political expression), traveled with the displaced and took root elsewhere. It is this rooting that interests me, the rhizomic quality of the African/Diasporic experience and reality that Edouard Glissant has so well described as a particularly Caribbean trope that I here extend beyond the Caribbean basin and articulate in this project as a dynamic, *virtual* space of cultural *knowing* the lakou (or yard) consciousness.

The *lakou* or yard, in Caribbean spaces, like their corollary in traditional African villages, originally served to delimit groupings of related individuals, either because they were related by blood (an extended family), or by kinship (ethnicity). Over time, such spaces became looser in their constitution, but belonging to a *lakou*/yard usually came to mean that one culturally and, more importantly, spiritually belonged to a community of like-minded folk. This space is one in which *filiation* and *affiliation* also become *redefined* cultural features or markers of association.

The difference between *filiation* and *affiliation* may seem slight but it is the nuance between the two that I seek to highlight. *Affiliation* means to associate with a group or structure in a subordinate relationship to a larger group identity or governing body (one is affiliated, for instance, with a church, or with an institution like a university or hospital); *filiation* means to be directly descended from a group or lineage (one is the descendant of a matrilineal caste of shamans originating in Peru, for instance, or the grandchild of Polish émigrés residing in the United States). Affiliation is more or less distant, nonaffective, while filiation invokes the affective bonds of blood ties, of heritage. A job or faith may tie us to an affiliation, a tie that can be severed when faith is broken or a job resigned, but a filiation is ruptured by very little, not even death. Thus, in this work, I redefine *affiliation* in such a way as to create a rapprochement between the linearity of *filiation* and the dynamism of *affiliation*—this is why, in places, I have come to use the term *af/filiation* to signal a constant flow between the two categories whereby disengagement from either a filiation or an affiliation may take place, or a reversal of the form of engagement may take place, across formerly distinct spaces or periods in time. In this sense, my understanding of the flexibility of these terms is cognizant of Lorna Burns's reading of Glissant's "assertion . . . that being cannot be understood apart from its becoming." By this, Burns means that Glissant is less interested in "filiation" because it "depends upon fixed being" (141) than he is on the fluidity of identity. However, my own approach does not focus on "difference" as the heart of identity (ibid.) within postcolonial Manichean dualities, as the rest of my introduction and Chapter 1 clarify. I am much more invested, as the concept of the *lakou*/yard consciousness connotes, in what Keith Sandiford has marked as a significant departure from both Glissant's and Gilroy's conceptions of "affiliation" in order to ascribe "to myth and traditional epistemic systems an immutable power to shape and determine the cultural imaginary" (155n25). Doing so means ascribing a certain weight to filiation in ethnographic terms, if not in terms of biology or heredity; the movement and transformation of these forms across the diaspora, however, contributes to the movement and dynamism of affiliation, allowing for a recuperation of identity that is not necessarily defined genetically (yet, may be—I return to this point in further detail in Chapter 1) or defined solely on the basis of colonial heritage. It is in this respect that my current project charts new ground. It is not, as one scholar termed Glissant's important work, a project in which "relation . . . is the project of a cure for unhomeliness" (Gallagher 269). It does not assume a lost home ground or origin(s) but argues for a constant reconceptualization of "home" from within *lakou*/yard consciousness.

Ritualized patterns of cultural/spiritual retention were rehearsed and repeated in such yards, giving each a particular feature and resonance, but, largely speaking, all such *lakou*/yards shared recognizable African Diasporic features that could be translated across yards, through which one could recognize "kin." In *lakou*/yard consciousness, the space of meeting operates simultaneously as "home ground" (akin to bell hooks's "home space"), meeting place, community space, sacred ground (for meeting with spirits and ancestors), crossroads, and recollection. It is a space of memory, of negotiation between past and present as much as it is, in the Americas, a space in which European, African beliefs confront each other and congeal into new, syncretic concepts and rituals. Yet, it serves not as a space of assimilation but as one of *reconfiguration* in which (African) cultural antecedents are guiding principles and aspiration(s), *alongside, rather than in spite of* concepts adopted and adapted from dominant cultures within hegemonic colonial systems that remain formative whether in postcolonial (in the Americas or Europe) or postcolony (in African, after Mbembe) systems.

As Mimerose Beaubrun explains in her text, *Nan Domi*, "For nearly 10 years, I have been interested in yard systems, 'a vital space, site of pluridimensional life where a number of families, or, rather, an enlarged family shares all aspects of life (spiritual, economic, cultural)'"[22] (31) and states, further, that "the *lakou* has three functions: conservation, protection, renewal." That is, it serves as a space in which the family or kinship/cultural group can gather, rest, know itself, refuse dispersion, and pass on knowledge from one to the other, horizontally, or across time, vertically, from generation to generation. Thus, in this text, I argue that the "yard" of African Diasporic thought/knowledge, of consciousness, resides in a virtual rather than physical space, even if some physical spaces of manifestation remain in discrete locations. I believe that the similarity of expression that can be traced across works by individuals of African descent from a variety of geographical backgrounds brings out this reality.

With this concept in mind then, *autochthonomies*, as a critical approach, functions as an intervention in fields concerned with "raced" identities in a global context, from postcolonial studies to African American studies, engaging contingent fields focusing on identity and subject formation such as philosophy, feminist/women's studies, political science, and anthropology, anchored in the interdisciplinary nexus of Caribbean studies. It becomes clear as one engages such texts that the process is not an easy one, that the disidentifications produced by difference and their social organization (such as race, gender, class, nation, and so forth) are extremely tenacious. Thus, how some texts overcome or negotiate this will serve to demonstrate both the limits and potentialities of "*lakou*/yard consciousness" and of the concept of *autochthonomy* as I engage them throughout the study. As such, they provide important *testimonies* bearing on crucial historical moments in the African Diasporic world and for humanity; they also serve to *transmit* the pitfalls and hopes of overcoming the constraints of national demarcations and their attendant raced realities. I suggest that the expression and practice of transnationalism these texts engage transmit useful tools of social and political testimony in the process of preserving and reconstituting codes of cultural af/filiation. Ultimately, my purpose is to focus on the substance of the exchanges the texts perform and to show how they facilitate and cultivate transnational identities in ways that illuminate the subjectivities of African-descended peoples transhistorically.

Methodology and Chapter Overview

My theoretical framework and analytical tools are necessarily interdisciplinary, multiple, and hybrid in nature. I draw from feminist and postcolonial theoretical paradigms, from advances in the disciplines of literature, philosophy, cultural studies, race studies, visual studies, performance studies, history, and anthropology. Within feminism, I look especially to the work of twentieth-century French feminists working with Lacanian psychoanalysis in order to reformulate gendered perspectives of identity formation,[23] late-twentieth-century/twenty-first-century postmodern and transnational feminists of color, and feminist philosophers working primarily in the areas of gender and race studies. From postcolonial studies, I draw heavily from scholars whose work focuses on power, racial construction, decolonization, and strategies of subversion/recuperation.

From across the disciplines aforementioned, I also draw from scholars who have questioned the methods and constraints of their disciplines, especially when these have proven to be outmoded or ethnocentric to such a degree as to be intellectually questionable. Historians and anthropologists appear to have been at the forefront of such disciplinary remappings. A handful of scholars trained or actively working in philosophy (such as Judith Butler and Emmanuelle Eze) have also offered new avenues for thinking through the nature of being from the perspective of bodies that are not conventionally thought of as occupying universal positions from which lessons about the human experience can be drawn. What these scholars have shown, along with developments in the fields of culture, visual, race, and performance studies—fields that are in themselves focused on the conventional "other," designated as such because of gender, race, sexuality, economic, or some other distinguishing marker forming a particular class—is the degree to which the "other" is not so much different but marginalized from the locus conventionally engaged as the overarching perspective from which to understand humanity. Their work of shifting focus to "the margins" or to classes not conventionally regarded as central to discussions of ontology has, of course, profoundly impacted my own approach.

Since I am trained as a literary scholar, I use the conventional tools of textual analysis to render meaning from the texts chosen for this study, whether literary or visual. As I do so, however, I apply concepts and ideas from a variety of fields to yield new approaches to analysis, to uncover a new reading practice that situates African Diasporic thought as instructive and crucial to understanding not only African-derived realities but the universal conditions of humanity—as I foregrounded earlier. Lastly, as I weave together a new reading practice for African Diasporic texts and engage an interdisciplinary methodology by applying a wide range of concepts and paradigms to the textual analyses performed throughout the chapters to follow, I simultaneously advance the dual theories of *autochthonomies* and *lakou*/yard consciousness progressively and *in process* from chapter to chapter. I do not "map" the two concepts onto every text from one chapter to the next but trace how we might move from a hyper-racialized cultural context in which race is essentially performed (i.e., constructed) but not acknowledged as such, to ways of rereading texts from these perspectives. I do this, having learned from various presentations over the years thinking through this project, that the ways in which "race" continues to operate as "natural" particularly in its most aberrant forms, makes it very difficult for even the most open reader to review known/canonical texts from new perspectives, de-racialized or decolonized, and reassembled through cultural vectors. As such, I have opted to demonstrate, chapter-by-chapter, the ideological steps necessary to arrive at this capacity. The chapters thus deliberately enact a process, moving from investigating "racial habitus" in Chapter 1, to moving to a politics of transhistoric and transnational af/filiative practices rooted in African Diasporic realities in representing contemporary genocides in Chapter 2, to a practice of textual (dis)identification to mobilize authority over one's subjectivity in Chapter 3, to practicing (Rancière's concept of) the "equality of intelligences" within intra-diasporic textualities underscoring *lakou* consciousness within *autochthonomous* perspectives in Chapter 4. In each chapter, interpretive practices shift from those focused on Euro-American dominance patterns and legacies of colonialism to perspectives centered in African Diasporic interpretive practices rooted in the reality of *autochthonomous* existence. I have also drawn from cultural studies with a particular interest in the works of scholars focusing on travel and mobility because I have purposefully chosen texts that engage ideas of mobility, travel, and border crossing, and those that can be situated as transnational even if they were produced prior to such concepts and terminologies. Such texts test our understandings of national identifications as well as our understanding of how cultural identities remain stable or shift as the borders of nation-states are revealed to be porous or permeable.

"Race . . . travels," suggests Hortense Spillers, elaborating: "It gains its power from what it signifies by this point, in what it allows to come to meaning" (137). In the investigations to follow, especially Chapters 1 and 2, it is precisely the *power* which Spillers recognizes as embedded in racial discourse that I dismantle. I am, however, not so much concerned in how racial demarcation has subjugated populations (the reasons why are explained earlier and they also have been sufficiently covered by other scholars) but in how those deemed subaltern subjects (a contradiction in terms) simultaneously escape such categorization by recourse to a competing or parallel existential reality. I am interested in the ways in which African Diasporic peoples have achieved—in the process of safeguarding their own epistemes and gnosis even through periods of colonial subjugation and in freeing themselves from both physical and ideological enslavement—a subjectivity that circulates at the same time as does their previous state of liminality in societies that do not recognize this subjectivity. Their relationship to "race" is coterminous with Spillers's notion of a "boundary of freedom" wherein the haunting of the slave ship operates as a metaphor more than a historical marker that, like "race," travels and signifies both difference and subalternity although the slave ship of today is more likely a 747 while, for others, it consists still of treks through spatialities (the desert, ocean, or even the plains of the American Midwest) as in the time of the Exodus. But since, as I argued earlier, my objective is to move the conversation beyond that of enslavement or of coloniality, I focus on narratives of travel that posit *another* mobility, that of subjects who are free to move from one space to another, who *choose* their mobility and, through it, observe the world, and themselves in the world, in a new way. I suggest, then, that the kinds of travel narratives explored in my study occupy a kind of "third" space, one that I define as the virtual yard/lakou space of consciousness in the African Diaspora. This space is thus one of indeterminacy, of hybridity, of multiplicity—an intermediary.

The idea of a postcolonial "intermediary" occurs in other, multiple contexts. For example, Kobena Mercer, in a discussion focusing on Black British citizens suggests that their identity emerges from the "conflicts and contradictions that arise in the relations *within* and *between* the various movements, agents, and actors" (425) of society. Similarly, Spillers suggests that African Diasporic communities reside "in the intimate *space* where the white man's almighty form is in fact forgotten" (144). Chela Sandoval, in her work on cultures of resistance within the United States speaks of Roland Barthes's analysis of semiotic mythologies as an investment in the "*interstices* between decolonial processes" and, taking Barthe's project as her starting point, argues for a "third view," or third form of subjectivity (32). Sandoval claims that that "third form" encapsulates resistance not as a counterforce but as an entity with its own spatial viability that is neither at the center nor the margin of popular or dominant discourses. Homi Bhabha, accused in response to his essay, "Postcolonial Authority and Postmodern Guilt," by an interlocutor of producing an "aesthetic of the fragment," counters as he does in the essay itself, and again in reference to Barthes in a neocolonial context, that he aims to uncover a "language of performativity" that emerges "from *in-between*" subject/other formations to create a third space so barely intelligible as to have no name. In the context of gender and sexuality, philosopher and rhetorician, Judith Butler also argues for a third space, one that exposes the performative nature of gender. What all of these theorists suggest is that beneath claims for the liberation of subalterns and explorations of resistance to authority, there exist gaps and fissures worthy of further definition and examination, interstices that function as indexes of the emergence of new (or, as I insist, preexisting or parallel) identities that can no longer be defined as they were before. Our categories of difference and diversity are worn and outdated. It is in the gaps between that which has been invested with power and that which has not (which creates both resistance and reinforcement of a status quo) that there exists an *exit* from our old ways of understanding and perceiving difference, one that requires that we abandon worn lines of demarcation. Such abandon (and I mean to invoke here the dual nature of the word: to give up completely as well as to lack in restraint) forces a compelling reconsideration of how categories of race, gender, sexuality, and class can come to function in a liberatory matrix in our present day.

Within these concepts, of particular interest to me will be Homi Bhabha's concept of "double-time" with regard to "natives" in postcolonial worlds (discussed at greater length in Chapter 1), that is, a doubleness in which the mechanisms of colonial hegemonies, which create seemingly homogeneous notions of national identities and flatten out historical processes of subjugation such that these appear to be natural and sequential, have to be negotiated and reformulated by "native" postcolonials, resulting in what may be productive interventions at times, while at others, remaining vexed and compromised by those very mechanisms. I reveal those moments when artists of African descent, unaware of the effect of "double-time" replicate colonial hegemonic tropes along national lines, but, when breaking with national narratives, they also break *through* double-time and expose its mirrored effects in ways that allow for the emergence of what Bhabha might call "native intelligence" and what I term throughout this project, *autochthonomy*.

Chapter 1, "(Re)Presenting Racial Permeability, (Dis)Ability, and Racial (Dis)Affiliations," begins the journey by investigating the discussion of racial "othering" and racial fluidity through the analysis of late-twentieth-century and contemporary conceptual art and literary texts that highlight the ways in which "race" continues to operate as a historicized fiction. I demonstrate how the focus of these texts on the interplay between the performance of race, gender, disability, and the interpellation of audiences in such performances (whether imagined within the text or positioned outside of it), sheds further light on the degree to which race operates as an overdetermined category that does not entirely define those whom it delimits. Utilizing recent advances in performance and feminist studies, in particular, I trace "race" within these texts as a traveling trope but also as a psychological effect that "travels" between performer and observer; I highlight here what philosopher Linda Alcoff has termed "racial animus" to explore the ways in which race is "performed" and "read" in the interplay of socially situated bodies transnationally and transhistorically, but more than this, to situate what the artists present as a potential to locate African Diasporic sensibilities despite or beyond such constructions. I show that African Diasporic artists focus on kinship ties and affiliations differently than those constructed through raced constructions and argue here that this is one manifestation of the practice of autochthonomy. After a discussion of conceptual art pieces (by Koons and Piper) that ask viewers to "see" race as constructs beneath which cultural identifications are effaced, yet remain, I turn to issues of disability, the law, and race in South Africa via the Pistorius case, as a bridge to explore two literary texts that expose race as social performance, yet demonstrate that kinship af/filiations exist cross- and intra-culturally: Octavia Butler's faux slave narrative, the science fiction novel, *Kindred* (1996), and ("white") South African playwright Pamela Gien's *The Syringa Tree* (2003). In Butler's text, time travel operates as a means by which the author seeks to have her readers rethink how race (alongside gender and class) are constructed and shift definition depending upon historical context. Gien's text, situated solely during the period of apartheid, does similar work as a one-woman play portraying twenty-five characters of differing ages, ethnicities, nationalities, abilities, and political convictions. By forcing viewers to be both complicit with stereotype and to break with them, the play, like the conceptual art pieces discussed earlier in the chapter, performs a new visual practice suggestive of a new "reading" practice. I conclude this chapter by beginning to trace the trajectory necessary to move from the space of racial overdetermination and binaries to the culturally specific yet globally diffuse *lakou*/yard consciousness space that enables a productive practice of *autochthonomy* expressed through understandings of kinship and subject identities articulated via African Diasporic points of view.

From having established the ways in which race discourse "travels" across time periods but is permeable if we shift historical periods, performance, and reading strategies, in Chapter 2, "Autochthonomous Transfigurations of Race and Gender in Twenty-First-Century Transnational Genocide Testimonial Narratives," I test the notions of *autochthonomy* and of *lakou*/yard consciousness by investigating late-twentieth-century texts that actively seek to *translate* seemingly discrete African/African Diasporic experiences across cultural divides through visual representations of the Rwandan genocide. Here, I am keenly interested in how visual representations of genocide have the potential to provide a new lexicon for a new reading practice that would engage African Diasporics as cultural agents actively performing their autonomy in a transnational, postcolonial world in order to bear witness for each other on a global stage. I refer specifically to textual media that relies on the visual: film/documentary, graphic novels, and photography. I show that the work of the artists analyzed in this chapter who productively abandon "racial" categorization in favor of a shared af/filiative cultural space come to rely on this shared space in order to articulate, for themselves and for others, how African epistemes are productively activated to consolidate cultural identities that travel across and beyond national boundaries—especially when "race" and/or "ethnicity" is abandoned in favor of a more wholistic approach to cultural af/filiation. I show that this af/filiative space, the space of the virtual *lakou*, is the ground from which *autochthonomous* identification springs. I also show that this identification shifts the discourse away from patriarchal, colonial givens to norms or representation that establish gender parity and de-hegemonize notions of the nation. From this gendered turn, I move to traveling African Diasporic subjectivities in the next chapter, "Subjectivity in Motion: Caribbean Women's (Dis)Articulations of Being."

Chapter 3 returns us to the late nineteenth century, when colonial paradigms were deeply anchored and seemingly unchallenged, via a reading of Mary Seacole's memoir *The Wonderful Adventures of Mrs. Seacole in Many Lands*, achieved through an analysis of Frantz Fanon's (mis)reading of Mayotte Capécia's turn-of-the-century novel, *Je suis Martiniquaise*. In this chapter, I propose that Seacole's memoir presages Fanon's philosophical findings in *Black Skin, White Masks*, in terms of his advancement of the psychic dislocation caused in Black subjects as a result of their confrontation with racism but also in its more obscure, least discussed assertion that this dislocation reveals, obliquely, the presence of a (nonracialized) subject unimpeded by social markers. I contend that the fact that Seacole wrote a popular, bestselling memoir and was multiethnic and multiply located as such in her time, resulted in her text being misread as no more than a mere record of a "free coloured woman" at the end of the nineteenth century; in fact, I contend that it is a significant record of a latent expression of autochthonomy, an expression of hybrid African Diasporic consciousness affirming itself through the vicissitudes of a text that, on the surface, appears to speak only to the European/white reader. I suggest that the work extensively practices a disidentification from imposed social raced and gendered categories in order to participate in their (dis)articulation such that an autochthonomous, hybrid identity becomes more and more evident. I explore Seacole's text through Fanon's (mis)reading of Mayotte Capécia to show *how* efforts, especially by women of African descent, came to be marginalized and dismissed. I contend that Fanon's reading of Capécia is a deliberate *mis*reading designed to cause dismissal by readers of Capécia because it allows him to make the point he wants regarding the place of women of African descent in the fight for (what Fanon perceived to be) Black (male) actualization in the hegemonic, colonial superstructure. But, if one looks closely at what Fanon dismisses in the text (over half the narrative) and otherwise ignores regarding its genre and purpose, we can also discern that Fanon did so because he recognized in it essential narrative turns that work their way into the more important aspects of *Black Skin, White Masks*. This analysis then allows me to read back into Seacole's text similar stylistic and thematic devices, showing that though Fanon may have come across these in Capécia, that they preexist both in a wider, African Diasporic literary tradition—in a literary *lakou*, so to speak. Chapter 3 thus serves to demonstrate the active presence of the African Diasporic subject and the strategies by which one pre–twentieth century African Diasporic traveler/writer sought to preserve and "perform" this identity against the social limitations of her time to present an *autochthonomous* African Diasporic reality.

Chapter 4, "Autochthonomous Ambiguities: Travel, Memoir, and Transnational African Diasporic Subjects in (Post)colonial Contexts," turns fully to narratives of mobility that move us into diasporic geographies and test the ground of intradiasporic af/filiation. In this chapter, I apply Jacques Rancière's concept of the "equality of intelligences" with notions of emancipation for African Diasporic subjects to suggest that *autochthonomy* must be premised on a liberation from outdated notions of freedom and common claims across humanity for autonomy from tyranny. From a consideration of these four texts, I conclude that the successful achievement of *autochthonomy* through the travel narrative genre can only be achieved when a certain sense of colonial identification is abandoned in favor of the af/filliation necessary to productively inhabit and work from the space of *lakou*/yard consciousness. I focus on literary works produced in the first decades of the twentieth century, during the Harlem Renaissance, a period in time when an intense wave of writings stressing African American autonomy emerged from the pens of African American writers, often in conversation with writers elsewhere, and across racial divides—in the United States, in Europe, in Africa, and in the Caribbean. Specifically, this chapter treats three works by African American writer, Zora Neale Hurston, and Jamaican writer, Claude McKay, both of whom found that their portal to creativity and to self-actualization was to be found in mobility. Both traveled widely throughout the United States, and the Caribbean (McKay traveled as well through France, Northern Africa, and the USSR). This mobility, at a time when African Americans did not have basic civic liberties in the United States, was nonetheless a mark of privilege. Yet, both understood that their mobility was intricately tied to the life force of African-descended communities elsewhere. For this reason, though I think a similar argument could be made by looking closely at the work of other writers of African descent of this time period situated outside of the United States, Hurston and McKay serve as productive case studies to examine the presence of "*lakou*/yard consciousness" within the United States and to examine the deployment of *autochthonomy* prior to the periods of post/de-colonial thought or literatures. My intent in doing so is to demonstrate that both these concepts, though articulated today, are foundational and ontological to the work of writers/artists of African descent, as already explored as nascent in the work of Seacole in Chapter 3. At the same time, situated in their historical moment of production, Hurston and McKay are not without contradictions and complexities worth exploring that suggest why such avenues have increasingly ceased and become illegible. My point is not to prove that such texts exist in an ahistorical vacuum but how they straddle space and, more importantly, how they might be productively reread in an interpretive practice that demands that we look away from the colonial as the only avenue for understanding. Hurston turned to the Caribbean for inspiration, writing her best-known book, *Their Eyes Were Watching God*, during a six-week period in 1937, while she was conducting anthropological research in Port-au-Prince, on Haitian vodou. As such, I investigate the novel as a travel narrative of sorts marked by a *kreyolization* (in reference to Haitian Kreyol, as I will explain in the chapter) that could have taken place only in the context of cross-national expansion, a kreyolization that has been misrecognized to signify other kinds of embedded marginalities in the text, notably around issues of women's solidarity. McKay, on the other hand, fled the racism of the United States to travel through Europe, finding in this displacement, as chronicled in his memoir, *A Long Way from Home* (also published in 1937), inspiration in the socialist-communist visions of the time that provided him with a sense of the possibility of achieving parity as a man of African descent in a "white" world without having to define himself within a set nationality. Read as a memoir, rather than as a straightforward autobiography, I show how McKay seeks to give voice to a particularly conscious, transnational identity that relies on mobility as its defining feature, while also remaining in touch with the "*lakou*/yard" space (grounded in Haiti). I then examine the politics of McKay's first novel, *Home to Harlem*

(1928), the notorious work "without a plot" decried by W. E. B. Du Bois for its ludic, unflattering, portrayal of black life in Harlem, for the ways in which McKay goes to some length to highlight the need for there to be a *filiation* between African Americans and Haitians, for the need to understand Haiti's history as a part of African American historical lineage. Constrained by the limits of their national and gender identifications, rereadings of these texts as *autochthonomies* allows us to reconsider the ways in which we might recast the literature of writers of African descent even when they seem well ensconced in a particular canon or literary narrative.

What has struck me in the process of bringing together these readings is that there is no linear progress in terms of how artists of African descent position themselves intradiasporically, transnationally, or even in postcolonial terms. In giving talks from the project, I have also encountered a great deal of resistance (even hostility) with regard to the potential of investigating texts on the basis of what they reveal of African cultural epistemes or practices, across geographies, and even across time. "What about white supremacy and continued racial oppression?" I have been asked. This project is not about denying the continued role of racial oppression and matrices of domination in the West. What it seeks to offer is a means by which to deconstruct our staid approach to the work of artists of African descent while apprehending in our cultural production intra-cultural discursive strategies that bespeak parallel realities grounded in African Diasporic histories and cultures. As the texts investigated within this project demonstrate, it is nearly impossible to completely break free of colonial vestiges; but, what interests me are those moments that demonstrate that these are not the only reality, and to suggest that it is worth taking our time to read not just for articulations of difference, but *differently*, such that what artists of African descent seek to reveal of their own communities, and of themselves, becomes a priority, a demonstration of cross-cultural competence but also an acknowledgment that people of African descent are not a priori "kinless," out of history, or only visible through narratives of oppression and subjugation. Those artists that engage the virtual sphere of *lakou*/yard consciousness through autochthonomy do so as subjects in their own right. The resistance to the notion of reading differently, or from within the "interpretive community" of artists of African descent as methodology, informs the project's arc as a process rather than as an easily deployable theory that can simply be mapped from one text to another; for one thing, we still reside in a time in which people of African descent continue to be perceived as "raced" and without a viable culture; for another, not all artists of African descent are interested in, or engage conversations with, others of African descent as an objective of their art. What I have attempted to do in this project is to develop a means of accessing the interpretive terrain that exists when that choice is made, demonstrating the process that one has to engage to get there if one is not already there, that there is a "there" but that it takes some work to be able to discern this reality in texts that have already been overdetermined and separated from the grounds of their intradiasporic production or meaning-making. Understanding that such is not a common interpretive practice, I thus take the time to demonstrate the necessity of deconstructing current patterns of assuming "kinlessness" for those raced as "black" and, from there, show how such deconstruction releases and reveals interpretive layers of perspectives affirming African Diasporic cultural tropes that add rich dimension to our understandings of texts, how these can be productively situated within African Diasporic (*lakou*) consciousness and reflect *autochthonomous* ways of being, still to be realized.

1 (Re)Presenting Racial Permeability, (Dis)Ability, and Racial (Dis)Affiliations

"Racial categories have a history and are subject to change," writes Eduardo Bonilla-Silva in his seminal work on the changing face of race in the United States (1), noting also that racial designations and identities are for the most part socially and politically overdetermined, even as they undergo continuous revision. This truism seems implausible given the ongoing ways in which, particularly in the United States, skin color or biological determinism appears to govern the material and psychic lives of the majority of those deemed "of color." Individuals may construct culturally and politically viable identities within ethnic communities separate from literally superficial physiognomic traits, but the racialized structures of U.S. society continue largely to dictate the meaning both of privilege and of difference, of exclusion and of inclusion. In many ways, this project proposes to answer the following series of questions: What might it mean to remove "race" from racialized categories of overdetermination, particularly for individuals of African descent? Is it even advisable to attempt to remove "race" from the social equation, given its role in determining social, political, and even economic societal roles? Having done so, what would it mean to understand the *cultural* production of artists of African descent beyond (albeit necessary) responses to structural inequity? What would it mean to understand such cultural production as having a *determination* of its own? What would it mean to reframe the discussion of such productions beyond the borders of U.S. nationalism, in transnational networks of representation and transmission? In this chapter, I suggest that a four-pronged approach is necessary to reform approaches to "reading race" in today's society, engaging the following concepts—"racial habitus" (Alcoff/Young), the post-human/cyborg (Haraway) and "assemblages" (more widely discussed), the phantom limb/amputation (Fanon), and subjectivity as "response-ability" (Oliver)—each to be explored further, in context, later.

We cannot move to new readings and cultural practices that sidestep or reconfigure "race" as such (this does not mean ignoring *racism* and its effects), without doing so. As Harvey Young, via the work of Paul Gilroy, asserts: "To uncritically employ the interrelated concepts of race, racism, and racial thinking without acknowledging their discriminatory origins would threaten to reinscribe notions of an inherent, natural, and biological difference that divides humankind into a set of distinct groups. It would be to accept a classification system that seeks to create difference and aims to develop a hierarchy premised upon the belief that particular groups are inferior and therefore deserving of unequal treatment" (7). To counter such a compulsion, Harvey Young suggests that "race" can be reconceptualized as "racial thinking." This perspective will inform the analysis to follow, in which I intend to demonstrate, via the concept of "racial habitus," how such "racial thinking" might be dismantled. I agree with Young, whose main focus is on how "race" is performed theatrically (as a reflection of social life), when he offers that, "*To conceptualize race in terms of embodiment* is arguably the most useful way of attending to the various manners in which it performs" (my emphasis 9). He asserts: "The concept of race is supported by a series of performances and enactments that give it a material presence and an experiential component in everyday life" (17). In my analysis of race-based works of sculpture, performance art, theater, and fiction that reveal how race is "performed" and "enacted," I will seek to show the *transparency* of race and the ways in which this transparency cloaks or dissimulates the "real" identities of individuals of African descent located *elsewhere* than in the space of habitus or racial thinking. I suggest that this "elsewhere" is to be located in place, space, and culture. It is through the material effects of which Young speaks, the *embodiment* of "racial thinking," that *how* "race" circulates as an ideological concept with real-world consequences or manifestations, that the alternate, constitutive space of culture (not to be defined as the space of the "other" constituted through disciplines such as anthropology, and so forth, as discussed previously), ancestry, and kinship can be reconsidered.

The purpose of taking some time to show the deleterious effects of racism on both black and white psyches via the works of artists of African descent, whether deemed white or black, is to show the extent to which "race" is both constructed and performed, the ways in which some of these performances have been naturalized, and the degree to which, as such, "race" can be reformulated and, at the same, time uncoupled from ethnicity or culture. In this, I aim to show that the degree of agency and autonomy that both "black" and "white" subjects can achieve in a racialized society is a function of the systems and structures that invigilate racial stratification. However, once parties are aware of their construction and systemization, through avenues that reveal that such organizing principles are neither natural nor inherent to individuals, then that which constitutes networks of belonging through culture and kinship can be differentially engaged in ways that break away from the naturalization of race as a means of separation and agglomeration. In other words, new ways of assembling human beings can emerge that run counter to already racialized societal systems.[1] The texts under analysis in this chapter demonstrate that truly awakening to the realities of racial constructions means that there is no other choice than to move to a place of understanding subjectivity from the point of view of those who have been refused access to the mechanisms of its oppressive deployment, but also to recognize that rigid, binary racial categories can be altered and alternative mechanisms not only imagined but employed in the service of altering the deleterious effects of colonial, that is to say raced, histories. The purpose, as the texts I ultimately look at for the latter, is not to *erase* these histories but to uncouple "race" from "culture" and to agree, as James Baldwin once suggested, to become the (oppressed) other— in cultural terms, however, these cultures have been modified by histories of injury and subjugation—in order to become more fully human and whole. Racial habitus, then, and its consequences, is only the portal by which we can begin to apprehend more egalitarian worlds in societies that have long been dominated by systems of racialization rooted in colonialisms that erase ethnicities and cultures in favor of fictive notions of identity based on racial demarcation whose only purpose is to service and prop up (post)colonial systems to maintain their foundations of inequity.

Further, I explore how artists and writers focusing on racial discrimination and apartheid have extended Fanon's metaphor of amputation from the impact of racism on black bodies, both male and female, to the psyches of those deemed "white," in both European and African societies impacted by colonialism. In doing so, they suggest that though racism may have a very real *material* effect on black bodies, and, therefore, by extension, on the psyches of those defined as "black," they also suggest that, due to racism's pliability, it also "amputates" the psyches of "whites."[2] I will demonstrate that the insights provided by disability studies, related to those provided by psychoanalysis, allow us to understand the effects of racism as psychologically disabling but also that we must be cautious of attempts to *rehabilitate those (physical) disabilities acquired directly through the violence of racist structures and systems.* The injuries procured via racial or other discriminatory violence cannot be naturalized. Some of my analysis to follow is a cautionary tale as to the reasons why we ought to uncouple the liberatory practices and discourse of disability studies from the ways in which *disabling violence* operates as a means to undercut and literally cut away the autonomies of "raced" and marginalized individuals. If racism is disabling, then the disabilities created through the violence of racism are not in and of themselves disabling even if they are designed to be so; they do not in and of themselves dehumanize, as some of the texts I analyze demonstrate, even if the object of such material violence has for aim to dehumanize. It thus remains imperative to consider gender as an integral aspect of identity impacting agency and autonomy when discussing race and disability within racialized contexts because the resulting effect of gender imbalance, in combination with the racialized state apparatus, at times combines and results in unexpected hegemonic equations.

Post-Raciality, Post-Humanism, and Cyborgs: False Futures?

Two pieces of conceptual art—a calling card, a sculpture—and a high-profile murder/femicide case in South Africa, entailing racial, disability, and gender issues, enable me to begin to suggest that if we cannot properly address the racialized dimensions of history, and our lived realities, the promise of racial harmony—and even dissolution—will remain largely unrealizable. My two conceptual texts are as follows: Adrian Piper's "Calling Card #1" from the "My Calling (Card)" series (1986–1991), and Jeff Koon's "Michael Jackson and Bubbles" (1988) from his series *Banality* (1988). Both these pieces allow me to explore the issue of race as performance and as fungible. This fungibility immediately brings to mind alternative constructs of the body via the post-human (suggested in Koon's piece) and the post-racial via cyborg constructions. The femicide case concerns para-Olympian, Oscar Pistorius, once dubbed the "Blade Runner" in reference both to his running on blade prosthetics but the superhuman quality invested in his athletic achievements such that he resembled the cyborg creations of the futurist film, *Blade Runner*. Found guilty of murdering his live-in girlfriend one Valentine's Day, after having first claimed that he was attempting to defend her from (black South African male) intruders, this example allows me to explore how the legalities surrounding ability in a deeply racially divided nation such as South Africa allow us to understand how the specter of race motivates action and deductions concerning how raced and gendered bodies perform in the material world. The case, when properly understood via gender, race, and disability studies set in the South African context, reveals how the fiction of race masks the violence of legally sanctioned white supremacy. Additionally, this real-life case provides the bridge to the literary texts to be analyzed in this chapter, Octavia Butler's *Kindred* and Pamela Gien's play/performance, *The Syringa Tree*, which both present race as performative, historically situated, and alterable through cultural shifts and exchanges; in both, violated and injured bodies of characters of African descent signal the urgency with which racialized violence must be addressed but also the importance of not looking away from the cause of such injuries. Ultimately, both suggest that cross-cultural af/filiations are the bridge out of such violent histories rather than, as in the Pistorius case, a continued, desperate attempt to both benefit from white privilege and to align disability with lack of agency. But, before arriving at these final text cases, I turn to the art works and the legal case, all of which underscore a need to confront misreadings of "African" bodies that continue to maintain the fiction of "white" versus "black" bodies. The fact that some bodies are neither and might still be read as African has much to teach us.

Scholars of race and representation in cultural studies are, by now, familiar with the subtly confrontational works of Adrian Piper, multimedia and performance artist, who, in 1986 commenced her now iconic "My Calling (Card)" series[3] through which she challenged U.S.-based conceptions of racial intelligibility through her identification with "blackness" (and rejection of racism). Calling Card #1 read, in part: "Dear Friend/I am black./I am sure you did not realize this when you made/laughed at/agreed with that racist remark." Through the business-size calling card, normally meant to provide the recipient with a name and contact information, Piper, described in press releases as a "light-skinned" African American woman, would "out" herself as "black," in the absence of other evidentiary markers, signaling to the ways in which racial identity is both constructed and illusory yet also very much culturally manifest and embedded, both on the part of those to whom race is assigned and for whom race, by design, differentiates between those who have the power to mete out racial type and denigration and those who are subject to such subjugation. Of the closing words of Piper's calling card, Doryun Chong writes: "*My Calling (Card) #1* . . . closes with a twist: 'I regret any discomfort my presence is causing you, just as I am sure you regret the discomfort your racism is causing me.' Irony and melancholia infuse the sentence, reminding us that it is precisely through discomfort that Piper's art cuts into the fortress of our injured consciousness, and such discomfort just might help to cure it." Chong's assessment is especially apropos because it points out that Piper's art is not so much personal as communal, her audience—a precisely American audience—forced to rethink its patterns of racial encoding and differentiation. Piper's embodied self and how it "reads," or is misread/misrecognized societally, serves as an index of how American society assumes racial fixity while denying the permeability of racial categorization. The "calling card" cuts through this false consciousness—to borrow a term from trauma theory and psychoanalysis—revealing the degree to which American society navigates a very long-standing but ignored facet of its traumatic, historical birth via the enslavement and subjugation of the ancestors of its African American population, the period in which stereotypes about what "blackness" signifies was born and then replicated in stereotype and visual codes.

In an attempt to escape stereotypes of black women as "pushy, manipulative, or socially inappropriate"—Piper, rather than address the racist remark she overhears, provides her calling (out) card. A passage in the text that is not normally remarked upon is her declared policy "to assume that white people do not make these remarks, even when they believe there are no black people present, and to distribute this card when they do." Piper's experimental work thus brings into *visibility* the ways in which visual cues (or Kant's "color division") are relied upon for social navigation while also underscoring their instability. Along with Young's idea of "racial thinking" and racial performance as embodied, we should here engage philosopher Linda Martín Alcoff's revisiting of Merleau-Ponty's concept of the "habitual body," which "is the concept of a default position the body assumes in various commonly experienced circumstances that integrates and unifies our movements though a kind of unconscious physical shorthand" (184). Alcoff utilizes the concept "to understand how individuals fall into race-conscious habitual postures in cross-racial encounters" (ibid.) in order to show that "[o]ur experience of habitual perceptions is so attenuated as to skip the stage of conscious interpretation and intent. Indeed, interpretation is the wrong word here: we are simply perceiving" (188).[4] Like Gladwell's "blink" effect or psychological and legal concepts of the "adaptive unconscious," Alcoff's rendering of the "habitual body" in racial theory works to show how perception and interpretation are so narrowly linked as to be confused one for the other. We perceive "others" according to constructed ideas and performances of "race" and "gender" and then "interpret" those bodies' actions based on how we perceive these to perform race or gender adequately, including stereotypically, in ways that satisfy and support the maintenance of power relations. Piper's work, in this sense, disturbs and disrupts easy notions of "race" and of racial embodiment, following Young, and others, to reveal the body as a terrain upon which to contest and reject given ideas of racial identity. She tests the means by which individuals or groups "read" herself/others and stage encounters or confrontations in which the person interpreting is made to face her/his *own* racial *habitus* at the same time as she asserts her belonging to a kinship group (those of African descent) otherwise racialized. In the simple assertion, "I am black," on the calling card, Piper makes clear her af/filiative alliances, not based on phenotype but inheritance. We do not need "proof" of genealogy (to provide it would be to doubt the force of the kinship alliance itself and to succumb to racialist patterns); it is made manifest in Piper's deceptively simple self-defining assertion. Her card also suggests that, if race is performative, and not visual, as we have been erroneously led to believe and re-encode, it is constantly subject to alteration and reformation; culturally, however, kinship affiliation is not so easily dispensed with. Although my intent in this chapter is not yet to broach the component elements of autochthonomy itself (this is shown in subsequent chapters), but rather to demonstrate how we must first understand and dismantle racial constructs through an understanding of their effects through time and their performativity, it is nonetheless the case that one can argue that Piper's affilliative performance could also be termed an af/filiative autochthonomy, simply because the performance exceeds racial habitus and persists in a zone of cultural exchange that racism itself cannot breach, and, furthermore, that recognizes itself as belonging to a network of African-descended cultures to which Piper freely inscribes her membership ("I am black."). In more recent work, dated 2008, Piper, in fact, consolidates this membership by tracing her genealogical routes to Catahoula Parish, Louisiana, to a white male slave owner, Philip Piper (54 in 1860) and his slave, Nelly Piper (35 in 1859). Nelly was mother to Philip's four children, ages 15, 12, 8, and 2; and paid Philip Piper $1,000 to purchase her children's freedom. Piper and Nelly subsequently married, in Pennsylvania, in 1860; Philip Piper, notes the artist, is listed as "colored" at his death in 1879, and Nelly's children, his former slaves, inherited his estate. The work, the last to be included in the retrospective, "Concepts and Intuitions, 1965–2016," testifies to the importance of place, inheritance, and genealogy in establishing af/filiation. It also reverses our sense of what it might mean to be autochthonomous, suggesting that freedom from racialization might also give way to freedom to af/filiate; Philip Piper's crossing the color line from white slave owner into an interracial marriage from which he would emerge as "colored" on his deathbed, suggests that his own identification shifted over time and gave way to a new understanding of freedom (from "race"), which Piper carries forward.

Jeff Koons's iconic pop art sculpture, in this respect, is equally though differently disturbing as it appears to reflect a desire to transcend race, so that the African American pop icon it depicts, Michael Jackson, becomes the epitome of passing into a color-blind future. Some critics and viewers of Jeff Koons's 1988, three-dimensional ceramic, "Michael Jackson & Bubbles," assume that the piece is simply ludic and a reflection of 1980s American pop decadence, while others see in the "cold, shiny surface of their snow-white faces . . . rather disturbing issues of race, gender and sexuality," a depiction of a "cultural icon whom we know to be a black man [who] has come to more closely resemble a white woman" (JCB).[5] Such a comment also conflates Jackson's perceived effeminacy as a gender crossing that cannot be readily detached from its perceived racial passing. When the piece was put up for auction by Sotheby's in 2001, at an estimated worth of between three and four million dollars, the accompanying curatorial write-up suggested that the piece has most often been perceived as the representation of the icon as "post-human"—thereby transcending racial/gender categories, and that its layers of lacquer and two-tone color of white/gold are meant to suggest an "opaque" meaning that frustrates any attempts at interpretation. If, like much of Koons's work, the Michael Jackson sculpture is ludic, how are we to know from where the piece extracts its humor—Jackson's well-documented eccentricities, or the fact that Koons has pushed Jackson's self-representation to its limit, as white/nonblack, and ultimately as de-sexualized?[6] If, on the other hand, the piece is read as an homage and post-human depiction, then it represents Jackson has having successfully outwitted social norms. Misreading or misinterpretation reveals the intransigency of race and the viewer's refusal to read Jackson as anything other than "black" while suspending interpretation or accepting the opaqueness of the piece renders both the race and the gender/sexuality of the subject beside the point. But does it follow that if Jackson is no longer physically readable as "black," that he is any less of African descent? The trajectory of his career, despite the changes in his physical appearance and representations, would suggest that one does not follow the other, that culture rather than social categorization supersedes. Koons, however, suggested at the time that he depicted Jackson as he did as an homage.[7] He sought to elevate Jackson to a demigod by depicting him as an Italianate statue; by doing so, he suggests, perhaps unwittingly, that this elevation consists of not-becoming-black. Koons, as Jackson, remains "white" while appropriating the markers of Jackson's eccentricities, perceived to be part and parcel of his musical genius; this is a form of mimesis that evades contextualization within African aesthetics. Koons's depiction is an interpretation with a racialized dimension inasmuch as he is able to project onto Jackson a perception that is at once ennobling as it is de-racializing in such a way that white supremacist visions of color-blindness are unwittingly integrated into the piece. As such, viewers of the piece are not so much confronted with the problematics of Jackson's "color" transformation in real life as they are with an affirmation of that transformation as positive because it appears to lead one away from "blackness," in terms of skin color, and into a futuristic color-blindness, which is overwhelmingly literally, alabaster white. Whether read positively or negatively, both interpretations suggest a desire to transcend race, to aspire to the "post-human," while sublimating both race and sexuality in a packaging that nonetheless remains identifiably European, if not white, and nominally heterosexual. In Piper's case, the *disruption* of racial habitus serves to underscore the latent presence of autochthonomy while, in Koons's case, the depiction of a subject of African descent as post-human leads to a non-identificatory appropriation. Yet, there continues to be intellectual investment in post-human, cyborg realities as the way out of racialization and its attendant social hierarchies rather than toward cultural affirmation.

We have, in the real-life case of "cyborg" para-Olympian Oscar Pistorius and his slaying of girlfriend Reeva Steenkamp in South Africa, February 14, 2013, a test case for such an aspirational identity in a context saturated with racial dynamics: at the time of his arrest and in the ensuing trial, Pistorius maintained that he killed Steenkamp mistakenly, thinking that there was an intruder in their fortified compound in an elite, presumably all-white enclave in Pretoria, South Africa. Though unstated, the implication in such a defense was that Pistorius was defending himself and Steenkamp from a presumed, South African, black, male intruder. Pistorius's defense rested on the notion of South Africa's urban violence (with one of the highest rates of murder and rape in the world—against black women), and, more particularly, though unstated, an ambiguous threat of black male violence turned against whites of the dominant classes (for which no statistical evidence exists). The Pistorius story is further complicated by the ways in which the paralympic athlete-embodied self was reconfigured from a *cyborgian* plus-ultra male, defying all conceivable odds as a childhood, double below-knee amputee, whose athletic skills were on par with, and may even have had the potential to exceed, with the assistance of prostheses, able-bodied athletes. Disability scholar, Kirsty Liddiard suggests in her article, "Reproducing Pistorius," that the "story" of the Pistorius trial comes to rest on the cultural production of two "characters": "the Supercrip and the imagined (black) intruder" (1). For Liddiard, Pistorius's construction as a cyborg, or more-than-human, is as fictive as is that of the (nonexistent) black male intruder. She suggests that we examine these figures through the lens of intersectionality in order to properly diagnose where and when the victim, Steenkamp, comes to disappear from the story. Liddiard critiques the social construction of the "supercrip" because it creates a mythical norm for people with disabilities: "Rooted in neoliberal and capitalist ideologies, the 'supercrip' valorizes individual effort, human resolve, self-control, competition, and success, only celebrating disability and impairment which can be normalized through exceptionalism" (2). She concludes: "Pistorius's freakdom is sanctioned and celebrated in dis/ableist cultures only because it disassociates him from dominant meanings of disability and impairment" (ibid.). Clare Harvey similarly argues about the case, in a 2015 article entitled, "What's Disability Got to Do with It?" that "non-disabled society was reassured as individuals ceased to be challenged about their own potential fallibility and bodily vulnerability" (4). As such, then, Pistorius's presentation as supra-human, or as a cyborg, appeared to engage a non-ableist discourse by celebrating his accomplishments (and his hybridized body) while actually subscribing to an ableist discourse of exceptionalism. Or, put more simply, as Peter Bansel writes in his 2014 article, "Assembling Oscar, Assembling South Africa, Assembling Affects," on journalist Adam Perry's *Time Magazine* cover story of the Pistorius case (with accompanying cover photo by South African photographer, Pieter Hugo): "When Oscar's prostheses are on his body he is assembled as a strong and powerful sportsman who has heroically overcome his disability; and when his prostheses are not on his body he is re/assembled as fearful and vulnerable, needing to shoot to protect himself and his girlfriend precisely *because* of his disability" (2). Assemblages, in this case, can run counterproductively and are not necessarily conduits for righting moral or social wrongs. As Bansel writes, with reference to Perry's *Time* article: "[in Perry's] assemblage of the event, Oscar (and his body with or without legs/prostheses) stands in the place of white South Africans who are vulnerable and need to protect themselves against the threat of the dissolute black other (when she is mistaken for an intruder). Importantly, Oscar does not say that he feared the intruder was black—but Perry's assemblage of the event as a racialized problem of post-apartheid South Africa means that Oscar does not need to say it—it is taken for granted" (42). Bansel underscores Perry's use of a colonial era fortification, the laager, an "enclosure [that] formed a defensive perimeter used by Afrikaner/whites for protection from black South Africans" (ibid.), to illustrate Pistorius's mind-set, seemingly without irony.

I would argue that Pistorius (the man and the constructed image) relied on a white optic that self-consciously excluded "race" while relying both on the celebration of a "new," post-Mandela, inclusive Africa, *and* Pistorius's heritage as a descendant of Afrikaners who benefited from the colonial, settler history of his predecessors. With regard to the latter point, Liddiard contends that the assumptions built around the "black intruder" defense "rest firmly on historical tropes of the indigenous black man as savage, violent, and criminal and the white settler as productive (thus wealthy), civilized and heroic (a heroism exacerbated by disability in this case)" (3). Pistorius, and his defense team, suddenly abandoned the "supercrip" discourse, which had surrounded Pistorius for decades, and subscribed to a more banal version of ableism, that of the incapable disabled body—incapable because of a bodily absence (or unenhanced feature; Pistorius had removed his leg "extensions" or prostheses at the time of the shooting) and was thereby *morally incapable of doing harm.*[8]

In this discourse, the disabled, white body is also bereft of consciousness: it can react only to (the fear of further) bodily harm. Doesn't this line of thinking eerily mirror the recent litany of defenses predominantly white police officers guilty of slaying unarmed African Americans have used in recent years? As Bansel opines, the Pistorius case can be read through the lens of affect theory, when affect is read "not [as] a personal feeling" but "as the effectuation of a power of the pack that throws the self into upheaval and makes it real" (Deleuze and Guattari qtd. in Bansel). Liddiard contends that focusing on South Africa's culture of violence "ghettoises South African cultures in ways that mask that misogyny and violence are global problems as well as socially, economically, and politically entrenched ones" (3); it also masks that that violence has historically been perpetrated by white male bodies in power, not by black ones. She goes on to add, however that "the disabled male (regardless of impairment, sexuality, age, or class) is (re)produced in a peculiar dis/ableist binary: weak, dependent, non-violent, and safe; and yet bitter, caustic, revengeful, and angry (anger positioned as emerging from an assumed resentment of disability). In Pistorius's case, his well-constructed *overcoming* and *becoming* (from impairment to sporting hero) and struggling against (assumed) adversity affirms him as of an inherently *good* character" (4).[9] During the trial, she notes, Pistorius is presented, and presents himself as fragile and sickly ("he whimpers, he places his head in hands, he wretches, and he vomits," (ibid.), so that "Pistorius' post-human masculine self is being presented ultimately, as human, emphasized in the ways in which it is experiencing trauma" (5; see also, Harvey 5). Ironically, though not noted by Liddiard, Pistorius comes to embody the *white male fragile self*, which has been discussed in the United States as part of the discourse of disavowal of state violence against (male) African Americans—one neither capable of understanding racial stratification, or of benefiting from it, and, even less, capable of harming, but always vulnerable to harm. Such belief stems from colonial discourse and persists. As Liddiard contends, disability "reappears" in the form of "dis/ableism" in media discourse surrounding the case, not limited to reducing the disabled body to incapacity of non-agency, but also as reflecting a damaged psyche, an always already dysfunctional individual. This "dysfunction" may humanize

Pistorius for jurists and a lay audience on which the defense depends for Pistorius's exoneration (not, apparently for having killed Steenkamp in cold blood, but for the "reasonable" fear of the nonexistent black male intruder) but does not de-racialize him; in fact, the "trauma" he is depicted as suffering extends from an imagined history of struggle against a fierce nature which includes the (black) natives of the land.[10] In the public trial, then, Pistorius, prostheses on but hidden, stripped of legendary status, attempts to win his case by appealing to an antiquated notion of decrepitude associated with the disabled body, while the court of public opinion (not the prosecution, which focuses on Pistorius's actions regardless of embodiment, and the cost to the victim for his actions) resorts to an entwined, and equally outdated discourse of disability linked to criminality.

Dis/ableism, then, returns to liberate the fallen hero. Liddiard, does not, however, fully uncover the raced implications of this resurgence in her article. Her purpose, as a disability studies scholar who is also disabled, is to uncover the ways in which ultimately ableist discourses serve Pistorius before and after his fall from grace. The complicity of the media in this, and of the defense, according to Liddiard, is to cover up the banality of violence against women as a global problem, to which Steenkamp also falls victim. This aspect of the case, though unmentioned by Liddiard, was spectacularly conveyed in the defense's collapsing of Pistorius with the figure of his victim when his counsel "compared Pistorius' disability as similar to the experience of an unending abuse of a woman by her husband" (Harvey 301); thus, despite evidence as to Pistorius's history of a violent temper, of encounters with police for domestic violence calls with regard to Steenkamp, an ableist discourse serves to both obscure the victim of the crime, and to replace the victim's body with Pistorius's: his disability, in this scenario, absolves him of criminality but also removes him from the signs of his privilege— "white" and male. Accompanying Pistorius's fall from grace following the killing of Steenkamp, is a modification of the disability discourse that had lionized Pistorius so that this discourse became both explicitly ableist and covertly misogynist as the former covers the latter. As Harvey suggests, "[p]eople with disabilities need to be recognised as fully human rather than as particularities with possibly different moral and psychological principles" (302); this means also recognizing that a person with a disability is no more or less likely than someone without a disability of being criminally minded. Other factors, especially sociocultural ones, come into play. In this case, what has been primarily overlooked is the role of gender and race in Pistorius's identity formation and the role these played in the incident of Valentine's day, 2013.

If we consider that the laager in Pistorius's life was not constituted at the moment in which he discharged his firearm at the closed door of this bathroom, thereby killing his unarmed girlfriend on the other side, in an attempt to defend both their bodies from an unseen, imagined, black male intruder, we have to determine where and when that laager was constituted. Adam Perry utilizes the image of the laager to suggest an ongoing need for white defense from black bodily harm, in complete ignorance of history, that is, the fact that the laager, whether in the African context or in the American, is a romantic notion of protection from harm from indigenous cultures which are transfigured as "uncivilized" and "violent" while simultaneously being plundered and violated by colonizing forces. We must, then, re-situate the laager from frontier discourse into its legal manifestation—not at the time of the trial but before it. In truth of fact, the laager of white (South African or American) culture is the letter of law. In the context of South African jurisprudence, Pistorius's white, middle-to upper-class, male corporeality supersedes whatever social vulnerability his disability may have occasioned. This is so for the simple fact that in South Africa, under apartheid (unlike in the United States, and perhaps elsewhere), *white, disabled* bodies constituted a *privileged* class *under the letter of the law.*

In an article published in 2013, entitled "Oscar Pistorius and the Melancholy of Intersectionality," Leslie Swartz has been the only disability scholar to point out the very tangible rights and privileges granted whites with disability under South African apartheid. Swartz's article title points out the difficulty of assuming a smooth trajectory of intersectionality between discrete categories of underrepresentation or "otherness-ness." Noting the ways in which the absence of emphasis on disability (rather than race and gender) in the South African media discussion of the case is erroneously read as "the success of mainstreaming," Swartz points to the entanglements of gender and race *privilege* that obtain here, noting that "the case reveals rather than obscures some difficult realities about disability and intersectionality in South Africa" (1159). I argue that the reverse emphasis in U.S. treatments of the case signals a similar reality, one in which racism has more and more been likened to having a disability (while ignoring the fact that people of color may also be disabled and suffer a double jeopardy of marginalization as raced and disabled subjects societally and under the law) and one in which disabled white bodies have been relegated to second-class status similar to that of African Americans. U.S.-based scholars have thus been, by and large, unable to reconcile their own reality—one in which race and disability have almost become synonymous in terms of states of liminality, with a context in which disability was not, by and large, subject to white supremacist logic in terms of legal apparatus. Whereas historically, in the United States, whites with disabilities acquired subclass status equal to that of racialized, economically depressed, or otherwise neglected sectors of the society who could not gain access to civic representation or various societal rights and services (for example, regarding education or health care), in apartheid South Africa, Swartz notes that "[t]he history of provision of services for disabled people in South Africa, as is true for all of other aspects of South African life, is saturated with issues of racial inclusion and exclusion, privilege and oppression." Tangibly, in terms of goods, services, and access rights, this means the following:

> One of the key reasons why South Africa, almost uniquely on the African continent, provides social security in the form of cash transfers for disabled people, whereas there is no general unemployment or poverty grant in South Africa, is that initially under apartheid disability grants were designed to support the interests of white disabled people.

The point of such policies was to "ensure [white disabled people] a standard of living better than that of their black counterparts" (Swartz 1159). This effectively means that white disabled bodies were given rights and privileges above that of black South Africans, whether abled or disabled, since, under apartheid, as under slavery in the United States, black South Africans had no rights that could supersede that of a white South African, able-bodied or disabled: the objective of such laws was to restore disabled bodies to perceived, social wholeness, to have more or less equal access to the quality of life of their *racial* equals—i.e., other whites. Swartz, then, complicates the facile ways in which intersectionality can be mobilized to uncritically align under-presented groups under the same umbrella showing that it is, rather, the intersectionality of race, gender, and *privilege* that were the elements that combined to make possible the tragic circumstances of Steenkamp's death (the forgotten *actual* victim in this racialized hall of mirrors).

Curiously, given the ongoing attention to the case in popular culture and its recycling in academic discussions of cyborgs in theories that focus on the post-human, Swartz's discussion has been taken up on these issues almost nowhere. This omission is not so difficult to understand, however, when we consider that the Pistorius case stands as national allegory in South Africa and that therein lies the potential connective tissue to discourses on race in the United States, where a *national* discussion on race is ongoing but largely obscured by a splitting along racial lines (resembling the "splitting" that psychologists and social critics claim occurs in the able-bodied confronted with the corporeality of the disabled), by which race as a national (his)story is recoded as a "story" (or reality) belonging *only* to people of color, especially African Americans (who represent less than 10 percent of the society). But, if Bansel is correct in asserting that the "assemblage" of Pistorius's rise and fall from grace is "told as a story of nationhood and citizenship [that] also assembles the reader within the spatial and temporal frame of their own sense of nationhood or citizenship *wherever they find themselves*" (44), then it would seem that Octavia Butler achieves a similar national allegory in *Kindred* wherein the time-travel device serves to confront readers with slavery as both a white/black construction that "assembles" citizenship and her readers' place within the nation's social-historical space in ways that also reflect on the limits of corporeality as an effect of gender, race, and privilege. That she does so through a complex vision of bodies that become disabled in the process of accessing the national construction of valorized identity speaks to her attempt to *disconnect* disability from discourses of underrepresentation (disabled bodies exist across all social categories) while instantiating disability as potentially productive, but not constitutively so, when the result of racial violence. As Saidiya Hartman asserts, segregationists viewed "black citizenship as a foreign appendage grafted onto the national body [to bespeak] the anxieties about amalgamation attendant to the enfranchisement of blacks" (165). In Butler, in contradistinction, the severing by amputation of a black woman's arm reveals the *cost* of amalgamation for people of African descent within the national body: if segregationists once viewed the presence of black bodies in the body politic as an appendage, for people of African descent themselves, becoming such an appendage required sacrificial, punitive, amputation of self and culture.

At the beginning of this section, I suggested that two conceptual art pieces (Koons's, "Michael Jackson & Bubbles" and Piper's "Calling Card Series") provide evidence of racial thinking as a social and psychological effect that can, by being elevated to consciousness (via scrutiny of the art object or the very physical act of confrontation in Piper's case), be contested, while also affirming African Diasporic identification as a nonracial effect (related to kinship, culture, or both). Beyond this, both pieces suggest that belonging to a particular cultural group can be based on something other than skin color (since Piper cannot be "read" as black but identifies as of African descent), but also that it cannot simply be appropriated (as Koons attempts to do with Jackson, who, despite his changing appearance remained associated with black cultural forms and aesthetics) without necessarily replicating the shallow ground upon which racial differentiation is based: it is more than skin deep. The Pistorius case demonstrates further that intersectionality through perceived membership in a marginalized group does not ensure cross-racial identification such that the effects of racialization become diminished because racialization is, indeed, the result of social technologies (as Weheliye has noted), such as the law and judicial systems. Indeed, the Pistorius case stands as a sobering example of how categories of race and gender can be utilized as markers of privilege to escape marginalization despite the appearance of membership in a marginalized class (in this case, disability). When legal codes serve as an escape valve from disenfranchisement but do not free those targeted for liminality, then it becomes clearer how kinship is itself abandoned in favor of membership in classes privileged by law.

Kinship, then, true affiliation, cannot be synonymous with race since societal race is truly only skin-deep but has real material value when legally encoded; kinship, as Piper's calling card calls into legibility, is a matter of af/filiation achieved through cultural knowledge, understanding, and exchange; as such, it is a feature of what I have been terming *autochthonomy* and provides the ground for exchanges within *lakou* consciousness. It provokes a redrawing of association and identification away from racialization. Kinship, as I will show in the following sections, then, is another avenue we should feel compelled to explore in thinking-through more productive de-racializing, sociopolitical arrangements. Kinship can, however, be useful only if it is used to de-hierarchize *and* denaturalize racial categorizations or, indeed, do away with them altogether.

Phantom Limbs: Kinship, Racial Performance, and Liberation

In South Africa, the Pistorius case demonstrates that the real-life confrontation with altered/tech-bodies in a racialized social landscape brings to light the ways in which the cyborg is a romantic/utopic figure that is tied to a notion of a color-blind future (much like Koons's sculpture of Jackson), which cannot lead to concrete social, restorative transformation[11] because the cyborg fails to be understood as already belonging to the racialized past from which it emerges while no strategies have evolved to dismantle that racialized history. Crucial to this discussion is a consideration of the presence of the "phantom limb" as a marker of that which cyborg bodies point to but cannot bring into being: an altered landscape, a disambiguation from social mappings. But, uncovering that disambiguation could, as Haraway begins to suggest, present a *space for regeneration*—not as she supposes, of a limb, but of something new in its absence, a social space that has always been present but which is unrecognized leaving only a trace of itself behind; the recognition of its present absence, not its replacement, provides the avenue for regenerative potentialities that are neither utopic nor hopeful, simply something more, not other, that the phantom limb gestures toward without being able to perform its movement. The phantom limb, then, could initiate a psychic shift or instantiation that requires loss for its activation and, in that loss, opens up a space for the recovery of untold futures. More importantly, Fanon tellingly utilized the term *amputation* symbolically, to signify the *loss* of subject identity/agency, to signify the impact of racism as a form of bodily violation, a dismemberment of sorts, psychic in dimension, qualifying the degree to which the *phantom limb* could be read as either utopian or as liberating.

My latter contention is aligned with, if not wholly emergent from, developments in assemblage theory, differently articulated across philosophy, postcolonial, race, and social theory to advance both ideas pertinent to identity formation and geography—more precisely, spatiality. Taken primarily from the work of philosopher Gilles Deleuze, who defined *assemblages* as "wholes characterized by relations of exteriority" (DeLanda 10), such theorists argue for the malleability of subject identities across ideological and physical structures. DeLanda ventures that assemblages come into play as a challenge to the Hegelian concept of "relations of interiority," by which wholeness of the subject is established through an organic wholeness or reciprocity between agents and structures that "mutually constitute one another dialectically" (ibid.). The theory of assemblages suggests that the component parts of any subject can be altered by virtue of their interaction with other assemblages, other structures or entities than those that constitute it, or which delimit its boundaries. Alexander Weheliye, within race/diaspora studies, finds theories of assemblage that take into consideration gender and race identities particularly helpful for the project of reconstituting social relations: "Assemblages are inherently productive, entering into polyvalent becomings to produce and give expression *to previously nonexistent realities*, thoughts, bodies, affects, spaces, actions, ideas, and so on" (46). Finding consonance between assemblage theory, Stuart Hall's concept of "articulation" in black cultural studies, and Hortense Spillers's "theorization of the flesh" via psychoanalytic studies, Weheliye argues further that the trajectory of enslaved black bodies "gives birth to a cluster of classifying assemblages that stands at the center of modernity" (50–51). In other words, we can read the "black body," which is essentially an ideological construct that has currency only when bodies encounter each other in social spaces and through institutions (legal, political, social) that enable the "marking" of bodies to accord or withhold them of social rights, in order to allow for the borders of certain bodies (black and female) to be traversed and violated materially. These social assemblages, which, as DeLeuze and Guattari explain, are the product of linguistic, machinistic, and territorial exchanges, but (as Weheliye argues) result in the forcible disappearance of black bodies (something which most assemblage theorists do not address) but, inasmuch as these assemblages conspire to disappear the black body, can also serve to recast the black body as presence and agent. My purpose is not, as Weheliye, Gilroy, and others have done, to recast the dis-investiture of enslaved bodies of their humanity as the primal scene of modernity (though I concur that it is also this), but to agree with these scholars that whether we call this stripping of the black body of its humanity a product of postcolonial (read historical) ideology, of performativity, or of assemblages, each prism suggests mechanisms that can be reversed, regenerated, and recoded. Instead, I argue that, taken with aspects of performance/embodiment theory, within which I situate Haraway's cyborg, when weaved through the works of women of African descent, provides the means by which to think through the latter's concept of "regeneration" (as opposed to a rebirth, which can never take place since rebirth would imply a complete annihilation of the previously constituted subject) as an expression of their autochthonomy, embedded within historically situated genealogies of kinship.

Within her cyborg construct, Haraway contends that feminist women of color's writing and political consciousness paved the way toward the cyborg reality she enunciates; within her manifesto, she argues that she, and others, missed an opportunity to grasp how women of color's writing—and specifically that authored by women of African descent—contested cyborg realities by demonstrating, through their imaginings, that newly configured identities that stretch the boundaries of the human remained constrained by the failure to redraw those of race and class. Haraway cites Chela Sandoval extensively:

Chela Sandoval, from a consideration of specific historical moments in the formation of the new political voice called women of color, has theorized a hopeful model of political identity called "oppositional consciousness," born of the skills for reading webs of power by those refused stable membership in the social categories of race, sex, or class. *Women of color*, a name contested at its origins by those whom it would incorporate, as well as a historical consciousness marking systematic breakdown of all the signs of Man in "Western" traditions, constructs a kind of postmodernist identity out of otherness, difference, and specificity. This postmodernist identity is fully political, whatever might be said about other possible postmodernisms. Sandoval's oppositional consciousness is about contradictory locations and heterochronic calendars, not about relativisms and pluralisms. Sandoval emphasizes the lack of any essential criterion for identifying who is a woman of color. She notes that the definition of the group has been by conscious appropriation of negation. ("A Cyborg Manifesto" 17–18)

Thus, Haraway concludes that women of color are in themselves a sort of cyborg assemblage: "This identity marks out a self-consciously constructed space that cannot affirm the capacity to act on the basis of natural identification, but only on the basis of conscious coalition, of affinity, of political kinship" (18), forming the basis for the futuristic cyborg that might move us into a more egalitarian present. Ironically, as is evident in the essay itself, despite this awareness of her models, Haraway failed to imagine how her own cyborg figure might be "raced" or failed to "de-racialize" her in such a way that the figure would not always already be read as "race-less," that is, as nominally "white." Consequently, as comfort with cyborg identities has grown, creating a space for altered and tech-bodies, it has been accompanied with a simultaneous *discomfort* with *ethnically* hybridized bodies, or bodies that can cross socially erected racial demarcations. Haraway, anticipating arguments now permeating animal and post-humanist studies wrote: "Perhaps, ironically, we can learn from our fusions with animals and machines how not to be Man, the embodiment of Western logos" (382),[12] but failed to anticipate the reproduction of the Enlightenment's fetishization of whiteness as its basis for the category of the human.

In advocating for a telos of "regeneration," imaged in the regrown limb of an injured, amputated salamander, Haraway concludes that the ultimate aim for the cyborg is to "require *regeneration, not rebirth*, and the possibilities for our reconstitution include the utopian dream of the hope for a monstrous world without gender" (386), echoing Fanon's call for the signification of the amputated limb and also what it leaves in its wake, not only absence but possibility. Haraway moves away from Fanon's masculinist discourse, through women of color's feminist approaches, to a future regenerated without gendered form but not formless. Haraway's "regenerative" cyborg is productive when taken *together* with women of African descent's imaginings of a future in which the past is reimagined and the bodily delimitations of the subject are reconstituted in a function of a past realized through a self-conscious, *performed* historicity and not through ideological constructions that attempt to efface historically gendered and "raced" realities, which I here reconceptualize as not so much raced as culturally embedded.

In Octavia Butler's *Kindred*, set in 1970s Los Angeles as well as the late-1800s antebellum South, the main character, Dana, is an African American woman who is called back in time by a predecessor, a great-great-great-grandfather, a white man, who inherits a plantation and its slave population. In the novel, Butler utilizes the imagery of amputation with stark effect. In the novel's prologue, Dana tells us: "I lost an arm on my last trip home. My left arm" (9). She also clarifies that this physical loss is accompanied by a psychic loss and a loss of self when she reflects upon her time-travel and its ultimate, violent ending with the rupture of her very body: Maybe I'm just like a victim of robbery or rape or something—a victim who survives, but who doesn't feel safe anymore" (17). Critic Therí Pickens suggests that scholars have overlooked Butler's use of disability in her works as a vehicle for productive transformation, that "Dana's missing arm literally writes her experience of enslavement on her body and connects the ability to remember with the experience of dismemberment" (4). Countering over-readings of the text that suggest that Dana's lost arm points to the nation's "brokenness," Pickens asserts that "the refusal to deal with the inherent inequality in the national narrative denies the human variance of disability and the social forces that create and sustain it" (5). Pickens thus wants to read the disability that Dana inherits from her violent collision with the realities of enslavement not as lack but as gain, thus applying a disability studies reading of her amputation as productive. She contends that in a work like *Kindred*, "Butler does not rely on disability solely to begin her texts. Rather, disability suffuses the novel" (9). The complication with such a utopic reading of the text is that it threatens to ignore the violence by which Dana comes by her disability and what the phantom limb indexes. Like Fanon's black man, Dana experiences a severing from self. The difference in Dana's text is that the violence she encounters and which dismembers her is part of the process of recovering the truth of a shared national history. If, prior to her time-travel, Dana believed that she understood herself as an African American woman, understood American history, overcame that history through her marriage to a white American male, and achieved freedom through the "wholeness" of her physical self and conjoining with a white "other," the wrenching back in time disturbs this satisfied sense of wholeness, cultural stability, and agency. In this sense, Pickens's appeal for reading disability as an important category of identification to be added to race and gender that reveals another reality is instructive, but when read through theories of assemblage and performance, it falls short. This is so because if we read neither race nor gender as stable categories, we are forced to do the same with disability.

Rather than read Dana's amputation as necessarily productive (as a disability, identity politics would impel us to), we might read it as multivalent—as producing a reality without which the future would remain devoid of potential for a true integration of the realities of the past in ways both liberating and transformative—but also one in which loss, of innocence, in particular, for all subjects, is impossible to ignore. More to the point, it is not so much Dana's ultimate disability that should be underscored, but the *process* of the accumulative violence by which she loses her limb. It counters a late 1800s reconstruction discourse, during which segregationist views were debated and denounced as based upon fictive racial lines erected "to perpetuate relations of mastery and subservience" (Hartman 165). Dana loses a part of herself that the novel constructs as already false and, in turn, gains the reality that enslavement imposed upon black bodies, especially female ones: loss of bodily integrity. Dana is configured as *already* a product of the feared future, and thus her loss of limb represents a partial loss of the otherness and blight that the nation has grafted onto black bodies. The lost limb symbolizes that physical disintegration Fanon so well describes in his reconstruction of the psychic effects of racist oppression upon "black" subjectivity; but it also describes an *a priori material, physical loss* suffered by the enslaved themselves, impelled by those who had the power to dominate and injure. As Dana explains about her time-travel, "Another fact: the boy was the focus of my travels—perhaps the cause" (24), "maybe he was one of my ancestors. Maybe he was my several times great grandfather" (28), and ultimately: "Rufus' fear of death calls me to him, and my own fear of death sends me home" (48). Across time, the characters are involved in *a process of becoming*, of understanding who they are, through a death drive, a fear that cements their kinship yet that fear is inverted; fear on the part of the white ancestor brings his progeny back to him, *into* memory/history, while fear of violence at the hand of her ancestors, its recognition and refusal, are what ultimately liberates Dana back to the future and away from the violence inherent in and inherited through this intimate blood tie. Despite the reversals of "raced" identities that Butler thus effects, this process is part and parcel of an African Diasporic autochthonomy through which kinlessness is eschewed in favor of tracing *through* the horrors of slavery's genealogies of kinship *across* otherwise discrete racial lines.

The intricacy of the way in which the process of time-travel functions in the narrative is Butler's way of testifying to the violent nature of kinship forged via the institution of slavery; the dependency of the characters upon each other, forged through an institutionalized fear of the other that is negotiated through affective sentiment is another layer of Butler's complex reconstruction of the effects of enslavement upon the present and future. Sentiment, as Saidiya Hartman has shown, was a means by which the ills of slavery were contained and belied. As she writes: "No less paramount in this conscription of blackness is the work of affect in muting violence and concealing injury"

(168). Though Dana appears to be generally aware of her ancestor's past, she is mired in a complacent memory complicit with a national discourse that has actively worked to conceal the injuries of the past. More to the point, as Achille Mbembe, has demonstrated in his work on the postcolony, the "conviviality" built into colonizer/colonized relations, relations comparable to that of the slave/master, only served to mask a violent venality of relations. Dana becomes acutely aware of how enslavement entailed a construction of identity suffused with fear and how the violence of cross-racial relations reified these identities. In another way, then, Dana's loss of limb represents a shedding of these constructed identities and how losing even these false identities must occur for a restorative justice to take place. In other words, I am suggesting that Butler hints at the fact that the recovery of history will compel reconstructing a sense of the meaning of "black" and "white" identities in the present and necessarily reconstruct the past through our *very bodies* and that this, too, is a feature of African Diasporic autochthonomy: such consciousness thus necessarily redraws cultural and racial mappings in view of a larger world perspective that integrates both.

Indeed, *Kindred's* importance with respect to my current investigation is the work it performs in exposing how racial and gendered readings are produced and performed within social temporalities while simultaneously affirming the presence of a consciousness navigating these temporalities with a sense of autonomy and historical situatedness. The novel uncovers the ways in which black and white bodies perform constructed roles that shift across time, but also plays with readers' ready-made constructions of gendered and raced identities and how these might interfere with their ability to transform such identities in the future. When I first taught the novel, in the deep South (Baton Rouge, Louisiana), to a mostly African American classroom of students, which included one or two white American students in a predominantly white university setting, most students assumed that Kevin, Dana's husband, named on the first page of the novel, was also African American. When I asked why, most said they assumed that a black author would be writing about black characters. When pressed, they revealed that Kevin could not be other than black because of the ways in which we are introduced to him in the first page of the novel. Butler writes: "When the police released Kevin, he came to the hospital and stayed with me so that I would know I hadn't lost him too," and "They began asking me about Kevin. Their words seemed to blur together at first, and I paid little attention. After a while, though, I replayed them and suddenly realized that these men were trying to blame Kevin for 'hurting' my arm" (9). Many readers, whether white or black, automatically associate criminality with black maleness—a social construction—and, reading these passages, assume that Dana must be subject to domestic violence. A chapter or so later, while Dana experiences one of her first returns to the past, she reveals to her white ancestor (then a child), and to readers, that Kevin is white, and the rest of the novel is the story of the process by which she lost her arm to a wall, that is, to the past—in trying to return to the present (which always suggests a possible forgetting that the loss of limb makes impossible). Why would Butler deliberately play with readers' racial mappings? Why would she pair an African American protagonist with a white male partner? Why would she let readers know of this loss of bodily integrity from the outset? I suggest that Butler does all three in order to reconfigure the *reader's* racial mappings and reveal them as *raced performances in time.* She intentionally pairs Dana with a white male partner to question the implied reader's racialized expectations but also to reveal how racial constructs affect white Americans as well; furthermore, she does so to compel a rethinking of the notion of blood ties and kinship, of what Hartman has otherwise called "networks of affiliation" (59). Finally, I contend that the revelation of bodily integrity at the novel's opening is less about the author's desire to have readers understand slavery than it is about her desire to invoke race and race relations as a temporal process that can be corrected only through other interventionist processes, in this case, that of lakou consciousness reflected in Dana's ability to cut through these processes via an understanding of herself as an un-subjugated Subject, as one contained within a history she can herself define related to the realities of similarly raced, African-descended subjects.

Butler imagines a process, time-travel, through which racial identity is contested as well as the historical and social contexts that seem to mire these identities as fixed and uncontestable. Dana is constantly negotiating her subject identity as she travels, as she comes to understand that, "Somehow, my travels crossed time as well as distance" (9), but she is never adrift, fragmented, or kinless. Butler thus effectively makes use of time-travel as a means by which to have her readers reimagine race and race relations as a construct or series of temporal performances that then compel a rethinking of modes of subjectivity as described by Kelly Oliver, a mode of subjectivity that I believe points to the space of autochthonomy. Oliver suggests, via the work of Judith Butler and Jacques Derrida, "no two iterations of social norms are the same because of the differences in their temporal positionality." And, as Ta-Nehesi Coates writes to his son in his recent memoir *Between the World and Me* (2015), "You can no more be black like I am black than I could be black like your grandfather was" (37). To be "black," or any other socially defined identity, at any given point in time does not have the same definition or parameters of another period in time, which is also to say banally that such identifications change and can be changed because none are natural designations. As Oliver states:

> The historicity of our experience of time, which is to say the individual-social context and subject positions that make any historical perspective possible, also challenge historical facts as universal. . . . It is the tension between our historical positions, which may be fixed at any one moment, and the process of history or experience that makes transformation possible. Subjective agency is the result of the tension between subject position at any one moment and the infinite responsibility that is subjectivity." (140–141)

Because Butler constructs a character who moves through time, she points to this theoretical supposition.

In the novel, as Dana materializes in her slacks in 1815 Baltimore, others enslaved on the plantation assume that she is a man (29); for her own protection, when she flees the plantation, and aware of the specter of rape/violence toward enslaved black women, Dana "decided to become a boy. In the loose shabby, but definitely male clothing I had chosen, my height and my contralto voice would get me by" (171). Her ability to read, and higher level of education than slave-owners, also remove her from 1815 categories of race/gender, but it is clear that she is still subject to the violence that ensures that she will perform subservience. Butler underscores this fact through Weylin, the plantation owner who cannot "read" Dana, but understands that the color of her skin is sufficient for her continued subjugation: "You're something different. I don't know what—witch, devil, I don't care. . . . You came out of nowhere and go back into nowhere. Years ago, I would have sworn there couldn't even be anybody like you. You're not natural! But you can feel pain—and you can die. Remember that and do your job. Take care of your master" (Butler 206). Rufus, the boy/ancestor who calls her back, Weylin's son, says: "I never know how to treat you. You confuse everybody . . . the kind of black who watches and thinks and makes trouble" (255). In both these passages, though "confused" by Dana's identity, Weylin and Rufus reveal their awareness of black subjectivity/agency, and their fear of it. They acknowledge that Dana "feels" and can be injured, that she thinks and can resist. They thus also reveal their understanding of the mechanisms by which to control and dominate subjectivity/agency. These characters reflect real-life actors belonging to American history that Ta-Nehesi Coates describes succinctly as a process through which to consolidate whiteness:

> It could only be the employment of carriage, whips, tongs, iron pokers, hand-saws, stones, paperweights, or whatever might be handy to break the black

body, the black family, the black community, the black nation. The bodies were pulverized into stock and marked with insurance. And the bodies were an aspiration, lucrative as Indian land, a veranda, a beautiful wife, or a summer home in the mountains. For the men who needed to believe themselves white, the bodies were the key to a social club, and the right to break the bodies was the mark of civilization. (104)

Coates's black nationalist discourse notwithstanding, he invokes the vulnerability of the black body when confronted with white fear. White domination, in fact, defines notions of blackness as well as of whiteness. But if Coates draws a straight line between black bodily vulnerability from the slave past to the present, Butler complicates this notion by demonstrating that Dana comes to this understanding by reliving the past, not by "natural" inheritance.

In this sense, Dana may be a cyborg—an *assemblage* of identities that cannot be made sense of by those inhabiting the cultural norms of 1815; she is a being outside of time and space—but her temporal presence and the color of her skin makes her subject to the sociopolitical context in which she finds herself. It is thus not her appearance or performance that needs changing, but the sociopolitical context itself. Dana realizes that she must perform the identity of an enslaved black woman in order to survive her forays into the antebellum South without, however, losing a sense of who she is. She admits that her knowledge of that past comes to her through reconstruction via books and film. She must act afraid and ignorant, the role relegated to black others under plantocracy: "I'm a poor dumb scared nigger until I get my chance" (Butler 48). In another instance, she states: "At first, I stared back. Then I looked away, remembering that I was supposed to be a slave. Slaves lowered their eyes respectfully. To stare back was insolent" (Butler 66). She "played the slave, minded my manners probably more than I had to because I wasn't sure what I could get away with" (Butler 91). Being made to witness violence toward other slaves teaches Dana about the precarious position of black life in early-1800s America but she sometimes questions what she perceives to be complacency on the part of those truly enslaved in that time. For instance, on the subject of teaching others to read and the fear that Dana will "infect" slaves on the plantation with dreams of freedom, one young enslaved man, Luke, retorts: "Like we so dumb we need some stranger to make us think about freedom" (Butler 74). Luke invokes his agency despite subjugation, demonstrating in this instance, as well as in others, that the enslaved were equally aware of social race constructions forging alliances based both in this knowledge and preexisting and developing cultural af/filiations. Dana does not fully comprehend the degree to which she herself has come to rely on a false sense of security through sentiment/affect, without understanding that these are the effect of learned entitlement post-slavery, having little currency in a vertical system of domination in which she is left unprotected by legal codes or social advancement. She convinces herself and Kevin that belonging to the future-present differentiates them from the enslaved. "I'm not property, Kevin," she says, "I'm not a horse or a sack of wheat. If I have to seem to be property, if I have to accept limits on my freedom for Rufus' sake, then he also has to accept limits—on his behavior towards me. He has to leave me enough control of my own life to make living look better to me than killing and dying" (Butler 246). Here, Dana is referring to sexual violence and freedom from it, assuming that she has a measure of freedom that others do not have by belonging to the future. This is, however, a false reading of structures of domination in the antebellum past, which Dana will shortly learn. The character reveals as much when she questions how she is able to navigate her time-travels. "But how do I come home?" she muses, "Is the power mine, or do I tap some power in him? All this started with him, after all. I don't know whether I need him or not. And I won't know until he's not around" (Butler 247). Ultimately, Dana will discover, when she kills Rufus in order to escape being raped by him, that she does not ultimately "need" Rufus; this killing also ushers the process by which she loses her arm and retains the past as a mark on her material body. Through this process, Dana fully becomes one with her ancestors—both white and black—assimilating the violence of past relations through her transfigured body.

Butler appears to suggest, then, that there is an interdependence between the characters by which both need the other but which neither can escape unscathed when the realities of the plantocracy system are fully exposed and understood. Extended to the present day, the novel thus suggests that systems of domination are in themselves always maiming and disabling and that consciously acquiring this knowledge results in a wrenching psychic loss of innocence that will serve to dissolve racial difference and antinomy. Entering that space is, in fact, entering the space of *lakou consciousness*, a space in which the memorialized repetitions of ancestral knowledge reside; the novel, in this case, points to the disruption from access to the ancestral lakou, and that it can be regained through embodied performance. More radically, Butler's novel suggests that the lakou, normally thought of as the space in which African-descended epistemes reside, may also be a space accessed by "whites" whose paths and histories are imbricated in the African Diasporic experience. If Rufus's or Kevin's understandings of themselves are altered such that their sense of self moves away from what constitutes them as "white" within the time periods in which they exist, and through their own "witnessing" (Kevin as an abolitionist who also suffers physical harm and Rufus as one who witnesses violence against the bodies of black people whom he loves as a child but over whom he is given power as he grows into adulthood, a power he could refuse), of the violence enacted against "black" bodies and even in a refusal to participate in racial logics could, then, lead to moving in and out of the space of the lakou where African memory resides rather than in the annals of "Western Man."

Kelly Oliver's notion of "witnessing" as a process that might take us beyond oppositional acts of recognition, is especially useful here. Oliver, via the work of feminists of color, especially that of Chandra Mohanty and Patricia Williams, as well as precursors in performance studies as applied to gender, suggests that "the notion of witnessing I am developing challenges the traditional notion of vision, which is at the foundation of theories of recognition." She states that "first, it is important that the witness is testifying to something that cannot be seen . . . the witness is bearing witness rather than testifying as an eyewitness" and "second, it is significant to remember that this experience does not exist in itself; it is not available for the witness or anyone else to access. Rather, the experience is constituted and reconstituted as such for the witness through testimony" (143). Read through Oliver's theory of witnessing, Dana's time-travels can be understood as Butler's attempt to imagine such a movement to transformative witness position—for *both* her African and white American protagonists—as an extension of lakou consciousness manifesting Dana's autochthonomy. But, if Oliver constructs the "witness" as a free subject—that is, one not subject to domination (in today's economy, one presumes Oliver's witness to be white), then Butler suggests that Dana's 1970 incarnation is such a witness who is able to go back in time to "see" what occurred then. Dana's 1815 incarnation, however, cannot remain impassive and, by virtue of her embodied self, is constrained by the temporal impositions of that time; she moves from being a witness to the past, to being part of the past, to being an eyewitness who can provide testimony even though, in the present, no one will believe her. For a time, prior to being subject to whippings herself, and threatened by rape, she withholds judgment as a witness, understanding that she is limited by lack of experience: "I had never felt the whip across my own back. I had never felt a man's fists" (171–172). Still, Oliver's definition holds here: "what the process of witnessing testifies to is not a state of facts but a commitment to the truth of subjectivity as address-ability and response-ability. Witnessing is addressed to another and to a community; and witnessing—in both senses as addressing and responding, testifying and listening—is a commitment to embrace the responsibility of constituting communities, the responsibility inherent in subjectivity itself. In this sense, *witnessing is always bearing witness to the necessity of its process and to the impossibility of the eyewitness"* (143; emphasis mine). But does this mean that Butler is suggesting that being a witness, even in Oliver's newly defined sense, is not enough, that empathy cannot be practiced without lived experience? As a science fiction writer, it would be fair to say that Butler contests the notion that we must feel another's pain in order to practice empathy; science fiction, as a genre, compels acts of the imagination to understand our present conditions in a new light. Dana's travel to 1815 is an attempt to reconstitute Dana's misapprehension of her degree of freedom in 1815 as a 1970s subject, and her inability to escape its effects into the present (her return to everyday life with a missing limb), is a product of relations of power constituted in the past but still active in the present. Her ability to survive her travels to the past are the product of kinship ties—both to black and to white ancestors—and dependent upon the shifting ground of racial identifications in time; her ability to traverse both is an effect of her understanding of herself as an autochthonomous Subject.

Dana's travails within the terrain of a spatiality that shifts through historical settings in which both race and gender have differing valuations that are shown to have a material effect upon the traveler's body, irrespective of race (but much more detrimental for the "black" body), raises the issue of what Butler means by the book's title, *Kindred*, given that these travels are provoked by ancestral, blood ties. Butler's novel provokes readers to revise and efface racial lines while reminding them to take into account the effects and affects of segregation. We are compelled to acknowledge the detrimental effects of racial constructions while simultaneously deconstructing their naturalization. In this regard, Butler's novel is especially prescient, underscoring decades in advance, recent discoveries in genomics that have conclusively shown the impossibility of separating humans into "species" as continental philosophers such as Kant were compelled to do in the eighteenth century.[13] Where once upon a time, pseudoscience served as a space in which to fabricate and contain racial fictions, today's scientific terrain appears to serve as handmaiden to yesterday's racial fictions. Nonetheless, genomics has punched holes into those fictions, revealing their falsehoods as well as the reality of human interconnectedness across visible physical difference; beneath the skin, we are more or less the same with insignificant biological differences between us. What this means, in effect, is that "kinship" must be rethought to encompass this reality.

In *Kindred*, refracted through Butler's time-traveling mechanism, Dana and her collision with kin across historical periods, compels us to rethink kinship so that it is *both* conceptually and genetically determined from an African Diasporic point of view. Dana is compelled into kinship with her

African American ancestors *not* by virtue of also being African American but by virtue of her lived experience as subject to enslavement's rules when she returns to the past, through a mechanism ordered by her blood ties to white, enslaving ancestors. In this sense, Butler compels us to rethink Dana's af/fili-ations in ways conversely to what we might expect: she is explicitly revealed to be inextricably related to her "white" ancestors through genetics, so much so that blood "calls her back" and to her "black" ancestors by experience, so that it is affect and material loss (the loss of the limb), rather than genetics, that solidifies her kinship to previous generations of African Americans. Put another way, Butler asserts through these inversions that kinship cannot be presumed on the basis of like *phenotype* but yet cannot be ignored in the presence of like *genotype*. Still and yet, in both cases, the discovery of these inversions occurs and they are revealed *in the process of exceeding corporeal performance in an affirmation of African Diasporic autochthonomy*. These are subject to spatial and temporal alteration and are the effect and product of performances of racial and gender habitus both imposed from without and manipulated from within. At the novel's end, Butler's Dana remains in a material body altered by her experiences in and through time. In Pamela Gien's one-woman play, *The Syringa Tree*, the main character, Elizabeth, along with audience members, become altered by *witnessing* Elizabeth's transforma-tion into other bodies than her own, such that their own bodily realities (as white/upper class/female) become subject to question and revision through autochthonomy: a subject position developed from an experiential, African-descended point of view.

Out of One, Many: Perceiving the World as a Subject "Other"

In her one-woman play, *The Syringa Tree*, white South African playwright, Pamela Gien plays with the ambiguities of habiti and their performance in order to ably manipulate audience responses to a single actor reproducing the identities of roughly twenty-four personifications consisting of South Africans of varying ethnicities, class, color, and language. The play effectively and sensitively illustrates the disparity of South African experiences across race/color and class lines without pandering to stereotypical notions of what it means to be "black," "colored," or "white" in South Africa. As *New York Times* book reviewer, Paul Gray, wrote in comparing Gien's novelization of her play with its performance, which he also had the chance to view: "In performance, Gien could shift instantly between playing young and old, white and black, English and Afrikaner, through alterations of accents and *postures*" (emphasis mine).[14] These shifts were so imperceptible and so convincing that Gien's quiet one-woman show became an off-Broadway hit, winning an Obie for best play in 2000. I saw the play performed by Gien in Vancouver a few years later, and then by another (biracial) actress in Northern California another year after that. In both cases, the productions were successful in that, utilizing the same pared-down, minimal sets and costumes, they enabled a suspension of disbelief while also actively engaging viewers in a more conscious, or transparent, exchange between performance and interpretation. Given that Canadian and U.S.-based racial structures differ in marked ways (the latter, though not without enslaved people of African descent at given times, not having developed its economy around a plantocracy system anchored around slave labor), I was curious as to the respective audience reactions in both settings and to the effect of having either a "white" or "of color" actress acting out the various characters on the stage. U.S. audience members with whom I saw the play reacted in a much more racially stratified manner to depictions of racial difference, preserving a sense of "us" vs "them," while Canadian audience members seemed much more prepared to "flow" with the play's portrayals and to be moved by them—judging from those times when the script called for laughter or pathos and respective audience's audible responses to either. By playing with audience expectations but also with the fissures of racial constructions, performance becomes the vehicle by which to get to the heart of the matter: the damage caused by segregation, or apartheid, and its operational devices.[15] In a society remaining racially stratified but less conscious of its racial stratifications, even the play's openly conscious representations of racial difference appear to have less effect. Nonetheless, the play remains instructive for what it attempts to deconstruct, even if the viewing audience cannot always meet these deconstructions all the way and serves as a powerful effort in "witnessing" such as identified by Kelly Oliver as a means of undercutting hegemonic hierarchies.

In *Witnessing: Beyond Recognition* (2001), Oliver, in fact, struggles with the following question: "Can we develop a theory of subjectivity by starting from the position of those othered within dominant culture?" I suggest that, in some ways, Gien's play answers this question in the affirmative. Though Oliver does not quite do this herself, she does move aside from "contemporary theories that propose a hostile conflict between subject and another and theories that propose that identity is formed by excluding the other" (6). Essentially, opposing the Hegelian conceit of recognition that occurs only within relationships of dominance and oppression, Oliver suggests that subjectivity entails ethical responses in relationships of mutual dependence that need not be organized hierarchically or in systems of domination/subordination. By and large, Oliver's work suggests a way by which to repair the damage of sub-ordination/trauma through the activity of "witnessing." As Oliver explains: "Through the process of bearing witness to oppression and subordination, those othered can begin to repair damaged subjectivity by taking up a position as speaking subjects" (7). Oliver's point is that "othering" *is not a subject position*; it is the result of oppression, a displacement from subjectivity. For Oliver, a subject is a subject by virtue of her/his ability to speak—to address and to respond. In her concept of "response-ability," Oliver also encodes an ethics to response; speaking subjects respond and are responsible toward others, thereby not reproducing the logic of objectifying those existing beyond themselves. For Oliver, "response" is not synonymous with "recognition." She asserts: "The very notion of recognition as it is deployed in various contemporary theoretical context is, then, a symptom of the pathology of oppression itself" (9). Eventually, it becomes clear that Oliver largely ascribes the work of witnessing to subjects privileged in today's society (as opposed to those who suffer trauma whose speaking subjectivity is testimony, as we have seen in Butler's *Kindred*, rather than witness). What is useful in her rejecting of "recognition" is that she effects an anti-Hegelian turn by demonstrating that the Hegelian ideal on which much of (post)Enlightenment theories rest are, in fact, the product of ideologies that are themselves pathological, that do not render an accurate understanding or analysis of how subjectivity is produced or maintained. Theories of recognition deployed within an organizational apparatus of domination are necessarily already corrupted by that organizational apparatus and do not describe subjectivity itself but its perversion in systems that are vested in unequal power relations and their naturalization. As Oliver offers: "Subjectivity is not the result of exclusion. If it is, it is certainly not only the result of exclusion but also of relationship through difference" (11). How "difference" is defined, however, need not be caustic or oppositional. It requires *a radical reimagining of relationality*: "if the world is not alien and the subject is not separated but essentially connected to the world and others, then domination is not a compensation for alienation" (Oliver 222). Elsewhere, Oliver warns, "The struggle is to make difference normal and natural without making it the same or homogeneous" (154)—I would add to this, also, without transforming that which is not the same into the abject/object. This process, then, entails ethics because, as Oliver explains:

> To recognize others requires acknowledging that their experiences are real even though they may be incomprehensible to us; this means that we must recognize that not everything that is real is recognizable to us. Acknowledging the realness

of another's life is not judging its worth, or conferring respect, or understanding or recognizing it, but responding in a way that affirms response-ability. *We are obligated to respond to what is beyond our comprehension, beyond recognition, because ethics is possible only beyond recognition.* (106)

Oliver's position offers the possibility of revisiting difference not as a wedge between individuals or social groups but as a plane through which world views negotiated through difference can be exchanged and accessed without presuming their hierarchized position in relations of power. Much like Luce Irigaray's argument with regard to gender difference as an area of social categorization that could be revised and redefined away from traditional Western codes by making the categories *sexuate* and invested with definitions that did not subjugate women to men, Oliver suggests that ("racial") difference, writ large, need not, by definition, presume a dominating center and its margins or norms and their opposites. To recognize another, in the Hegelian sense, is to supplant the other with oneself so that the other is always already subordinate; when two encounter each other, they thus necessarily struggle over whose agency or identity will govern the other's. Oliver admits that it is possible *not* to recognize the other, even to mis-recognize the other and to *not* have one's identity or agency threatened. Indeed, she argues that to move "beyond recognition" could solve the very issue of dominance/subordination by replacing the politics of domination with an ethical practice of acknowledging the other's presence and that person's difference without the need to supplant or dominate their reality. This would also mean that the need to construct the other's identity in relation to a socially dominant norm (whether racial or gendered) would no longer be necessary. Such a position also allows for the increasingly recognized pliability of race and sex (Young 16), the mobility of class, and the ways in which dis/ability is being continuously revised, reread, and redefined. In this respect "legibility" to others becomes less important than acknowledging that difference is a part of social reality and that each one's reality differs in important respects yet retains its own integrity. Difference becomes legible socially through its performance of distinct types of identity formations, but such performances are also subject to projections, misreadings, and revisions, as can be evidenced in the performance/reading of a play such as *Syringa Tree*.

Despite great care taken in the mise-en-scene as well as stage directions designed to mitigate against projections of race/gender from the audience onto the actor/actress (or actors/actresses if the play is performed with an ensemble rather than solo cast, as the original play was designed), what the play's/playwright's hyper-awareness of racial codes and stereotypes reveals are their potential malleability but also the ways in which their seeming fixity are social fictions. This is to say that the play, as performed by solo artists can be "read" very differently by audiences who may have South African members but who are largely made up of non–South African, (white) Canadian, or American members with distinct historical legacies with regard to race and racialization in North America. One assumes that audiences attending *The Syringa Tree* are self-selecting, progressive, and antiapartheid. Reactions to particular scenes when the audience is interpellated in "suspending their disbelief" because the body on the stage does not match the body it performs, whether in terms of race, gender, or age, reveals a great deal about the ways in which racializations circulate unseen. At the same time, the effectiveness of these performances (which can be judged by the play's overwhelmingly positive reception—at least from white audience members) reveals, to some extent, the degree to which the naturalization of race can be overcome and racial habitus revealed to be as much an effect or social conditioning as it is also an effect of ethnic, cultural, and geographical factors. Indeed, what I want to suggest here is that *The Syringa Tree*, performed as a solo play, challenges the former and opens up the door to the latter.

In her author's note to the play, Gien situates the play in a physical/imagined space, her grandparent's farm "Clova," even though much of the action of the play, which centers on the character of a little girl named Elizabeth, a proxy for Gien, takes place almost entirely at the home of Elizabeth's parents. We are initiated to the complex politics and social hierarchies of South Africa through a child's eyes and through a family that is progressive, inclusive, attempts to defy the constraints of apartheid without, however, defying them so profoundly as to endanger the lives of the most vulnerable individuals with whom they share the house and surrounding property (indigenous housekeepers, gardeners, nannies, and so forth). Gien speaks to her heritage but also emphasizes that the play is a recomposition of her memories, an elaborate fiction meant to invoke a specific time and place, as seen through the most innocent of perspectives in a non-innocent time.

Gien also emphasizes that though the play is autobiographically inspired, she borrowed from the lives of those she encountered while growing up in South Africa; she also emphasizes the multiplicity of ethnicities and experiences to which she was exposed. Salamina, Elizabeth's nurse and the housekeeper, Gien states, "was inspired by several women who took care of me." Of this collective of women, Gien writes: "They were of different origins, some Sotho, some Xhosa or Zulu, and I've tried as much as possible to accurately reflect tribal differences in the language, but some of the sounds were so strong and poetic in my memory that I wanted to include them" (9–10). Whether this means that distinct ethnicities and their performances were conflated to produce a stock "type," is unclear, as Gien elsewhere explains: "Vocal delineation among characters, through variations in pitch and tone, give each a distinct voice. These are further assisted by chosen psychological gestures for each character. These choices become crucial in the audiences' ability to quickly identify one from the other. As there are no costume changes, and no props, the actor has to convey each character with speed and depth, and the psychological gesture functions as an invaluable shorthand" (11). Gien then goes on to offer specific examples as to what she means by these descriptions and explains the psychological states of some of the characters—Elizabeth's hyperactivity, and Salamina's "robust" physicality (12).

At times, Gien's attempts to emphasize the ethnic, class, social or psychological makeup of her characters become romanticized. For example, she describes Salamina as a "warm body seemingly part of the rich earth around her," inadvertently repeating a (colonial) trope that conflates native women with territory/land, fecundity (not to say sexuality) with the very ground from which such women have been dispossessed. Nonetheless, by utilizing the child's innocence, who is guided by a keen sense of observation throughout the text of the play, Gien is able to achieve a racial sleight of hand. Heavily racialized topics such as color, racial contamination, and prejudice, are noted but not analyzed. Elizabeth may notice color difference, even her own "whiteness," and its association with purity/cleanliness, but, as Gien writes, her lines are written (and delivered onstage) without "any political awareness": "She is a witness, and her words are her simple way of trying to make sense of what she sees. There is never a value judgment, only fear, matter-of-fact observation, excitement, curiosity, joy, the simple feelings of a child" (ibid.). This simplicity, both in the mise-en-scene, and in the writing/delivery of the main character's lines (as is the case with all of the other characters that appear on the stage throughout the staging), compels viewers into that space of analysis, judgment, and reasoning. Gien's stage notes are "given in the hope that the audience will supply their own thoughts and feelings" (ibid.). And though one cannot control or even truly measure what those thoughts or feelings might be, Gien's attempt to strip down "race" in her examination of the late period of apartheid in South Africa, as experienced through many eyes and sensibilities, through different bodies, ethnicities, genders, and ages, clarifies the importance of understanding habitus as a conduit for reforming racial dynamics, whether in South Africa or elsewhere.

If anything, *The Syringa Tree* is a play about masking un/masking. As the solo actress narrates the story of "Clova," or apartheid South Africa in its final years, through the embodiment of twenty-three different characters, she transforms and transcends, while also reinscribing "racial" types—though every attempt has been made by the playwright to negotiate or even negate racial stereotype or prejudice. The physicality of the characters—the movements that come to define and identify them for the audience—as well as their reactions to one another—all refracted through one, representative body—provides a mirror for the audience to reflect upon their own *preconceived* notions of race, while also being led through a particular narrative of individuals struggling to coexist with dignity within a world structured to deny the humanity of some while affirming that of others. I also suggest that the physicality of the performance can be understood as residing in the space of what Homi Bhabha has termed the "double vision" of mimicry, in which the representation of hybridity (which Bhabha uncommonly defines as an opportunity for productive differentiation from colonial binaries and hegemony) is akin to a photographic "transparency" by which the "real" is never quite what it seems.

On the one hand, the transparency would seem to provide a clear access to a representation of the real, yet, in actuality, is a reverse image of the scene being represented. Using for example the presence, or "surface" of the English book, Bhabha argues that "despite appearances, the text of transparency inscribes a double vision: the field of the 'true' emerges as a visible sign of authority only after the regulatory and displacing division of the true and the false." He elaborates: "From this point of view, discursive 'transparency' is best read in the photographic sense in which a transparency is also always a negative, processed into visibility through the technologies of reversal, enlargement, lighting, editing, projection, not a source but a re-source of light. *Such a bringing to light is a question of the provision of visibility as a capacity, a strategy, an agency*" (emphasis mine, *Location of Culture*, 157). As such, Gien's play/performance presents a variety of entry points into representative values through the discursive qualities of gestures and utterances that reveal, in and of themselves, and through interplay with the viewing audience (and their stock of cultural arsenal), that the "real" cannot be easily or directly accessed. Gien's representation of twenty-three identity positions within apartheid South Africa, then, through the solo performance, operates as what I thus term a kind of "transparent doubling" of identities through which no one identity stands out as more "real" than the rest. Only through their interactions in the structure of apartheid and their reactions to one another as they struggle to transcend that structure is the structure's constricted, oppressive imposition of racial codes revealed for the ugly dehumanizing (yet manmade) machinery that it is. In this, the performance(s) also reveals their temporality, their situatedness within the confines of a nation/state with a particular historical span of time, enacting what Bhabha has termed a "double narrative movement." Writes Bhabha:

> We then have a contested conceptual territory where the nation's people must be thought in double-time; the people are the historical "objects" of a nationalist pedagogy, giving the discourse an authority that is based on the pre-given or constituted historical origin *in the past*; the people are also the "subjects" of a process of signification that must erase any prior or originary presence of the nation-people to demonstrate the prodigious, living principles of the people as contemporaneity: as that sign of the *present* through which national life is redeemed and iterated as a reproductive process . . . the very act of the narrative performance interpellates a growing circle of national subjects. (208–209; first emphasis mine)

Interestingly, Bhabha's theory of the ambivalent present-tense of the "nation" appears to suggest that the nation qua people are, in themselves, an erasure of the indigenous, of any prior claims, either cultural or territorial, upon the land that the nation sits upon, invoking here my own discomfort with Gien's conflation of Sarafina, for instance, with the "fecundity" of the land, a colonial trope. Sarafina, then, as imagined by Gien, is the product of a colonial imaginary process and does not emerge as her own true being, *except through the postures of the characterization itself*. In this, Gien's play unconsciously produces Bhaba's double vision such that the "true"—whoever Sarafina might truly represent—is hidden behind the authority of settler logics, which Gien has not completely undone in her stage direction.

In a postcolonial, African context, Bhabha's concept of "double-vision" is apropos, since the indigeneity of Africans within their own continent is hotly contested or displaced in favor of a complete erasure of antecedents. The "people," in the postcolonial/nation, Bhabha contends are "a complex rhetorical strategy of reference" (208). Gien's play, through its explicit use of gestural, iterative, and cultural references as a means to convey both cultural and moral references to its multiply situated audiences, demonstrates this truism in layered fashion even if it does not completely arrive at this self-reflexively. Still, as a product of an African territory, it ironically contributes to the archives of South African lakou consciousness in which the realities of South Africans of color inform and, in fact, delimit the realities of their white South African counterparts attempting to narrate them in part and in whole.

In keeping with my arguments regarding the performativity of "race," whether conscious or not, Gien moves beyond racial stereotypes by giving key characters distinguishing *physical* attributes and gestures that move them out of the space of settler logics and stereotype into a space of exchange between testimony/witness and racial reversals. In these exchanges and reversals, race dissolves in favor of shared or interpretable cultural encodings, some hinging upon physical disability wrought by racial violence making the violence of raced mechanisms visible. In some cases, the characters are recognizable by physical handicaps that in no way perturb their ability to see the society in which they reside clearly, but, when read against recent scholarship on white privilege and the racialization of rights for the disabled in South Africa via the Pistorius case, discussed earlier, serve as a means to individualize characters and, as such, render their humanity legible against the greater tapestry of apartheid within which individualized victims and perpetrators become indistinct. In Gien's play, the performance of disability reveals a societal fissure with regard to bodies that matter socially and those that do not, but also reveals how disability may not function in the same social spheres or under the same regimes of domination as does race *except when disability is attached to "black" bodies.* One such character is Zephyr, the elderly Zulu gardener of Elizabeth's Afrikaans next-door neighbors.

Elizabeth alerts us to the violence Zephyr has endured when she tells us who is about to enter a scene, one including Zephyr, and tells us, "he's very, *very* old and somebody cut his fingers off." (28). The absence of these fingers is later suggested by the actor's gestures in stage directions: "*(Zephyr reaches down and takes Elizabeth's hand with his mutilated fingers.)*." Later, even, Elizabeth recounts that Zephyr lost his fingers as punishment for singing South Africa's unofficial, indigenous national anthem of liberation (rather than the official anthem in Afrikaans): "But if you're very lucky fish, after supper . . . Zephyr might sing you the prayer song . . . (*Imitating the slicing off of Zephyr's fingers.*) the forbidden song!" (30). The forbidden song, its singing, and its mnemonic in Elizabeth's recounting are all veiled signs of autochthonomy—as it reflects the cultural salience, resistance, and lived reality of indigenous Africans in their struggle for freedom; Zephyr's "prayer" song gestures toward the lakou space, which Elizabeth accesses via memory, the affect of fear, and her incorporation of the memory of Zephyr's punishment as a sign of the state's authority against evidence of autochthonomy, an alter-reality subsumed by the violence of settler colonialism. In the scene that follows, between Elizabeth and her neighbor, Afrikaan Loeska, Gien reveals an astute understanding of the difference between imitation and identification that reveals that the play's action intentionally means to bring the saliency of black African lives to legibility.

When Elizabeth openly mocks Loeska's patriotism by repeating the words of the official anthem: "We will live, we will die . . . we for you South Africa!"

(*Imitating Loeska, marching and saluting*)" (31), the performance reminds us of the slippage evidenced in colonial mimicry, of the difference, as discussed by Diana Fuss, between an unquestioned identification and an imitation that is meant to save one's life (for the colonized, with whom, Elizabeth, as a child, identifies). Gien's play, as one produced by a playwright who has relinquished (or, at the very least, puts at the service of the disadvantaged) her privilege as a white South African, exercises the reversibility of colonial power by situating the performance of the soloist enacting several different lives affected differentially by apartheid in Bhabha's double-time as explained earlier. Throughout most of the play, the actress must *identify* with the characters she embodies across racial lines, and thus across space/time continuums, rather than imitate them. When she "imitates" characters, it is to create a sharp distinction between her own physicality and that of another body, that is, character. Here, for instance, she mocks Loeska while, in contradistinction, later on, she will imitate Zephyr's physical handicap as a means of homage, identifying Zephyr with ancestral knowledge and rights to the land, in a gesture, again, to what I have identified as African Diasporic autochthonomy:

> She's got Zephyr's blanket on her, *(Imitating Zephyr laying the blanket over her.)* . . . the one that he always wears at the fire, *(Imitates Zephyr's gestures at the fire.)* to sing the prayer song. Zephyr says . . . the spirits of our ancestors *fly* into the trees when they die . . . into the leaves and the berries and the bark. *(Imitates Zephyr again, creating a tree in the air with mutilated fingers.)* And that's why when you carve your mask out of a piece of wood, you can't choose the face *you* want, because the face is already there, and you just open . . . it . . . out . . . *(Like carving with Zephyr's hand, no fingers.)* into the world to see *who it is* . . . like being born. (57)

Zephyr's individualized identity is thus related to life but also to a long continuum of departed ancestors and hopes for a better future. But more than this, Elizabeth's imitation of Zephyr, distinguishable through a physical handicap, underscores what Bhabha has called the necessary "splitting" caused by colonial double-time. He states: "In the production of the nation as narration there is a split between the continuist, accumulative temporality of the pedagogical [or prescriptive], and the repetitious, recursive strategy of the performative [or iterative]. It is through this process of splitting that the conceptual ambivalence of modern society becomes the site of *writing the nation*" (209). In this sense, Elizabeth's imitation of Loeska's jingoism mocks the pedagogical/prescriptive aspects of the nation-state while that of Zephyr invokes the *performative* as iterative and therefore consciously recursive, disruptive, ambivalent, within the former's cataracted vision of who does and does not belong to the nation, confirming, in the final analysis, the former's belonging to the nation through the violence etched on her/his very body.

This "splitting" has a further consequence: unveiling for the privileged, the mechanisms securing that privilege. Though we are told that Gien's central character, six-year old Elizabeth, brings "no political awareness" to her observations, it is also clear that she understands that something is amiss, that she has rights that others do not have, and that being in a "black" body has consequences related to bodily freedom. Though she identifies the markings on Zephyr's body as a "writing of the nation,"[16] she comes to understand that writing as illegitimate against Zephyr's invocation and recitation of the "forbidden song." Literal writing, rather than bodily markings, come to signify the signs of the nation's illegitimacy, which attempts to discard indigenous South Africans from their own land and their natural rights to that land. More than once, Elizabeth expresses an awareness of the need for "special papers" and is fearful when she believes that someone is missing the special paper needed to circulate within South African borders; at times, reflecting a true sense of lack of political awareness, she is uncertain who needs the special paper and is not clear as to whether such papers are race-related.

The very first line of the play is related to the issues of identity papers and brings the awareness of free circulation (or lack thereof) to the audiences' attention so that observing the performance becomes at once an observation of a play and an exercise of how bodies performed under the duress of policed conditions, both physically and psychologically (that is, if they believe that they are being policed or not). Elizabeth's opening line (also the opening line of the play) is as follows: "You not allowed to go in there" (we are never told to what "there" refers) "You have to have a special paper to go in there" (21). As the action of the play advances and police arrive at the Grace's farm (ostensibly to see after something that Elizabeth's father may have done against apartheid dictates), Elizabeth frets over the housekeeper's daughter, secretly delivered by her father on the farm, and, as such, unregistered. "Salamina's got a paper," she says, "but you've got not paper. *(Exasperated, runs off, singing.)* Hide away . . . hide away . . . !" (36). As she listens to her father and mother arguing about how to maneuver apartheid society for their daughter, given their left-leaning positions and antiapartheid activities, Elizabeth explains the importance of identity papers, and her fear, to the audience, in this way:

> Something's happening outside! If you look under the shutter, where it touches the window sill . . . you can see the police van is coming back again. It drives up and down the road all night long, looking for people who've got no paper,

and in the lights, shining on the road, they've got somebody down, and they shouting at him . . . "*Fokking kaffir!*" . . . (*Outside, over the garden wall in the street, the shadows of men, policemen caught in the headlights of their van, hold a black man down on his knees in the road. Shouting "Pass!" and "Jou fokken Kaffir!" muffled by the closed window. Dogs bark incessantly.*) *Heee* didn't think! . . . He's supposed to be at his home! If they catch you, without your special paper . . . and you don't have time (*Trying somehow to tell the man.*) climb up into the Syringa tree, under Salamina's bed. . . . If they catch you, they put you *down*, on the road . . . and they beat you . . . very much. (40–41)

In this scene, Elizabeth, reveals that she is learning the process of apartheid ("he's supposed to be at his home!") even if in her childish innocence, she believes that the absence of a special paper can be saved by climbing up a tree or under a bed—actions she most likely has seen work for black South Africans in the past despite the simplicity of those acts. She is also aware that the consequence of being found is a brutal beating, or worse. Thus, Elizabeth learns from a very young age, as all those around her must, whatever their position in the system, that scripts (identity papers) control movements as well as fate. Later on, it is clear, however, that Elizabeth has not yet quite grasped that such papers are only needed by people of color, especially those determined to be "black." Elizabeth inadvertently confuses a fear of blackness by those in power with her own elemental fear of *darkness* and those things that go on under cover of night (police pursuits, beatings, and so forth). When Salamina's daughter disappears after being taken ill to a local hospital, Elizabeth is fearful of letting her mother go into the darkness: "When Dubike comes nearer to help Salamina get up I say *(To her mother.)* You not allowed to go *in* there! *(Dubike shrinks back.)* And he jumps back in a puff of dust! He thinks I'm talking to *him*, but I'm telling my mother" (48). Understandably, Dubike, Salamina's cousin, responds to the white child with fear and apprehension. Elizabeth records Dubike's reaction but understands it as a miscommunication; for the audience, the physicality of the movement conveys the degree to which even an innocent child of six can have structural power over others bestowed upon her, beyond her understanding, within such a system. Elizabeth persists in warning all of the danger, regardless of race, of entering the darkness. Still later, as her father pursues another lead to find the baby, Moliseng, Elizabeth is frantic with fear: "When I got to the kitchen door with my blanket, and my sweets for Moliseng, the lights of the car going, going . . . going . . . and the gate closed! *(Highly distressed.)* . . . I hope my dad has that special paper . . . ! *(She runs around the house, frantic, and inside, climbs onto her bed, trying not to cry.)*" (55). In short, though Elizabeth will not be subject to the physical violations she so fears in the absence of the right "papers," social structures of power at play in her lived universe have made clear the latter's importance. She thus is aware of the imperial/colonial process that Fuss states defines identification as "a form of violent appropriation." Her own mimesis, however, her identification with the powerless—both as a six-year-old and as one who witnesses the violence born against black bodies, some of whom she loves and knows intimately— inverses the role intended for her by the society. Though she cannot ever fully "be" the other—no one can; she acquires identification with those casts as "others" in the system of apartheid through the traumatic processes of fear and violence instigated by the State. Within psychoanalysis, such a loss is figured as the loss of the symbolic "Other," of a rupture of human relatedness; but it might very well be that the trauma of recognizing the loss of the Other as human, within human space, is the jolt that awakens the Subject to the reality of the social construction of both categories. Writes Fuss, "Trauma is another name for identification, the name we might give to the irrecoverable loss of a sense of human relatedness" (40). In Gien's play, the playwright goes somewhat beyond this by suggesting that the mimesis at work in the play, and within the viewing audience, is a *retrieval* of that sense of human relatedness that only trauma can uncover. As such, in an attempt to make violated and disappeared bodies live again on the stage, though partial and incomplete, the identifications produced through mimesis creates a sense of relation, a *kinship*, which the colonial (and psychoanalytic) order has sought to displace and effectively disrupts.

Thus, though the play might well underplay the harsh realities of apartheid through its use of a child protagonist and the explicit policing of black bodies by simply differentiating the situatedness of one or the other within the (imagined) borders of the nation, it highlights rather than effaces them. By using the child as interpreter, the play emphasizes the psychic and psychological effects of the violence of apartheid as a lived and manmade created reality in ways described by Diana Fuss in *Identification Papers* (1985). In the latter, Fuss makes use of psychoanalysis to explore issues of power and identification, concluding that though long represented as universal and unalterable (through Freudian archetypal tropes) identification is, rather, a process with a politics and, more precisely, in terms of psychoanalysis, one with a colonial, imperial history. Fuss writes, revising alterity and identification via Fanon that "identification is neither a historically universal concept nor a politically innocent one" (141). Subjectivity and Otherness come to symbolize two sides of the same coin, one that identifies "whites" while always excluding non-whites. This is so, Fuss argues (again, via Fanon) because "the white man . . . monopolizes otherness to secure an illusion of unfettered access to subjectivity" (142) such that the black man is "relegated to a position other than the Other" (143). She elaborates: "The colonizer can claim a sovereign right to personhood by purchasing interiority over and against the representation of the colonial other as pure exteriority" (145). Thus, Fuss comes to consider mimesis (through the example of the un/veiling of Algerian women during the Algerian war as Algerian women in the resistance passed as "white" women in order to infiltrate white French sectors of Algiers), as an alternative to "prescribed identification," whereby an imitation does not necessarily indicate identification or acceptance of an imposed identification. For Fuss, this capacity of mimesis to perform a mode of resistance is meant to overturn certain givens in psychoanalysis: "When situated within the context of colonial politics, the psychoanalytic *assumption* that every conscious imitation conceals an unconscious identification needs to be carefully questioned, read for the signs of its own colonizing impulses" (148). Keeping Fuss's approach in mind in reading Gien, then, we can best understand her text as belonging to a "context of colonial politics," situated as it is in apartheid South Africa. Though Fuss is attempting to read resistance on the part of the colonized of color, I propose that Gien's text allows readers to perceive—through performance—the extent to which someone positioned as having power in such a context, i.e., as white or noncolored, can uncover the limits to identification through a mimetic process that might serve to overturn the very structures of power that invest certain bodies with sociopolitical power while stripping others of their access to such power and, more than this, allow those otherwise privileged in such systems to enter the epistemes of the formerly disenfranchised without needing to re-create racial hierarchies, indeed, to enter them as potential subjects (or in Oliver's parlance, "witnesses") of these epistemes, which I identify as autochthonomous, in other words, as reflecting African and African Diasporic kinship and cultural networks, histories, and lived realities.

Conclusion

It is plausible to read Pamela Gien's representations as bordering on the stereotypical or, as Rey Chow argues about certain kinds of cross-ethnic representations as an "appropriation in the guise of an embrace," as we might also say of Jeff Koons's rendering of "Michael and Bubbles." It is certainly possible that some audiences who are least aware of the social constructions of power and race and their material effects, in particular in the United States, could easily miss the ways in which the play both reconstructs and deconstructs such categories in laying bare the power dynamics of apartheid-era South

Africa. As my earlier analysis of Gien's stage instructions signaled, the playwright herself, when writing the play, occupied an ambivalent space which, at times, unwittingly reproduced certain kinds of primitivist discourses while attempting to disrupt—or at least, question—racial power dynamics. My analysis can neither disprove this ambivalence nor demonstrate that the play succeeds in deconstructing apartheid era politics. What I can claim is that the play's performances enact, through such ambivalence, the trauma that such racialized politics impose both psychically and physically upon *all* who must exist within regimes of power, regardless of racialization. The traumatized white girl child as witness is the antithesis of Fanon's boy child deforming the black man through a denigrating speech-act of othering: she embodies Oliver's "witness" who effectively engages a theory of subjectivity from the point of view of the "other": she assimilates alterity because she cannot yet differentiate herself from it, which, in itself, is a thought-provoking positionality with which audiences must grapple. It is in this crossing of racial lines into a political alterity, signified by violated bodies that in themselves become disabled but not ineffective (as evidenced in the representation of Zephyr) that Gien's work provides us with some insight into the ways in which power, realized through racial othering, must be read in more complex ways contextually and in ways that cannot be easily collapsed intradiasporically. This is to say that though "black" bodies are similarly violated both in the South African context and in North American contexts (as I showed earlier in my analysis of Butler's *Kindred*), *disability* must be understood as impacting black and white bodies, as well as gendered bodies differently within racialized political contexts in which legal codes may not penalize or effectively index disability for marginalization (as in the Pistorius case and the South African legal context more generally). Octavia Butler's novel, *Kindred*, also serves to underscore the ways in which disability in and of itself, is not necessarily a category of alterity that can easily be assimilated to racial or gender difference.

In both Gien's play and in *Kindred*, we see that disability is the result of racial violence in the effort to dehumanize violated, "black," bodies; in both texts, those bodies disabled through racial violence have their humanity made legible *through* their disability in that these disabilities are an index of the human relatedness lost through imperial/colonial violence. It is not the disability that renders humanity legible but an understanding of how such disability was occasioned; in both texts, the loss of a limb or physical function creates empathy in the reader/viewer, an identification, as well as a means by which to distinguish one character from another, while recognizing through this disability the ways in which the phantom limb is a marker of a loss of freedom, of autonomy. But, since "white" bodies are not perceived as having lost legal status or autonomy through racial violence, both texts reflect the ways in which white bodies, in particular geographies and historical time—in this case, apartheid South Africa, and, to some extent, the antebellum Southern United States—were not subject to disabling physical violence. Even Dana's husband, Kevin, though physically violated when lost to the past, does not lose his social status as a "white" man. Through physical violation, he comes to grow world-weary and enters the "double-time" of the colonized; he takes this understanding into the present like viewers of Gien's play might after understanding the play's mimesis as one that transcends or, at least, points out the ways in which racial demarcations are man-made and legally constricted.

As readers/viewers, we have been transformed along with these characters so that our "reading" practice has been redirected away from conflating the *naturalization* of race with its animus; we come to better understand or detect the transparency of "race" as performative. Dana/Elizabeth have shed the "habitual body" of race/gender of their own time and taken on the accouterments of the *habitus* of previous generations on both sides of the racial fence in two very different locales: both have become assemblages of past and present configurations of race/gender/disability (when the latter is attached to a black body—in which case the phantom limb becomes synonymous with the loss of humanity of the social order that violently disfigures such bodies and renders them disabled while the society itself becomes nonfunctional)— while also coming to represent an ability to free themselves from imposed (racialized) categories. The caveat in all this is that neither Gien nor Butler, in the end, assert that we can ever be altogether free of the damaging effects of raced categories: they persist and injure as we witness through Elizabeth's fear and anxiety and through Dana's loss of limb. Yet, and in particular, through Dana's imagined embodied transformation, Octavia Butler signals that the power of interpretation and shifting reading practices remains available to us as a means of redirecting our concepts of identity markers. Gien similarly indicates the same in the multiple performances her play enacts. In both cases, we are engaged in reading/viewing practices that are designed to redraw the parameters of our understandings of race as politically situated and of culture as functioning separately from and beyond race (to return to the work of Piper's calling card). As seen in the texts explored in this chapter, "race" reveals itself far more as a marker of the European imagination and of colonial history, than of African or African-derived cultures. Yet, in both cases, shedding the Western/Euro-American site of the nation and its settler history engages the reality of African/Diasporics in such as a way that renders lakou consciousness detectable, possibly accessible, even to those who are not of African descent and even if this consciousness is latent; still, as Gien attempts through physical representation and Butler demonstrates through the mechanism of the time-travel, a shared reality having its base in the realities and embodiments of people of African descent, rather than the point of view of oppressors, serves as a grounding for cross-cultural identification and a basis for another sense of the real. It also signals the importance of realizing that ground through which African-descended people(s) enact their free will as reflected and embedded in cultural practice and rites (such as the singing of the unofficial South African anthem), rituals, and memories particular to African/Diasporic experiences (these I term autochthonomous in the chapters remaining).

If, in this chapter, I have largely been preoccupied with exploring the ways in which racial habitus is performed and reveals itself as a manifestation of social hierarchies organized around fictions of race, in chapter 2, I show more explicitly how artists of African descent actively employ ontological principles emerging from "lakou" or yard consciousness. This is in order to reveal how kinship functions as a reflection of shared cultural tropes, and aspirations, rather than fictional racial ones imposed via historical hierarchies born through imperial or colonial settler histories. Indeed, in assessing cross-cultural representations of the Rwandan genocide, I seek to show that assuming a perspective of transnational autochthonomy such artists—who are not necessarily phenotypically "black"—assume the cultural/political perspectives of kinship consciousness as a means to reveal the intimate ground of the devastation in such a way that reader-interpreters must assume a similar interpretive capacity, a *relationality* to the subject matter, that refuses a dualistic separation. I also demonstrate that such an engagement is also feminist at its base or advocating for listening attentively to African women's realities within the lakou space, while also refusing the "pornotroping" (see Spillers) so prevalent in colonial, patriarchal models that exploitatively seek to represent genocide but are otherwise unsympathetic to the African basis of the experience, leading then to distortions in representation.

Alternatively, autochthonomous representations do not seek to claim that they can do the work of representing all aspects of such genocide; indeed, to the contrary, they leave a space open for that which cannot be mapped or represented, especially pertaining to African female bodies. They also advocate for a mode of representation that reflects a larger political body as well as intra-cultural interpretations that yield more nuanced approaches to understanding the effects of such violence beyond the confines of their Euro-colonial legacies.

2 Autochthonomous Transfigurations of Race and Gender in Twenty-First-Century Transnational Genocide Testimonial Narratives

The Photograph does not necessarily say what is no longer, *but only and for certain* what has been.

* * *

The important thing is that the photograph possesses an evidential force, and that its testimony bears not on the object but on time.
—Roland Barthes, *Camera Lucida*

A genocide is a film which unfolds every day before the eyes of he who came through it and it is pointless interrupting it until the end.
—*Sylvie Umubyeyi*, qtd in Jan Hatzfeld, *Into the Quick of Life*

At no other time has there been more access to information or have artists of all backgrounds, but especially of African descent, have the means (and mobility) to comment on world events in their own and other communities. The events of 1994 in Rwanda are one such event. Depictions and representations of the genocide in Rwanda both visually (in photography, film) and in print (in this case, graphic novels), provide rich material to examine how *autochthonomy* as well as *lakou consciousness* make themselves manifest in global/ transnational contexts and what we can learn from their creative deployment. Each of the representations of the genocide in this chapter examines the partial exposure of a silence that appears to be symptomatic of trauma. Trauma scholars have argued that trauma can be narrated only by proxy: it is always related in its aftermath and can only be a fallible, if "true," recomposition. That recomposition suffers from victims's "semiotic incapacity" (van Alphen 26), a failure of words, of narrative containment, of the proper signs to enunciate the mechanisms of trauma and its pain. Cathy Caruth emphasizes, "the historical power of the trauma is not just that the experience is repeated after its forgetting, but that it is only in and through its inherent forgetting that it is first experience[d] at all." She continues: "a history can be grasped only in the very inaccessibility of its occurrence" (Introduction 8). Such inaccessibility suggests an entry point into not so much a silencing of history but of a silence that is constituted within trauma, and which exceeds it. It is the silence that Haitian historian, Michel-Rolph Trouillot writes of when he speaks of the Haitian Revolution's entry into history as "unthinkable," expanding upon Pierre Bourdieu's twin concepts of the "unthinkable" and "unnameable." For Trouillot, the erasure of the violence the Haitian Revolution committed against Western racialist epistemes, amounts to the West's "failure of narration" (90), which would have demanded a "fundamental rewriting of world history" (106, 107).[1] Although I return to Trouillot's reading of the denial of the impact of Haitian history on world history (after Hegel) in my treatment of Raoul Peck's film on Rwanda in particular, for most of this chapter, I am more interested in the concepts borrowed from Bourdieu and how these might be of further use in understanding the representation of the implicit "silence" of trauma. What I ultimately come to argue is that artists who consciously emulate African Diasporic aesthetics in their representations of the Rwandan genocide—by utilizing African/Latin American Third Cinema tropes or by utilizing autochthonomous feminist approaches to representations of gendered violence—also engage counterhegemonic modes of representation such that victims of state and gendered violence can be represented, even if obliquely. In doing so, they diminish the gap between Self/Other or Subject/Other instituted through Manichean dualism and take part in that "fundamental rewriting of world history" of which Trouillot speaks. By approaching representations of others through autochthonomous, lakou/yard consciousness, they assert that Self/Other and Subject/Other dualities should be diminished in favor of understanding that those made victims of state/colonial violence remain fully autonomous, humane, and worthy of our consideration as mirrors of ourselves.

In this respect, Bourdieu's claims are instructive. He elaborates several useful concepts in his *Outline of a Theory of Practice*, in which he criticizes the disciplinary pitfalls of anthropology and demonstrates that the relationship between the interlocutor and his/her informant embeds gaps and fissures; these observations, I argue, are transferable to the fields of photography and film, which dominate the fields of documenting historic moments. As Bourdieu explains:

> Invited by the anthropologist's questioning to effect a reflexive and quasi-theoretical return on to his own practice, the best-informed informant produces

a *discourse which compounds two opposing systems of lacunae.* Insofar as it is a
discourse of familiarity, it leaves unsaid all that goes without saying: the informant's remarks . . . are inevitably subject to the censorship inherent in their
habitus, a system of schemes of perception and thought which cannot give
what it does give to be thought and perceived without *ipso facto* producing an
unthinkable and an unnameable. Insofar as it is an *outside-oriented* discourse
it tends to exclude all direct reference to particular cases.

And concludes:

It is understandable that anthropologists should so often forget the distance
between learned reconstruction of the native world and the native experience
of that world, an experience which finds expression only in the silences, ellipses,
and lacunae of the language of familiarity (18).

Bourdieu goes on to explain that the anthropologist's error reflects a larger
constitutive power of those in dominance by which certain discourses are
authorized and others de-authorized, in a process he calls "officialization"
or an "aspect of the objectifying process through which the group teaches
itself and conceals from itself its own truth, inscribing in objectivity its representation of what it is" (21). The dominant group accrues what Bourdieu
terms "symbolic capital" and infiltrates all kinds of exchanges, especially gift
exchanges, which appear to be freely entered into but mask an exchange of
power, while others are relegated to the arena of the "self-interested" and
denied currency. This is similar to Paulo Freire's analysis of "cultural invasion" by which conquest is achieved through cultural infiltration: "In this
phenomenon, the invaders penetrate the cultural context of another group,
in disrespect of the latter's potentialities; they impose their own view of the
world upon those they invade and inhibit the creativity of the invaded by
curbing their expression" (133).

Though Bourdieu means these terms to be applied to exchanges between
and within societies, I want to extend their value into the sphere of the
transnational and especially with respect to traumas lived on a monumental
scale. In this respect, what becomes "unthinkable" or "unnameable" are the
details, or traumas, as well as their numerical scope. The attempt to bring
such details to light appear to be "self-interested" because they often have to
do either with restoring the humanity of the victims, assisting in their healing, or achieving justice for those harmed from governmental bodies who
are often loathe to enact effective redress. As part of the dynamic of having
their discourse silenced, shame, fear, and even retribution can accompany
breaking with silence and *naming* the trauma, or the memory/experience
of it. Part of the process means, also, breaking with the idea that the event

is what I would call the *unimaginable* or the *(in)imaginable*. By this, I mean to insist, via Bourdieu's claim, regarding the effacing or silencing of subjects in classic anthropological discourses, that the culture(s) and subjectivities of the subjects remain, even if otherwise disregarded and thereby rendered unthinkable or unspeakable.

These "remains" (the unimaginable) are what I term the (in)imaginable, which, by a play on language (in French, the "inimaginable" is literally the unimaginable or inconceivable), are thus to be thought of as contained *within* the imagination, as suggested by the bracketing of the prefix *in* serving here as both an index of impossibility and of enclosure. Given the evidence remaining of desacralized bodies, indeed, scarred and mutilated bodies, traumas cannot be unthinkable but they hover within the space of the unnameable to the degree that those beyond the desacralized bodies (i.e., who have not experienced it themselves) refuse to *imagine* the terror of trauma itself. It is within this space that I call the (in)imaginable that the representations I seek to examine reside: they defy notions of unthinkability, of the unspeakable or unimaginable, in a double-sense. They posit that the trauma survived or witnessed can acquire a language, a narrative, a representation, that it has a semiotic capacity, but they also refuse to visually represent the site of trauma or to reenact the trauma itself, especially when the violated body is female or feminized (specifically, that of a woman or child). In this latter sense, representation becomes gnarled, and though it can appear to lapse into rendering a silence rather than a telling, it shifts the ground of enunciation in the visual sphere to one of narration, defying the popular notion of trauma theory that argues for trauma's essential forgetting. Though it may be true on a collective level that national traumas are forcibly forgotten in order to forge a sense of a unified nation-state or culture, despite violations from within or without the state of these codes of unification (indeed, new codes for national coherence may have had to be created as a result of the cataclysmic event), it is seldom true for individuals who must contend with trauma's persistence at somatic and/or psychological levels.

Gendered, visual narratives of the Rwanda genocide, those that focus on women's bodies as overwhelming and explicit sites of trauma reveal that such representations are always mediated by the shadow of a silence that exists beyond the silencing effect of dominant discourses as explained by Bourdieu, whether they are those of resistant official agencies, or of those individuals of communities that want to "forget" the event, to move forward, as if it never happened. In this case, "dominant" discourse asserts itself as both a male domain and one of hegemonic discourses of the State, of postcolonialism, and of the making and disseminating of representative images themselves.

Nondominant discourses therefore reveal themselves both implicitly and explicitly as pertaining to the feminine domain inasmuch as they are rendered powerless and are most often attached to actual female (or feminized, that is, disempowered) physical bodies and their violation(s); strikingly, it is only when such narratives have been engaged by Rwandan women themselves or African Diasporic artists that such representations have been deployed.

For most non-Rwandans, knowledge of the Rwandan genocide of 1994 has been filtered through the circulation of images of State-directed carnage that left over 500,000 to 1 million dead in a man-made slaughter that lasted approximately 100 days: photographs of dead bodies amassed by the side of roads, or of bones blanched by the sun found months or even years later in the naves of churches where victims huddled together in the hope of a rescue that never came. Of these, most circulating quasi-anonymously via worldwide AP services, those of South African, Pieter Hugo, and Brazilian/French, Sebastiao Salgado, have perhaps been the most haunting and the most recognizable, owing to each's authorial "stamp" in the framing and composition of their photos. Hugo, throughout his work, tends toward the spectacular, the grotesque, while Salgado toward the epic yet restrained depiction of (dis)humanity and nature. By focusing on Hugo's work specifically here (in contrast to South African, Gien's text analyzed earlier), I explore further the notion of *autochthonomy* as nonracialized but as an act of identification with cultures of African descent.

I begin by suggesting that the politics, cultural background, and social position of image-makers impacts the resulting image(s) produced. We all know by now that, as powerful as the photograph is in conveying "reality," images (even prior to our digital age) are manipulated from the moment of their making in what is designated as worthy to be a subject and framed, what is left in and out of focus and in and out of the frame (Sontag, *On Photography* 133; Barthes, *Camera Lucida* 89). Often, these manipulations occur in order to create empathy between the viewer and the photographed subject. But it is in the arena of empathy that notions of interpretive capacity come to bear, especially across cultural difference. Yet, when trauma is documented, especially in large scale, empathy often fails. Perceived *cross-culturally*, and within matrices of power hierarchies, the impulse to identify *with* others (that is, to empathize with them) is often supplanted by a counter-impulse to view those who suffer as ultimate Others, in an exteriority that can only summon sympathy rather than empathy. Sontag, for one, calls photography the "inventory of mortality" (70). For her, the relationship between the two is related to photography's "evidentiary" work, as she notes, "the very notion of atrocity, of war crime, is associated with the expectation of photographic evidence. Such evidence is, usually, of something posthumous; the remains, as it were," (*Pain of Others* 83), allowing us to enter and investigate those elements that contributed to the event archived, with the assumption that the viewer seeks to evade death and those with its associative markers. Though such images may assist our understanding, Sontag argues that they do not humanize their content: photographs "[allow] us to participate, *while confirming alienation,*" she argues (*On Photography* 167); emphasis mine). The trick of the photographer is enmeshed with "*a disavowal of empathy . . . a claim to be invisible*" (77; emphasis mine). On the other hand, yet similarly, Barthes writes, "the Photograph then becomes a bizarre *medium*, a new form of hallucination: false on the level of perception, true on the level of time: a temporal hallucination" (*Camera Lucida* 115). He goes on to argue that the viewer virtually becomes the object photographed, thereby by-passing the photograph's actual content and any atrocity it may index: "I [pass] beyond the unreality of the thing represented, I [enter] crazily into the spectacle, into the image, taking into my arms what is dead, what is going to die" (117). The photograph embalms the past for future use and even as it alters time cannot speak for it. "Such is the Photograph," writes Barthes, "it cannot *say* what it lets us see" (100). An image can come to mean anything, or almost nothing, according to Barthes. Entering the stage of the photography, "what is dead, what is going to die," does not, for him, necessarily mean that the scene depicted is accepted or even less understood, but that viewers make it their own, transform it into their own terms. This is where the work of interpreting the photograph, or translating its visual language into text, becomes both crucial and a potential minefield for limiting affective responses.

We have simultaneously grown accustomed to the idea that if a photographer clearly indicates his/her intent, especially a photojournalist, and if that photojournalist is documenting his or her own culture, that their assessment of the content of their images should be taken at face value; we assume the same for photographs of human suffering, especially of man-made cataclysms. Yet, philosopher Georges Didi-Huberman suggests that despite the photographer's manipulations, the viewer still reacts to the content of the photograph in such a way that invokes emotion that displaces the viewer's narrow self-interest (recall Bourdieu's critique of anthropologists and their distortions of the cultures they study). Drawing upon the findings of Sartre, Merleau-Ponty and Deleuze, Didi-Huberman asserts emotions are passed on through *gestures* (recall the content of Chapter 1 and notions of racial habitus and their potential defeat or reframing once understood as constructed responses to difference) that take us out of ourselves, and that such gestures, via photographs, are passed on transhistorically, that is, through time and history (37–39). He argues that such gestures are embedded in the visages of those photographed and it is *they* that communicate to the viewer, not so much the photographer or his intent; such gestures are primal and evocative, and by reacting to them, Didi-Huberman suggests, they become part of us: an exchange takes place that is emotive, even, at times, empathetic. But such assignment of authenticity becomes more complex when we begin to think across cultures and transnationally, when it is no longer quite so clear who has the authority to make, disseminate, and interpret images—who has the responsibility, even—to do so. When there are competing notions of what constitutes membership in a particular culture whether because of "race," economics, or some other marker delineating differences in and among the social groups of a particular nation, matters become even more complicated as the ability to participate in the making of images, rather than only being caught as its subject/object, becomes an issue of power and privilege.

In the perspective drawn by Didi-Huberman (drawn in turn from findings in Darwinian evolution), cultural history is what permits us to understand each other's emotions and to be drawn out of ourselves. Didi-Huberman contends that emotions, like fossils, are always in movement (he rereads the word *émotion* as *é, ex-motion—hors* [out of] motion [30]), stating: "Ils [emotions] ont une très longue—et très inconsciente—histoire. Ils *survivent en nous*, même si nous sommes incapables de l'observer clairement sur nous-mêmes [they (emotions) have a very long—and very unconscious—history. They *survive in us*, even if we are unable to clearly observe them within ourselves]" (40). Bridging Didi-Huberman's contention with that of Barthes's and Sontag's, then, I argue that what emotion is drawn out from the viewer is largely dependent not only on the photographer but on the culture within which they are embedded, from its "interpretive communities." Sontag, Barthes, Didi-Huberman, like Fish, all assume that imagery is archetypal while situating such archetypes in Euro-white contexts unmitigated by questions of racial/ethnic or national power dynamics; as such, their findings are Eurocentric but do not necessarily mean that the theories they espouse cannot be read anew from a different ground. If we read the photographs of the Rwandan genocide from within the interpretive community of African Diasporics, then we may find that the "gestures" of photographs reveal something more than a European viewpoint. Only by contrasting images taken from differing starting points can I make this latter point clear. In the remainder of this chapter, I seek to test these findings by examining representations of Rwanda that are meant to draw empathy from their viewers. In what follows, then, I pursue the notion that it might be possible to overcome the short-circuiting of empathy, that critics such as Barthes and Sontag invoke as endemic to photography, through the process of identification engaged through autochthonomous and lakou/yard consciousness. Those artists whose practices reflect the latter draw upon aesthetic choices steeped in both dimensions as one way to counteract what some perceive as the affective limitations of visual genres. My findings will show that though Sontag and Barthes are correct in assuming that the photograph operates as a "dead" image in the Euro-white imagination, this is less the case for those working in photography and film out of an African Diasporic point of view, one in which, epistemically, all things remain living, even beyond corporeal death. In this sense, Didi-Huberman's contention that emotions travel is on point, even if he does not situate this sense of emotion's travel as being constitutive of particular cultures, as I intend, but, rather, as universal.

All "Our" Kin: Representing the Rwandan Genocide

Pieter Hugo, is invariably described in interviews and reviews of his work (and even by himself) as an "improbable" African due to his over six-foot frame, blond hair, and blue eyes, working in various parts of the African continent, ruled, it seems, by both a political and aesthetic agenda dominated by a desire to photograph liminal populations of the continent (albinos, "hyena men," the disappeared) and producing a significant body of work in the last decade that is as arresting as it is disturbing. His work recalls that of pioneering independent photographers working among the demi-mondes of New York or Paris, such as Diane Arbus (whose work he admires). Unlike Arbus, and others, however, Hugo does not *participate* in the cultures he photographs, other than the insertion in some of his later projects of contrasting self-portraits with those of his subjects; he keeps himself outside of such frames of reference, and by maintaining a strict divide between the Subject (positioned in his work as the photographer) and the Other (the object of the photograph). Says Hugo: "I've travelled through Africa, I know it, but at the same time *I'm not really part of it....* I can't claim to [have] an authentic voice, but I can claim to have an honest one," he says in one interview (Montgomery 2; emphasis mine). This is most pronounced in his albinism project, indicating more of a grappling with "whiteness" as a construction or aberration by the artist, than with the liminality or marginalization of his subjects affected by albinism. This series reveals Hugo's awareness of his privilege but also his limited understanding of the erasures abjection entails. As Leah Ollman writes, "[t]he problems raised by Hugo's work are fascinating, even if the images themselves are not" (1). Widely acclaimed, and only rarely reproached by critics for "exoticism," Hugo is largely hailed—despite his protestations—as a faithful documentarian "[challenging] stereotypes of Africa with his controversial take on the continent's subcultures" (Montgomery 2). It is not clear, however, if Hugo's work has been successful because it reveals unknown subcultures, or if they present "Africa" as a continued construct, as an enigmatic locus of quintessential difference. Within the larger scope of his work, Hugo's series, "Rwanda: Vestiges of a Genocide, 2004," is worth a second look not only because it appears to be a stark departure from his other series but because it features no actual human beings, only remnants. What effect does providing photographic "evidence" of genocide have upon viewers? Can it be beneficial for us to imagine only those whose lives were taken in the slaughter, to believe that the violence was, indeed, "unimaginable," beyond witness? Or does it serve to reinforce the notion of exceptionalism that surrounds mass atrocities, preventing us from believing in our ability to engage the mantra of "never again" we have heard recited actively since the Shoah and, now, again, after the Rwandan genocide?

In notes accompanying a part of the series, photographs taken in Ntarama Catholic Church grouped together in *Afterwards: Contemporary Photography Confronting the Past*, editor Nathalie Herschdorfer relays that Hugo claimed that he "wanted to preserve a certain distance from the victims," that "he chose to adopt a distant and rigorous approach. All that is left of the victims are a few remains and some personal items. The images are so similar and repetitive that they almost take on the quality of an inventory" (42). That quality can also lead to a collective forgetfulness, an approach to death disembodied from real people who were made to suffer and lost their lives; it can lead to a decrease of empathy. On the other hand, the silence captured by the photographs, especially those of sacred, personal objects once owned and cherished by the dead (since these are the few objects they gathered in futile acts of flight as they sought refuge away from the killing brigades) can lead viewers to project themselves into the space left behind by the disappeared, to an attempt to imagine our own objects, our own exchanges in the material world and its tactility. In either approach, empathy is either lost or gained but neither ensures one or the other. Like the engagement graphic novels and film demand from readers, these photographs rely on the active participation of the viewer but, in so doing, may also produce their disengagement.

Within Hugo's "Rwanda" series, there are two variants. One has Hugo examining the remnants of corpses preserved by acid down to the bone at a Murambi site. These photographs show the corpses in what appears to be a death pose that reveals the agony or simplicity of the subject's passing, even in the absence of clothing and muscle-mass, but often without context. One particularly gruesome image seems to show an individual screaming, with a stream of sputum frozen to his/her lower "lip." It almost seems as if the corpse is frozen in time, at the moment of being slain. It is more likely that the acid has had some effect on distorting the physical mass and the preserved sputum is a remnant of the chemical reaction between the acid and body mass. It is hard to tell. Hugo's close-up shot doesn't allow us to understand the photograph's materiality though it does convey, in an abstract way, the agony of the slain, even though this effect is fabricated postmortem. In another photograph, suitably used as the cover of Boubacar Boris Diop's novel, *Murambi: The Book of Bones*, the close-up shot is of a child, in a fetal pose, quietly extinguished. For Barthes, the essential basis of the photograph is the "pose," which has been stilled "in front of the tiny hole and has remained there forever" while "in cinema, something *has passed* in front of this same tiny hole: the pose is swept away and denied by the continuous series of images: it is a different phenomenology, and therefore a different art which begins here, though derived from the first one" (*Camera Lucida* 78). The tension in these portraits is that none of the subjects have posed, but Hugo's tight framing suggests that they have, that each has given up his/her life in order to leave behind some vestige of their existence and pain in death. Barthes also contends that photography's testimony "bears not on the object but on time" (89), past time, that "it is *without future*" (90). In this sense, Hugo's photographs join the skeletons in freezing time, past time, and accentuate the impossibility of a future for those whose remains they enshrine. The "gestures" they portray are without affect; they are simulacra of emotions that we project onto the images but they do not draw from the repository of available facial gestures that Didi-Huberman discusses in this work on emotion. These are literally remains. More than this, what "gestures" or emotion we may read into them are produced through scientific manipulations of the bones that have little to nothing to do with the human beings they once were and what they were subjected to, felt, and, ultimately, did not survive.

The other strain in the series is of everyday objects, remains found in and around a genocide site of Ntamara church, prior to the creation of the massive, concrete burial vaults that have more recently housed remains (some remaining open to accommodate more findings of bones in the countryside): a comb, a shoe, faded fabric, a rosary. Here, the object becomes a subject, its pose of repose a comment, again, on the "without future" of its prior owner. These photographs are essentially images of found objects that seem to speak of an obliterated past. They necessarily engage the viewer to create contexts that may or may not be true, to reflect on the humanity reflected in the objects by way of our own relationship to material things and our own affective attachments, our phenomenological relationship to our environments. In the end, however, we do not so much reflect on the human beings who once made use of, or cherished, these objects, we reflect on our own fears of loss and annihilation.

The photographs appear to create an *empathetic* reach into the lives of others but we really can only muster an ambivalent *sympathy* that relies on our own survival as a stay against what the remnants represent, what we imagine is the worst of humanity's inhumanity. We are not asked to reflect on how our own "tribes" enact, have enacted, or might enact such violence; it is beyond the purview of the frame, beyond access. The reality of the history behind the objects, who owned them, and what occurred at Ntamara Church is obscured. Again, by utilizing a tight frame and close-ups, Hugo achieves intimacy with the object photographed but cuts out context, thereby elongating time, making it far from our reach. Barthes concludes that "the Photograph flows back from presentation to retention" (90) but it isn't clear what has been retained in Hugo's photographs. It is as if aesthetic beauty has been derived from forensic evidence. I am not certain that this is what we would want a photograph of violent carnage to do. Still, the images powerfully hold a restive silence, one that allows viewers to approach the remains closely without yet violating them. And yet, it isn't so clear that what Barthes calls the "Operator," the photographer and his/her intentions, has done the same. Even if a photograph or a portrait is, too, a composition, the particular silence that envelops victims of genocide is concerning not only for the sheer scale of the killings, the calculated nature of their engineering, or the crude manner in which so many are slain, but for the details of the tortures many suffered before their deaths, and that, despite these, many thousands have survived, many of those women and children. Such statistics escape the potential frame of the photograph, as they do that of the graphic novel, but do not lessen the empathetic response they can elicit from the viewer willing to look beyond themselves, and, if they are Western (read white/European) willing to lose "being the privileged decoders and ultimate interpreters of meaning" (Gabriele 39). If Hugo, then, fails at creating images that create empathetic responses because, as the photographer says of himself, he is a non-African and can only "see" Rwandans as Others, then, to some degree, we are one step closer to understanding what we seek in autochthonomous representations: representations that bring out what is "beyond imagining," beyond the European "universal" that cannot see itself in those it deems as others.

Moving Pictures: The "Co-mix" of Politics and Empathy in Documentary Graphic Novels

It would seem almost counterintuitive for genocide narratives to take the form of "comics" given their subject matter, but modern graphic novels have been at the forefront of tackling difficult, even "unspeakable" events in modern history; in fact, some critics argue that the development of the genre coincides with a postmodern realization of the incapacity of traditional formats to encompass traumatic events of a national or global scale. The graphic novel has increasingly found its niche in the representation of the seemingly unrepresentable; among the best-known examples are the Holocaust in Spiegelman's 1991 groundbreaking genre-defining, *MAUS*, and the depiction of the Iranian Revolution from an exile's point of view in Satrapi's 2000–2003 French serial, *Persepolis* (English translation 2004/2005). Spiegelman, himself, distinguished the work of the graphic novel from conventional comic strips by referring to his work as a "comix," which he defined as "to mix together, because to talk about comics is to talk about mixing together words and pictures to tell a story" (1999, 74). The potency of the "comix" is in its insistence in the relationship between its parts from image to word to the gutters (white space between boxes of image/text) and the role of the reader in making sense of the interplay between these components. As Michael Levine writes, "[o]nce the medium is activated, the individual picture windows are no longer read primarily as discrete units, but rather as links in a chain of signifiers. Each panel itself becomes a kind of gutter, an interspace, a self-different image whose relative value is determined only through its relation to other 'inter-images'" (320). Thierry Groensteen has presented the cognitive process of reading graphic novels as a process called spacio-topia, in which Marie Thorsten summarizes, "both space (espace) and place (lieu) facilitate complex simultaneity of reading and looking that greatly expands story-telling." Thorsten argues that the "activation" of the graphic novel lay not so much on the interplay between parts but what these parts attempt to depict, that is, contributing "to current affairs book and film collections, serving as accessible introductions to humanitarian struggles" (222). For her, in the accessibility of the genre lay its potential for actively sensitizing, educating, and transforming the consciousness of the medium's readers: "To the extent that current affairs comics provoke public conversations and opinions in classrooms, coffee shops, or book clubs, they are more constitutive of a transnational public sphere than any nation's particular 'soft power'" (225). Furthermore, following Sacco, the Palestinian author of several graphic novels, on the question of Palestine, 9/11, and other topics, she contends that "current affairs graphic novels and animations question the truth claims of conventional, seemingly detached reportage and photorealism" (226). The genre thus has the potential of countering the limits I have considered above in the work of documentary photography. Notably, the leading figures of historically based graphic novels (some cited earlier) share the cultural and ethnic contexts they seek to recount.

Generally speaking, critics of graphic novels consider that the medium allows for readers' active participation in the creation of the text's ultimate meaning: "The text is understood according to the reader's negotiation of tensions and harmonies between visual and verbal signifiers" (Watkins 12). The medium is also considered to be more accessible as a result of "styles [that] are more iconic due to their simplified forms and are therefore 'universal,' as opposed to representation styles which narrow the reader's ability to identify with characters due to the exclusive detail of representational illustration" (Watkins 12; McCloud 31). Scott McCloud, in his *Understanding Comics*, goes further to say that comics are even more universal than photographs or realistic drawings because "when you look at a photo or realistic drawing of a face—you see it as the face of *another*. But when you enter the world of the *cartoon*—you see *yourself*" (36). The benefit of such identification, one assumes, is that it is necessary to be able to see the other as oneself to create a sense of shared humanity, or to invoke affect; it also assumes that to see another as one's self closes the gap between sympathy and empathy: cartoons should allow one to walk in the other's shoes. But cartoons are not realistic and the projection onto the cartoon image of one's own image implies a form of narcissistic identification that returns the reader's gaze to oneself rather than the condition of the other, bringing us back to the potential pitfalls of the abstractions of documentary photography. The danger in this, in the case of representations of the genocide of Rwanda in particular, is that the identification in most of those depicting the genocide force the reader to identify not with victims but with perpetrators. There is irony in this transference of empathy toward perpetrators in that it confirms that the energy of understanding is to be directed toward the colonial matrix rather than toward a decolonial one: readers are led to empathize with perpetrators who belong to a power hierarchy that resembles the presumed reader's own: a white, patriarchal gaze that sees only its own projection into postcolonial space rather than its effects.

Stassen's *Deogratias* conforms to the standard elements of the comic strip, as described by Scott McCloud, moving the action forward from panel to panel to create a sense of mood, time, and space. Movement between time-periods is primarily established through the demeanor and clothing of characters, and the space between the panels, or "gutters," simply advance the plot. There are no tricks here or a calling of attention to the artifice of the medium. If, as McCloud suggests, the comic panels "fracture both time and space, offering a jagged, staccato rhythm of unconnected moments" so that "closure allows us to connect these moments and mentally construct a continuous, unified reality," Stassen's "closure" in this case, the process of his main character, Deogratias, progressively mutating from man to dog, relies less on the reader's ability to "construct a continuous, unified reality" of the panel's fragments but on previous iconographic knowledge of African subjects conflated with animal imagery. This is quite different from Spiegelman's use of animal equivalents in MAUS in which all ethnicities are depicted as animals (human bodies with animal-heads) "to convey . . . his elderly father's experiences in the Holocaust—Jews were mice, Nazis cats, and Poles were pigs . . . thinking of the cat-mouse metaphor of dehumanization used in anti-Semitic Europe; he wanted to critique race and class oppression and at the same time mask his own incapacity to enter his father's world" (Thorsten 227). Or, as Michael Levine advances, these representations of human beings with animal heads operate as a means of suggesting "that the human faces one expects to find beneath the animal masks are themselves surfaces for projection" (322). The initial effect of equating Jews to mice can be only an uncomfortable one since we know that the Nazi propaganda machine readily imaged Jews as rats or mice, but, by playing with the ocular spectacle of animal-headed human beings that replicate the anti-Semitic sentiments and power relations of the time described, Spiegelman reveals his awareness of such constructions and signals to the reader that they must "read" past this artifice as well as recognize its operational function during Nazism. He also refuses to single out one group in particular in order to demonstrate how each ethnicity was forced to interact in an "animalized" or dehumanized relation within the power hierarchy created by Nazism. Stassen does not engage in these kinds of self-reflexive gestures, nor does he force the viewer to have to rethink what s/he knows about the history of colonialism and the dehumanization of Africans; neither does he depict white Europeans or "Westerners" as dehumanized or animal-like, even if their words reflect callousness or dehumanizing points of view. They, themselves, remain human.

Madeleine Hron observes in her review article of texts seeking to re-present the 1994 genocide of Rwanda, which she refers to by the Kinyarwandan nomenclature, *itsembabwoko*, that most non-Rwandan depictions of the event have great difficulty in deciphering both Rwanda's complex colonial history and the postcolony present in which the events themselves took place. She notes, "[m]any opted . . . to deal with this difficulty by adopting a child's perspective and the Bildungsroman genre, a tactic deployed from early colonial writing to current child-soldier narratives." She thus situates Stassen's Rwanda text in this tradition, rather than that of the graphic novel, in which "the child-hero is part Hutu and a killer," aiming "to humanize the representation of the 'enemy'" (165). By universalizing their message, however, such texts deny or silence the fact that "during *itsembabwoko*, there was no generative or neutral "in-between" or "third space": one was either Tutsi or Hutu, a perpetrator or a victim, dead or alive" (66). Hron goes on to assert that the exclusion by critics of assessments of Rwandan-derived narratives says as much about "the ethics of *reading* about genocide" as it does about "the failures of our imagination and our reluctance to imagine the horrors of genocide, in solidarity with its victims and survivors" (173). Such tales of genocide "instruct" the reader on how to "read" the genocide and reveal that graphic novels are not, by virtue of their usually self-reflexive nature, in any way freed from social constraints and constructions. If anything, the "graphic" nature of the genre, its slippages and gaps, can enable intentional misreading.

Another area in which *Deogratias* falls short is in its attempt to depict sexism as incidental rather than genocidal. Sexist attitudes are presented as precursors to genocide as when "Boss," a Belgian sergeant who becomes an innkeeper post-genocide, now a tourist, accidently meets Deogratias in a bar after the genocide and comments on Tutsi women walking by: "Man, those Tutsi girls! You know what I mean, right, Deogratias? That's what I missed the most. . . . And it's such a shame, when you think about it. All those beauties who won't be sharing their soft little thighs with anyone anymore. All those sweet pieces of ass hacked to bits with machetes. . . . What a waste!" (Stassen 3). Boss's only understanding of the slaying of Tutsi women is that he and others like him have lost access to these women as prey. When Stassen then turns to depicting the violence in Boss's description visually, it is to show Venetia ("the African prostitute"), recognizable only by the clothing we have come to associate with her throughout the text, beheaded, legs parted and bloodied, a beer bottle suggestively positioned before her genitalia to suggest digital rape (74). On the one hand, this depiction is consistent with illustrating Venetia as an object, but it unfortunately does not relieve this objectification in the mind of readers. Elena Coundouriotis understands this depiction of Venetia, a mother of two school-age daughters, Appolinia[2] and Benina, more generously as a rereading of the corpse of Mukandori at the Nyamata memorial, who is featured in a number of African-authored texts on the genocide, as an "appropriation and recasting of the figure of the impaled woman as the death of a Rwanda that had been shaped by its colonial history and the Rwandans' continued entanglement in its ideology" (384). Although the genocide is undeniably an effect of colonial entanglements, I would have to disagree with Coundouriotis's generous reading of Stassen's appropriation of the Mukandori image. For one thing, Mukandori was not a prostitute;[3] secondly, Venetia is a minor character in Stassen's story, therefore it is impossible to create an emotional tie to her. She is an object both in life (as prostitute) and in death (raped *Interahamwe* victim); at no point in the story is she fully humanized, except in a brief exchange with one of her daughters in which she explains to the daughter her life choices: "When we came back here [from Zaire], of course I'd have preferred to grow bananas and beans! But our plot of land had been stolen!" She continues, in the next cell, as she lights up a cigarette (in keeping with her bad-girl representation): "All I did, I did for you! And all I do is still for you! How else do you think you were able to go to college, study your books, become somebody?" (42). This is not to say that women like Venetia do not exist, but it seems peculiar that Stassen would resort to such an established literary trope (the African migrant as prostitute) in order to "humanize" the only African mother in the text; such a choice, given that Africans continue to be stereotyped does not seem to advance issues much. Thus, when Venetia's corpse is visually presented on the page, it is difficult to ascertain how Stassen wishes to position the reader's gaze. Her daughters seem to be those who are looking upon the remains. The sisters say, "off camera," as the image shows a guilty Deogratias in the background and the Interahamwe in civilian clothing in the foreground, smiling diabolically, "Deogratias, what have they done to her? What have you done to Mom?" The Interahamwe's response suggests that Deogratias is then forced to rape the girls but the images of the text stay silent on this point. Soon after, Deogratias witnesses dogs feasting upon corpses as the liberating forces enter Kigali. Visually, from left to right, as Deogratias is questioned in the rain by a liberating army soldier, his physiognomy shifts in the drawing from that of a crouching man to that of a dog. "Another madman," says the soldier, "all that's left are corpses, madmen and dogs." (76). Told in medias res, in flashbacks after the end of the genocide, readers have been experiencing Deogratias as a mad-dog all along, but it is at this point in the narrative that we see how he transforms into this man/dog: he has seen too much, been complicit in violence, perhaps even participated in killing and raping Venetia and her daughters. In the movement from one cell to the next, from the representation of Venetia as an object to that of Deogratias traumatically transmuted into a dog, readers' sympathies are drawn away from the former and toward Deogratias, who is, after all, our story's protagonist.

Other than the imaging of Venetia as a violated corpse, it is Deogratias who otherwise narrates women's violations but he does so in a state of "madness" such that it is impossible to tell whether he should be read as a reliable narrator. Deogratias can no more differentiate between memories of witnessing atrocities and his own nightmares. "The insides of bellies are blending into the inside of my head," he states at one point, then the text has him speak disjointedly, without context, "and sharp, sharp blades plunge into women's genitals" (Stassen 53). What is the effect of having a perpetrator/witness speak these words? For whom are readers meant to have empathy? Victims here disappear and the violence enacted against women's bodies become a wounding of the perpetrator, with whom we become complicit as we absorb the "story of Rwanda" through his troubled eyes. In fact, just prior to the panel cited earlier, we are subjected to Deogratias's tortured mind-set as he becomes and un-becomes a dog. Throughout the text, whenever Deogratias drowns his sorrows in banana beer, it is under cover of night and Stassen inserts a panel of a star-lit sky over the Rwandan hills. It is alcohol that keeps Deogratias from descending into a doglike state, as if he is attempting to escape a form of spiritual possession. This might remind us of Colin Dayan's invocation of the figure of Ovid's Hecuba who is transformed into a "roaming haunt," a "She-Hound": "Changed into a dog, at once mystified and historicized, ghostly and corporeal, she brings us to the interstices of human and animal, person and god, living and dead" (The Law Is a White Dog 17). Stassen repeats the images of a star-lit light throughout the novel but especially in the closing panel; there, it is preceded by a panel of Brother Philip stating of Deogratias, "He was a creature of God" (78). Through these continuous transformations, then, Deogratias is both reduced to an animal state and elevated to the status of hapless victim or anointed one. But note that Brother Philip calls Deogratias not a "child of God" (which would be the usual Catholic designation) but a *creature* of God, so that Deogratias, from beginning to end, remains conflated with the animal. Having to make Deogratias's ordeal central thus deflects us away from what he has witnessed, from the violence and pain physically amassed on the corpses we see the dogs eating. We see Deogratias as such a dog, and we lament his descent into madness. Ideologically, this naturalizes Deogratias's predatory behavior yet still depicts him as a victim of colonialism in such a way that those he victimizes are given little such consideration.

If, then, Colin Dayan draws sympathetic parallels between the treatment of dogs and men through Anglo-American (juridical) history to the present, to argue: "The image of the dog body that encases the spirit of a dead person can be related figuratively to the *civil body*, the artificial person who possesses self and property, and to the *legal slave*, the artificial person who exists as both subject and object, who is both self and property" (41), I argue here that Stassen's depiction of Deogratias as a dog is rooted less in an understanding of how dogs appear as specters in both Western myth and Anglo-American jurisprudence and more as a powerful, residual symbol of colonial power. Here, we should recall that dogs are not only linguistically symbolic as synonymous with beings of a lower order in popular speech (comparing humans to dogs to discredit their rights or valor via the phrase "like a dog") but, especially in the Americas, dogs were systematically utilized to track, police, and punish slaves. In the United States, legal statutes concerning dogs and slaves made the equivocation of the two a question of slippage between the human and animal, between what was considered humane regard for one or brutish disregard for the other. "Once tamed," writes Colin Dayan, "a dog gains legal value, even if not the status of *absolute* property" (212); not absolute because their status was ambivalently secured in jurisprudence because dogs were considered "neither wild nor domesticated, neither profitable nor worthless" (214). This ambivalence, however, was not granted to the slave. As Dayan writes: "If they had no value as instruments of labor or procreation, then they literally had no reason for being and no legal protections against neglect or mutilation, maiming or death." She continues: "Slaves had no legal personality in civil law but gained it in criminal law. Dogs, on the other hand, had no property value in criminal law but were granted it in civil law. What both dogs and slaves have in common, however, is their standing outside the concerns of civil life" (214). Slaves were considered "chattel" and hence had property value, but only acquired the status of the "human" when it came to punishing "crimes" derived from their de facto, yet structurally denied, humanity (from attempts at flight from slavery to the killing or poisoning of whites); dogs could not be held responsible for "crimes" (though their owners could), but acquired property value once their loss was established as causing injury to their owners (Dayan examines dog theft to explore this particular point). Dayan's insight here has high relevance to my reading of Stassen as, though Dayan does not ultimately term the equivocation of "dog" to "slave" in the way that I do here, it could be argued that her analysis ultimately shows not just that both dogs and slaves were contained as "outsiders" to civil life but that dogs were *raised* in status from the "wild" to the "domestic" according to their usefulness (i.e., for their protection or to hold their owners responsible if they were destructive) while slaves were *lowered* from their status as "human" to that of the "domestic" (read *animal*). The latter is consistent with the colonial relationship described by Achille Mbembe when he asserts that such relations are "based on the distinction between the wild and the domestic animal" (*On the Postcolony* 237). Stassen's projection of a Hutu victim/perpetrator/survivor as animal-like unto his creation, Deogratias, accurately reveals the macabre aspects of how the colonial relationship remains intact despite decades of attempted decolonization. This is to say that because the depictions in the text do not step away from stereotype but reinscribe these in a simplistic equation of genocidal complicity to animalism, and the effects of trauma to madness, the text is less an account of "what happened" during the genocide of Rwanda and more, a reflection of the social matrix of its creator: it rescripts the colonist perspective in a strikingly spatial way that induces the collusion of the reader in ignoring its wholesale fabrication as an ideological effect. The reader literally must inhabit the "gutter" of Western, colonial thought: we are given no choice but to accept the animality/savagery of Deogratias as inevitable.

If, for Dayan, the law is a "white dog" that is a supernatural entity, a ghost in the machine, then that "whiteness"—that is, the colonial imagination—is what haunts Stassen's depiction of the Rwandan genocide. But one would not have to look far to understand that Stassen's graphic novel is also a part of a tradition of French "bande dessinée" which has long replicated colonial thought in its visual compositions, from Hergé's 1931 *Tintin au Congo* (Tintin in the Congo) to Liquois's 1943–1944 *Vers les mondes inconnus* ("Towards Unknown Worlds") serialized in a children's illustrated magazine called *Le Téméraire*, both "influenced by eugenicist ideology" or the myth of the West's "civilizing mission" (MacLeod 60).[4] It speaks sadly to the degree to which "we" accept the depictions of people of African descent as depraved or as animals that few, if any, reviewers of Stassen's work have taken the time to consider or analyze in historical context. It might be that Stassen did not give much thought to the socially embedded signification of conflating dogs with (African) men; he may have been attempting to avoid a conflation of Rwandans with "the racist depiction of the black man in simian form" particular to Hergé's depiction of the Congolese (73n10). Unfortunately, in the end, not only do Rwandan perpetrators perversely benefit from "victim" status, but the targets of genocide, the true victims and the history of their victimization, remains obscured; understandably, the place of gender and tools of genocide, such as rape, can appear only in such representations as spectacle. Without proper contextualization, they are silenced altogether.[5] Tragically, then, Stassen's graphic novel fails in realizing what Groensteen termed the "spacio-topia" of the genre; the text fails because the "space" and "place" of the genocide are not fully rendered (or even, understood) because the representation remains anchored in colonial tropes and clichés regarding Africans more generally. Because it does not (and cannot) engage lakou consciousness—in other words, a spacio-topia reflective of Rwandan realities, consistent with how Rwandans see and understand themselves and the event of the genocide, it fails to inspire a "co-mix" of *moving* the reader toward empathy. It is not enough for the text to designate a Rwandan protagonist and it is not enough for sexual aspects of the genocide directed toward Rwandan women to be rendered as incidental and regrettable, rather than central to the genocide.

Sometimes in April: Transnational Parallels of Forgotten Histories and Women as Carriers of Traumatic Memory/Healing

In her work on photographic depictions of rape (in the aptly titled chapter, "Has Anyone Ever Seen a Photograph of a Rape," from her text, *The Civil Contract of Photography*), Ariella Azoulay argues that rape in particular "isn't accessible to the gaze in any of the discursive frameworks in which it is posited" (218).[6] That is to say that though "rapes" might be found in some forms of pornography, as Elena Coundouriotis has written: "The caution that leads us initially to read along the grain of the indirect reference to rape stems from the anxiety that a more explicit narrative is potentially pornographic" (372); this, in turn results in both the occlusion and misrepresentation of rape as the "collateral damage" issuing from situations of armed conflict in which political power is at stake in a national context, inevitably defined as male/patriarchal. Azoulay suggests, however, that the choice not to represent acts of gendered violence can have the paradoxical aim to uncover them. She discusses the ways in which rape has been nebulously defined both in contemporary, popular discourse and legalistically (conflicting definitions of what constitutes or does not constitute rape), while also obscuring the depiction of women who have been subject to sexual violence (the displacement of photographs depicting rape/gender violence from war archives to sites for and of pornography[7]). Azoulay pointedly asks: "What are these images that the codes of knowledge who treat rape as unrepresentable have effaced, and what is the meaning of this effacement?" (246). Her answers to this question are ultimately complex but she concludes that image-makers must be held and hold themselves to a moral standard by which choosing or not choosing to represent rape is a choice made in order to, as she says "pry rape free from its last grip on worlds in which women are yet subject to the norms of the frater-patriarchy," in order to "challenge the clear demarcation between those images that are allowed to be shown and those that are not—the line of demarcation that distinguishes rape from the other horrors that afflict humanity and preserves women as the exception to the rule" (281).[8] Her point is that the way in which images of rape have circulated such that the violence of rape is misrecognized or rendered unrepresentable must give us pause as to the ways in which such violence could be effectively depicted so that not only are acts of rape made legible but recognized for the trauma they inflict on the victims of rape and on those who either witness the rape or its effects on survivors.

Turning now to my analysis of Raoul Peck's film, *Sometimes in April*, I suggest that Peck's visual work goes the furthest in attempting to reconcile the unbreachable silence around inhumane acts of violence directed specifically toward Rwandan women this is an act of *autochthonomous* identification. He demarcates rape from other horrors by choosing *not* to show a rape on screen and instead creating a space in which a *narrative* of rape can emerge and still be given voice. The film refuses "pornotroping"—Hortense Spillers's term for the reduction of the Black body to both a dominated and sexualized form. Peck instead interrupts or suspends these forces as part of his *autochthonomous* representation of the genocide. In fact, choosing to create a space for the testimony of rape, a testimony that effectively altered international law, Peck's film continues in the vein of "militant" or "Third" cinema—in opposition to Western modes of cinematic representation—in such a way as to recover the remainder that has normally escaped the legal order so that viewers are compelled to experience the shift in the legal order in their own imaginary structures. My discussion addresses how Peck's representations ride the edge of silence to *create* the space of the (in)imaginable as derived from African Diasporic realities, and that we can thus situate this space within the virtual ground of lakou consciousness because it is one drawn through an understanding of the realities of African Diasporic experience, and, through this understanding, a consequent incapacity (or refusal) to view those of African descent as "Others."

Raoul Peck is a Haitian filmmaker brought up partly in Haiti and the Congo while trained in Germany and France. His work is informed by these geographies and their histories, giving rise to a hybrid identity and hybrid forms of expression, which I argue in my introduction, to be constitutive of autochthonomous points of view (after Stuart Hall's concept of "new ethnicities"). When contemplating *Sometimes in April*, a film that specialists of the area consider to be among the most accurate and convincing representations of the genocide and its aftermath, I sought to see what Peck's biography might have to do with his sensitivities to the "ethnic" divides that culminated in the violence of the genocide in Rwanda. There are, in fact, striking similarities between discrete Haitian and Rwandan histories. Although both these histories are the product of colonial interference, the ways in which Peck appears to draw upon them for inspiration in the making of his film on the massacre reveal his *autochthonomous* subjectivity precisely because his main focus is not the force of colonialism but what African-descended people themselves understand of their realities and complex histories. The understanding of colonial histories as formative is rejected in favor of a preceding consciousness of *autochthonomy*, of an autonomous subjectivity that preexists colonial disruption. It is an affirmation of the life force of the subjugated as well as the retention of a lakou or African Diasporic consciousness, which valorizes the need to constantly recreate kinship ties; in short, it is an avowal of (dis)affiliation (discussed in Chapter 1 and explored further in Chapter 3). Intra-cultural affiliation is affirmed across African Diasporas while colonial dictates are disavowed; what is more important is how the future of preexisting *autochthonomous* subjectivity can be preserved and passed on. I would not go so far as to suggest that Peck consciously tracks or indexes the similarities between Haitian and Rwandan trajectories in the film; he does not.[9] However, I want to claim that, informed by them, he is able to go further in his depiction of that which others have found "unthinkable," "unnameable," and thus unrepresentable, which we must concede by now also includes African Diasporic outlooks themselves, in order to render this material, and that pertaining specifically to gender violence, (in)imaginable.

As noted, the similarities between Haitian and Rwandan histories are striking: both countries share entwined legacies of French imperialism, and both, previous to efforts to render them perpetually dependent colonies of Europe, were composed of more-or-less homogeneous ethnic groups. This homogeneity is what made the Haitian Revolution the only successful slave revolt in the Western hemisphere possible. Previous to the Berlin conference in the 1880s through which the African continent was carved up among European powers, Rwanda had been left untouched by the slave trade and unexplored by European expansionists. Writes Paul Gouveritch, "when the explorer Henry M. Stanley, intrigued by Rwanda's reputation for 'ferocious exclusiveness,' attempted to cross that frontier, he was repulsed by a hail of arrows" (54).[10] In this time, like the inhabitants of Hispaniola, Rwandans had a deeply unified character; indeed, Kinyarwanda remains the unifying language of Rwandans and, is second to Swahili in popularity in Africa.[11] Of the patois of the Caribbean, Haitian Kreyol is the only language to have been recognized as one to become a codified and officially recognized national language. Further, the twentieth-century ethnic division between Tutsis and Hutus in Rwanda is similar to the division between Haitian and Dominicans during this same time period. In Rwanda, the Belgians forcibly reified the Hamitic myth that held that certain tribes of differing ethnicities were believed to descend from Ethiopians whose features were deemed Asiatic or more refined, who were cattle herders while the darker tribes tended the land. The fact that this myth had little to no basis in fact was immaterial since the division of the population would serve the purpose of controlling the nation for colonial exploitation. The fact that the Belgians needed to utilize phrenology as a means to distinguish between Hutus and Tutsis in order to emit identity cards supports the evidence that ethnic divisions were not stable; to the contrary, relationships between the ethnic groups were as porous as they were between Haitians and Dominicans prior to the closing of the borders between Haiti and the Dominican Republic in the 1930s. Interestingly too, Tutsis, like Dominicans, were cattle herders while Hutus and Haitians were traditionally agriculturists, divisions in labor which were class-based and which, in both geographical areas, have served to sustain an underclass of darker-skinned appearing inhabitants. However, due to the porous nature of relations in both areas and intermarriage, it was common to find these roles inversed or shared so that the perception of an upper class due solely to ethnicity was often baseless. Indeed, in the border zones between Haiti and the Dominican Republic, as Lauren Derby has conclusively shown, Haitians were perceived as wealthy, while Dominicans were not and, increasingly, in Rwanda, with the assistance of the Belgians post-1959, the Hutu became wealthy in ways that belied the monopoly of Tutsi power that the Belgians had installed in the late 1890s when Tutsis, like Dominicans in the early 1800s, losing their class status, "collaborated with the colonial overlords in exchange for patronage."[12]

In the case of the Tutsis, such patronage lasted for only a time, while for the Dominicans, it has remained to this day. The Belgian's shift from supporting Tutsi eminence to Hutu power is explained only by their desire to maintain a neocolonial hold on the country. When it became clear that the Hutu underclass was rising, the Belgians simply switched sides, because their role had been to impose a class difference in order to control Rwanda, and they did so through a mechanism they all too well understood, ethnic division. Supporting the Hutu ascendance even at the cost of Tutsi lives allowed for the maintenance of the fracturing that made the Belgians, seemingly, the only power that could intervene (though they failed to do so when it most counted since their interest was never humanitarian but extractive). What the Belgians had cultivated in the Hutu masses, however, was a deep distrust of European aid, which can—beyond the fact of colonial oppression—be understood also in terms of the Belgian's use of forced labor against Hutus, which led many to flee to the Congo or Uganda in the 1920s; this is paralleled in the postrevolutionary period in Northern Haiti when the mulatto leader, Christophe, reinstated the French *corvée* in order to build monuments to his kingdom that still stand today and which led to Christophe's demise. In both areas, this reinforced a sense of oppression and inferiority in the lower classes and a distrust of European and mixed-race elites.

It comes as no surprise, then, that after a hundred years or so of such exploitation and divisiveness, of the employing of indigenous myth to turn otherwise kindred groups against themselves, that those seeking to reign in the rage of the underclasses would turn to the peasant classes in order to legitimate their rise to power. Says a Kigali lawyer, François Xavier Nkurunziza: "In Rwandan history, everyone obeys authority. People revere power, and there isn't enough education. You take a poor, ignorant population, and give them arms, and say, 'It's yours. Kill.' They'll obey. The peasants, who were paid or forced to kill, were looking up to people of higher socioeconomic standing to see how to behave. So the people of influence, or the big financiers, are often the big men in the genocide. They may think that they didn't kill because they didn't take life with their own hands, but the people were looking to them for their orders."[13] These comments could just as easily describe the thirty-year regime of terror of the Duvaliers in Haiti that began as U.S. gunboat diplomacy in the region waned. That regime could have taken hold only through the co-optation of the male peasantry who were promised wages and goods, and more importantly, were provided arms with which to "rule" their communities. It was also the means by which, in the 1930s, Trujillo sought to rid darker-skinned inhabitants of the Dominican Republic through "el corte," where peasants were given free rein to cut down with machetes "Haitians"—though the evidence to date suggests that Haitians were not the primary targets of the *blanqueamiento* movement.[14]

Suffice it to say that this all too brief sketch of the similarities between the two countries suggests a malignant, postimperialist legacy that it seems to me can only be countered by a continuous resurrection of a collective memory that insists on nondivisiveness. Raoul Peck taps into this collective memory in *Sometimes in April*, the story of two Hutu Rwandan men, two brothers, one a former army officer married to a Tutsi, whose wife and children are ultimately slain, and his brother, a radio commentator, inciting violence against the Tutsi's, who nonetheless attempts to use his clout to get his brother's family past checkpoints during the genocide. Ten years later, in 2004, the radio journalist stands accused at the UN tribunal and asks his brother to come to see him. The brother and main character, Augustin, now in a common-law marriage to the former teacher of one of his three slain children, Martine, goes, only to find commiseration with a secret witness, Valentine, who, through her testimony, allows him to face his (and the nation's) losses. It is the confrontation with this female witness's words that proves to be the hero's healing agent and thus the film's unlocking as a text of collective memorializing. Interestingly, this scene focuses on a prisoner who did not wield the machete but the ideology that made the carnage actionable.

The key scene, which appears at least two-thirds into the film's storyline, follows an exchange between Augustin, and Valentine, through the wall of their respective hotel rooms. In this exchange, Valentine tells Augustin that she is a secret witness and then requests Augustin's presence during her testimony; sight unseen and underscoring that she will not be able to see him in the court, Augustin agrees to attend. In the crucial scene, then, we hear the witness's testimony of rape and sexual battery before we are allowed to see her (only her voice was utilized in the hotel room scene, filmed from and featuring Augustin's perspective), as the camera focuses on Augustin sitting in a room lined with empty chairs, behind a double-mirror, the only witness from the public to the testimony being given. The camera then shifts to the room in which Valentine is recounting her rapes at the hands of Rwandan genocidal militia, but the audience is still prevented from seeing her. We see, instead, the judges presiding over the tribunal, the blue-and-white UN logo hung behind them on the wall, a row of lawyers for and against the accused sitting below them, and the accused and interpreters sitting in the far background of the screen. Slowly, the camera pans from the back of the room toward Valentine, viewing her from above so that she seems small, even defenseless, in the courtroom; the film then jump-cuts to a midrange shot of Augustin, now sitting back, slumped in his chair, as he listens to the testimony, breathing deeply as he absorbs Valentine's words; a quick jump cut back to Valentine finds us closer to her yet, as she continues her narrative, arms crossed protectively across her chest, her face grave and resolute. She pauses, shakes her head in remembrance, and speaks of one particular soldier's humiliation of her and the gang rape she then suffered. As she details the minutiae of her assaults in a flow of narrative, the scene shifts back to Augustin, now seen from the back, his reflection in the one-way mirror before him, uneasy with the knowledge he is forced to absorb. He listens and looks up as Valentine confesses that she wanted at that moment, only to die. The scene shifts back to Valentine on the stand as she momentarily breaks down. As she wipes away tears, the camera focuses on her in a tight closeup still, at no point does the filmmaker attempt to stage or reimagine the trauma endured through a cutaway or flashback scene—such a scene will come only later when Augustin, emboldened by hearing Valentine's testimony, meets his brother to hear his version of what happened to his family; he will hear, then, a similar story about his wife, Jeanne, and the film will attempt a reconstruction of a rape scene of a group of women by *Interahamwe* men in which rape is only suggested via the facial terror of the actresses, half-clothed, and the stoniness of the men whose acts of terror are indexed by the gesture of zipping up their flies: rape itself remains un-imaged. Valentine narrates her story and that of other women like Jeanne who did not survive. She refers to her assailants as *Interahamwe* as she is questioned, gently, by a white male judge, while we are shown female lawyers, both white and of color, crying and weeping discreetly at the testimony. Realizing that she had to save herself and her own baby, Valentine recounts leaving the rape house to hide in a field. Asked by a judge why she decided to testify at the International Crime Tribunal for Rwanda held in Arusha, Tanzania, she answers, "I felt responsible to testify about this man's betrayal of the people who were entrusted to him." She continues, "When a man leads assassins," pausing to look directly at the accused again, "he is also an assassin." As she turns away from his stony gaze back toward the judges, the camera eye stays with her, at level distance, but the focus subtly shifts from the background of the scene where the accused sits, to the foreground in which she resides, filling most of the screen. The scene ends with a crystal clear view of Valentine's profile, no longer speaking but, by this point, restored to dignity by her courageous act of providing witness for the crimes visited upon her and other women during the genocide.

The camera work of the scene subtly suggests a shift in power as the narrative is taken over by Valentine; it also suggests a giving over of the director's framing to accommodate the storyteller or altered point of view. We no longer focus on Augustin as the main victim or "hero" of the film but on his wife, Valentine, and others like them; when Augustin is forced to look at himself in the two-way glass protecting Valentine's identity as a secret witness, he is forced to look upon his own image, a subtle reflection of the very male nature of the national discourse around the events of the 100-day genocide but also of the necessity to look at the male privilege that engendered the forms that violence took. In a 2005 interview with NPR's Elvin Mitchel, Peck reveals that the scene is drawn from the historical "Witness JJ," who testified before the Arusha International Tribunal, and whose testimony recategorized the use of rape as a war crime to that of weapon or arm of genocide in the landmark "Akayesu" case of 1998; ten years later, the United Nations Security Council (UNSCR) adopted Articles 2, 3, and 4 of the 2008 Genocide Convention. Article 4 notes, "that rape and other forms of sexual violence can constitute a war crime, a crime against humanity, or a constitutive act with respect to genocide." Because Witness JJ's testimony was so influential in changing international law, and because so many victims/survivors of the genocide were women who endured sexual acts of violence, Peck chose to highlight her testimony and to virtually reenact the scene at the tribunal, using the judge's actual responses and the emotions displayed by tribunal lawyers in the original case.

The inclusion of the testimony, the desire to *reenact* rather than *rewrite* the scene, and the camera work utilized throughout the scene to underscore shifts in authorial power speaks to Peck's Third Cinema approach.[15] In the film, Augustin, passive and reflective, acted upon and observant rather than acting or even reacting, stands in for the collective Rwandan experience; other narratives are related or hinged upon his own in order to reveal the multitude of Rwandan realities through, and as a result of, the genocide of 1994. As Peck says of the character, "he's an anti-hero." Peck composed the film in collaboration with Rwandans, both in terms of the real-life accounts he collected in the three to four years of his preproduction research and threaded through the film's narrative but also in the use of local Rwandan actors, most untrained (except in the case of the lead actors), throughout the film, as a means of "telling their story with them" (Peck via Mitchel). In this, Peck echoes Paulo Freire's "pedagogy of the oppressed," wherein productive action is expressed by speaking not *for* but *with* the oppressed. Freire reports: "Political action on the side of the oppressed must be pedagogical action in the authentic sense of the word, and, therefore, action *with* the oppressed" (48)—lending the film its grounding and political authenticity. For Freire, this is a form of praxis by which he terms revolutionary leaders: "If they are truly committed to liberation, their action and reflection cannot proceed without the action and reflection of others" (107). In fact, the final scene of the film centers on Augustin's present-day love interest, Martine, herself also a survivor of the genocide and witness to the slaying of Augustin's daughter along with her other students; she denounces those responsible in a *Gacaca* court, a system of community justice through which localities decide how perpetrators are to be dealt with within the community and outside of European-style legal systems. This is a powerful instance of lakou representation through which Peck demonstrates that the possible outcomes from both systems might yet be the voicing of African women's voices and, in both, patriarchal models are silenced, muted, or vexed so that that the truth can be told from feminized autochthonomous points of view: these are centralized for the viewer and given authority over future outcomes that the film cannot yet imagine. These are scenes reflecting aspects of reality not often represented on screen; Peck is able to discern these avenues by accessing his own biography and that of his subjects, after having conducted multiple interviews and excavated the local site for the stories there to tell. Rather than impose a European point of view upon the tragedy, he unearths the stories of the locals because he already knows that these exist. His autochthonomous stance allows for a more wholistic representation to emerge, one which does not seek to humanize the inhuman (as does Stassen) or to derive sympathy from inert objects (as does Hugo); instead, he feminizes his subjects—male and female—knowing that it is there that the strength of the culture resides (which is why it has been so violated) while illuminating the obscured corners of the genocide through

African sensibilities through which notions of "kin" and "justice" are reconfigured in narrative lines that seek to examine the complexity of present-day reality that, though having seed in colonial exploitation, is far removed from this ground. Lakou consciousness, or the similarity of experience within other African Diasporic grounds, provides Peck with the necessary insight to go further in his investigation than the surface treatment provided by Stassen and Hugo, who assume the impenetrability of the present-day Rwandan context or assume that it can be unpacked only in European terms that fail in advance by assuming the inhumanity of their (African) subjects.

Another aspect of Peck's authenticating details is his photographic handling of sets and framing throughout the film; as he reveals in the interview with Mitchel, he, set designers, and costumers relied on period photographs to reconstruct many of the scenes so that they would reflect as accurately as possible the 100-day genocide period. Though Peck observes that very little archival material exists past the first two weeks of the genocide, given that foreign journalists had left the country by then, there exists enough post-genocide documentation and documentation by Rwandans themselves of the pre-genocide period to piece together, for instance, the difference in appearance between a rural roadblock and one in Kigali, or one manned by the Rwandan army or another by UN forces. Peck's photographic elements are not confined to reliance on evidentiary photographs but on the periodic use of long shots to establish the scale (as in the scene of refugees amassing in a church or the opening and closing sweeps of Rwanda's chains of lush, blue-green hills) of the "pose" (recalling Barthes) to frame a character in an especially tense or revealing moment, as in the scene highlighted earlier of Valentine's testimony, at which end the camera comes to rest alongside her as if framing her for a portrait, or in the instances when Augustin must accept the unacceptable—his friend Xavier being shot before his eyes—or even his brother, as he watches Augustin's family being attacked in their car, their death imminent. These "pose" shots suggest to the viewer that they must give over his/her gaze to the character's—that is, we must relinquish point of view to the Rwandan individuals who fill the frame and whose stillness in the face of atrocity reveals both their humanity and the inhumanity of that which they witness. These "poses" are also utilized to index trauma responses in the face of horror, not Marlowe's horror in a reimagined Congo that is of an invented and distorted Africa on which the "West" projects its "rests," but of the horror that collectives inflict upon fabricated "others," which is the history of humanity. As Peck underscores, the stasis that such moments in the film reflect are not due to an absence of affect but, in fact, its presence; the impulse not to flee, he surmises, is an effect of hope. Peck gives for comparative example the refusal of some Rwandans to believe in their endangerment, whether Tutsis or moderate Hutus, and their refusal to flee, to the refusal of Holocaust victims to flee in mid–twentieth-century Europe, especially Poland, because, as archives of Holocaust survivors and witnesses tell us, they hoped that whatever was sweeping the land would not be worse than what they had already endured or seen ("you can't believe that horror," says Peck, speaking of Holocaust victims who refused to believe that they would be next); the disbelief, then, that they and thousands, millions of others could be slain in order to justify the alienation of an entire group of people—an ethnicity or "race"—seemed unfathomable, implausible, especially given the fact that the annihilation of any group based on a perceived difference that is wholly, socially, and politically fabricated and reified to seem natural is in and of itself irrational. This disbelief, then, is both an attempt to hold on to reason (the rational) and a tenacious refusal, albeit misplaced in the face of escalating violence to preserve power in the hands of a select few, to give up hope (affect).

As in Peck's previous African film, the documentary, *Lumumba: Voice of a Prophet*, in which the narrator continually tells the history of Lumumba's rise and fall through his mother's memory with a refrain that begins "My Mother tells the Story . . .," Peck ultimately and deliberately relinquishes his authorial voice to women in *Sometimes in April* through the key scene of Valentine's testimony and the final scene in the *Gacaca* court, which makes possible the telling of other women's traumas within the narrative scope of the film and to turn these traumas into the foundation for better futures. This, in turn, suggests that in women's memory resides the (in)imaginable of collective history and that these ordeals are not unthinkable but are stories worth telling, narrating, if not always visualized. In this, Peck's narrative moves away from phallogocentric nationalist discourses but also shuns the idea that trauma cannot achieve "semiotic capacity"; he demonstrates that by changing the terms of how a medium can function, that is, by utilizing a visual medium in order to frame an auditory story itself not visualized in the form, it is possible to shift sign systems in order to provide trauma a capacity that has been denied. Also notable is that, aside from its multiethnic cast, *Sometimes in April*, refuses to tell the story only of Tutsis or only of Hutus: it advances a vision of a shared loss, shared history. It testifies to a unified Rwanda desecrated from without that viewers must acknowledge and seek, somehow, to restore (given the ongoing impasse between Haiti and the Dominican Republic, it is a message that implies other restorations).

I have spent some time delineating how Raoul Peck's Haitian background may have provided him the means by which to navigate an able representation of the Rwandan genocide in his film that encompasses presumed "unthinkable" or "unspeakable" violence toward women, to suggest, in contrast with the photography and graphic text examined earlier, that cultural formation and political inclination are key to cross-cultural depictions of seminal historical moments. As a Haitian (Congolese) director, Peck already had within his arsenal the knowledge of various phases of Haitian (and Congolese) history that had been denied by official history, thus rendered unthinkable and unnameable. That knowledge, in turn, makes possible the opening up of the field of the imagination, to defy the notion of the unimaginable that, as I showed in my analysis of Hugo's photography in particular, presents itself as unrepresentable. Though the film does not "stage" scenes of abject violence, thereby not contributing to the desensitization of viewers to such violence, it not only refuses to make women's narratives secondary but centralizes them so that they unlock the arc of the film and of the futures viewers might imagine for both the characters in the film and the real human beings they are meant to represent, both in the Rwandan context and elsewhere. Relying on African Diasporic transnationalism, Peck's work *presumes* the *thinkability* of African discourses situated in formerly colonized, yet original, space; provides their semiotic visibility by providing the *language* for their representation (nameability); and by rending these narratives legible, renders them (in)imaginable for the viewing audience. In every way, then, Peck's film defies the notion of the unspeakability of the extreme violence suffered by Rwandan women during the genocide and makes us realize that all of humanity, and our hope for it, I argue, resides in what we allow ourselves to know, principally, of African women's lives, as undergirding truly universalist humanist concerns.

I wrote in my introduction that this project enacts a process, one by which we apprehend how to rethink and revise our interpretive practices from within the interpretive community of artists of African descent interested in intradiasporic conversations, in tune with their own autochthonomy and also participating in lakou/yard consciousness. These last two chapters show that such a process must begin in deracialization and a subsequent redirection toward identification with African cultures, realities and sensibilities. It is lack of identification, rather than solely ethnic or kinship membership, that results in the reproduction of silencing and effacing narratives situating Africans as others, as we have seen in the case of both Hugo's and Stassen's representations of the genocide, whereas, in Peck, the representation consciously engages a project that is, at its heart, as decolonizing as it is affirming of African autochthonomous points of view that also include women, not as objects, but as subjects both of transgression and of modes of storytelling. This chapter thus came to focus on the importance of autochthonomous African women's perspectives in Peck's text in particular. In the next chapter, I turn to a late-nineteenth-century text by Mary Seacole, by way of mid-twentieth-century intertextuality between Fanon and Capécia, to demonstrate that though there has been an interruption in the discernibility of African-descended women's perspectives and positionality, there is evidence that a commitment to lakou consciousness and to a nascent autochthonomy was indeed present even then, though we have been unable to discern it. The chapter demonstrates why it has been difficult to unearth Caribbean women's contributions to ontology specifically through their texts, both because these contributions have been misrepresented and because their modes of address simultaneously hide and reveal the positionality I seek to bring out of the texts. Autochthonomy, in such texts, is nascent rather than fully evident and must carefully be unpacked to be revealed. Once exposed, however, it becomes difficult to un-see it, providing another layer to texts otherwise narrowly read as only reflections of black women confronting white dominance. Instead, I argue that though the latter is present, an underlying subtext reveals itself as giving voice to a transnational African Diasporic reality situated in the virtual space of lakou consciousness, which itself becomes the very ground from which *autochthonomy* can be deployed. It is this subtext that I make clearly discernible in Chapter 3.

3 Subjectivity in Motion

Caribbean Women's (Dis)Articulations of Being

Should one postulate a type for human reality and describe its psychic
modalities only through deviations from it, or should one not rather
strive unremittingly for a concrete and ever-new understanding of man?
—Frantz Fanon, *Black Skin, White Masks*

In *On Reason: Rationality in a World of Cultural Conflict and Racism,* Nige-
rian-born philosopher Emmanuel Eze argues that reason is produced by and
through the reconciliation of difference rather than existing simply as a tool
by which Western thought annihilates epistemological claims outside of itself.
As such, Eze concludes that, historically speaking, "there is neither in the
purest conceptions of human rationality nor in the language of any cultures
evidence that reason or language escapes time and sociality" (125). He goes
on to argue that experience is "an essential attribute of humanity" and "[by]
way of language, it is memory and history that, dialectically, constitute the
subjectivity of an individual . . . the conversation of the soul with itself" (126).
Thus, all societies, all individuals, undergo a dialectical coming into being,
through their experience of the world and their reflection upon that world.
This ontological process, argues Eze, though being constituted by a variety
of aims or epistemes that are culturally, socially and historically specific,
remains largely similar in its unfolding. Eze posits that diversity constitutes
"the act of thought," that is, that there is "diversity in reason" (2) and, thus, that
"diversity constitutes a necessary condition of thinking in general" (3). From
these gambits, Eze goes on to argue that Western thought does not constitute
a universal rationality (13). Via Kant, Hegel, Husserl, Sartre, Fanon, Gadamer,
and others, Eze demonstrates that African and postcolonial philosophical
perspectives are not so much at odds with Western thought as they rework
the very ground of what the West has posited as universal (while subjugat-
ing other ways of thinking to itself). In a nuanced treatment of the subject,

to which complexity I can only give a bare nod here, *Eze* goes on to argue that, in the postcolonial African context, he "can see no less than an intense struggle over the life and death of the mind." He writes: "Postcolonial African philosophy remains one of a few accessible arenas in which to stage the *embodiments* in thought of the humane struggles of our souls against forces that seek not only to silence our internal conversations but also to negate the historical shapes of our freedoms" (144; emphasis mine). Eze's own survey of the vast array of concepts regarding agency, subjectivity, and freedom within continental European philosophy demonstrates its variegations. He does not argue for an alternate understanding of subjectivity or appeal for the place of African subjects in the West, but argues that the West's imposition of its own formulation of subjectivity is a local impulse, one borne of colonial impulses (much as Bernasconi has argued in his discussions of Kant).

Saying so, however, does not preclude what Eze ultimately discusses, the formation and deployment of subjectivity in the dialectical relation, a relation inherent in Monique Wittig's transformation of Jacques Lacan's formulation of the divided subject, the "j/e,"[1] or the articulation of a complete self, unifying a first-person consciousness with one's self-awareness as a social object, into a body-consciousness (or consciousness with a body) that necessarily and forcibly exceeds its socialization in order to find itself, in order to enter into that conversation of the soul with itself (qtd in de Lauretis, 250–252). Given that, as Frantz Fanon has noted, the effects of racism are known to give rise to what psychologists call "cognitive dissonance," the inability to assimilate into one's cognition evidence that is contrary to or in conflict with one's beliefs so that the disturbing event or person is continuously foreclosed or rejected, my discussion in this chapter takes inspiration from Eze's refusal to subjugate African realities to Western ones and from Wittig's lead to refuse gendered and sexual subjection, in suggesting avenues for exploring the "excess" or "eccentric" presence of African, mobile, gendered subjectivities. I thus suggest another "cognitive practice" in the form of new avenues for reading, providing a means of resituating the works of African Diasporic writers specifically in contexts that reflect their own epistemic systems.

Through the situating of specific Caribbean texts in this chapter at the crossroads space of intra-cultural, diasporic exchange, I engage a reading practice that uncovers the importance of understanding such texts within the cultural, political, and transnational contexts of their production and dissemination, following Stanley Fish's concept of "interpretive communities" and the competencies for rendering meaning embedded in the particularities of the communities producing the texts at hand. Such a reading practice goes beyond the idea of discursively producing "a post-colonial discourse within which [writers] construct counter-discursive rather than homologous views of the world" (Ashcroft et al. 191). Though such texts can be construed as counter-discursive when read as responding only to the colonial, hegemonic past, here I suggest that the texts in question exhibit an *imbrication* of cultures forced to coexist through the colonial matrix while also privileging and highlighting the importance of remaining traces of African Diasporic cultures. As my analyses will show, however, these traces are, at times, difficult to uncover, due to the long history of colonial domination, its disruptions, and the manifest cooptation of the formerly colonized into cultures that are themselves colonial in nature such that formerly colonized individuals and groups can find themselves participating in the oppressive structures of the dominant society in which they figure as marginal.

I focus here, primarily on literature, and, in particular, travel literature or literature of mobility, precisely because "literature was made as central to the cultural enterprise of Empire as the monarchy was to its political formation" (Ashcroft et al. 3) in European/British contexts. We can argue today that the participation in the production of literature (and other discursive practices) by descendants of the formerly colonized (and often of the colonizing as well) is no longer simply or only a practice of resistance or of counter-discursivity but an assertion of subjectivity, agency—in short, of autonomy. In some instances, this literature is not only counter-discursive but it forms the corpus of dominant, indigenous cultures reflecting the amalgamation of the inhabitants of postcolonial territories such that, as I discussed in my introduction, certain works and authors can be understood as autochthonous to those places and spaces. I follow in the footsteps of earlier critics who have suggested that postcolonialism offers us reading strategies by which to examine any text for its underlying institutionalized, social assumptions and presuppositions while also suggesting that we examine the texts for evidence of traces of a previous order, of af/filiative connections that transcend space and time. If, in the past, such practices focused on displacing, reshaping, or questioning the composition of literary canons, this study side steps such questions, or builds upon them, by assuming that the utility of the text resides in what it can reveal best about human nature while engaging with the same care and advocacy of the epistemes and gnosis of African Diasporic cultures. Reading across texts of the African Diaspora transnationally and as a product of af/filiation, allows for a new mapping of imaginative and political spaces and of history, that can potentially provide models for reading emerging transnational cultures. The producers of these texts do not see themselves engaged in minor, marginal or marginalized cultures but in engaging urgent discussions of hemispheric or global importance hinging upon tracing, remembering, or releasing the agency of a group of people defined variously, depending on the text, by their gender, race/ethnicity, or nationality. In short, the concern of these texts is not resistance to a dominant force, or the state of one's "otherness," but how to reflect an African Diasporic subjectivity that can unhinge itself, at least partially, if not wholly, from colonial definitions of subjectivity. They do so by engaging subjectivity from African Diasporic perspectives, by seeking and revealing af/filiative kinship connections, and by working through the ways in which an imposed colonial heritage has disrupted access to the former without, however, being able to completely extinguish these.

(Dis)Identifications

Diana Fuss's signal essay, "Interior Colonies: Frantz Fanon and the Politics of Identification," discusses how politicized mimicry does not simply replay scenes of identification but ironizes dominant forms of representation (300). Fuss underscores, via Fanon's analysis of the torture of Algerian detainees, that it is "politically imperative to insist upon an instrumental difference between imitation and identification" (308), that "imitation alone is not sufficient to produce an identification" (309). In her essay, Fuss goes on to show that Fanon's own analysis collapses when it comes to gender because he readily assumes that "black women are essentially mimics and black men are essentially not" (309); that is to say, that black men "imitate" but do not identify whereas black women inherently are that which they mimic. Fanon's gender incongruity inherently undercuts his findings regarding the nature of ironic mimicry in the postcolonial context. What, then, can we conclude occurs when a postcolonial author who belongs to more than one social class simultaneously—none of them privileged—expresses herself utilizing a genre situated in dominant discourse (the novel), while her liminal status (as "black" and "female") serves to mute her contribution to advancing alternative forms of representation inconsistent with the genre? This chapter addresses this central question by reframing the work of early Caribbean women writers via the *politicized* form of mimicry that Fuss insists exists across and despite gender difference by first advancing an analysis of Frantz Fanon's *(mis)reading* of Mayotte Capécia's turn-of-the-century novel, *Je suis martiniquaise*. To do so is not, to echo Rey Chow, "to belittle the epochal messages of a seminal political thinker" (41), but to uncover the ways in which Fanon's work demonstrates a *denied* understanding of the power of Caribbean women's narrative strategies. His forceful analysis of Capécia's work, as I will show, becomes an *admission* of *what* he seeks to willfully ignore in the work. I assert that it was Fanon's recognition of the strategic textual and authorial framings in Capécia's text, which he himself was either simultaneously engaging or borrowing from having read Capécia and other black women writers whose works were circulating in French literary circles at the time, which motivated him to mischaracterize and denigrate the work, its author, and others of her gender, to such an extent that the novelty of its first-person narrative voice as a rhetorical strategy of (racial) dissimulation would eventually fail to be recognized as attention to her text waned and attention to his rose. I thus show how Fanon misread Capécia's work, first as memoir then by only devoting his analysis to a partial component of the work, a component, as it turns out, that was written, in part, by yet another writer, as a memoir, now integrated into Capécia's novel as a kind of pastiche. In contrast to Fanon's mischaracterization of the novel as a memoir, careful examination of the arc of Capécia's representation of her protagonist, "Mayotte," reveals how Capécia positions her character's authority by using a first-person narrative in such a way as to categorically shift the ground on which Caribbean women writers asserted their cultural identities in a social/cultural milieu that sought to silence their voices; in so doing, though this is less my purpose to show here, Capécia engages an autochthonomous subjectivity. My main focus here, however, is to consider how we might recover in Capécia (and others) an important model for subversion—in other words, a decolonial, counter-discourse, that Fanon himself replicated, yet dismissed. This may be a contentious and difficult reading for Fanon scholars to reconcile, who find a great deal of value in his *Black Skin, White Masks,* a seminal text for critical race and postcolonial studies as generative for its claims on race as it is misogynistic. However, I believe mine to be a careful analysis: its point is to make such scholars rethink first, why they fail to critique Fanon and take him to task on his gender issues; and second, why they persist in misreading Capécia (or not reading her at all) such that Fanon's misreading stands as the *only* reading of her work.[2] My analysis demonstrates that once one has engaged with Capécia's *actual* text, not Fanon's recasting of the work, it becomes evident that he both felt threatened by it and utilized some of the same textual strategies (the first-person narrative and memoir-like genre) to make his own claims on race. He did so for the advancement, specifically, of black men, to the complete abandonment of black and mixed women in a race for authority and dominance in the terrain of decolonial thought and struggle. My purpose here, then, is not to position Capécia's text as one engaging liberally in autochthonomy or in lakou consciousness, nor is it to argue that Capécia's novel does more than it attempts. My purpose is to demonstrate how, in accepting Fanon's misreading of the text, we lose an important gendered, if not entirely feminist, intervention in the terrain of textual decolonization. This is what Capécia's text attempts, through its personalized, quasi-autobiographical, first-person narrative. But being neither a memoir nor an autobiography, it advances a story of a woman who first attempts an (unwanted) assimilation in order to find her "kin." The story thus traces the main character's process of (dis)identification to reveal itself as a counter-discursive text that thus *exceeds* its semblance as memoir, situating the protagonist as autochthonomous insofar as she comes to assert her autonomy as a free, female subject of African descent. I then turn to an earlier text by British Caribbean writer Mary Seacole, *Wonderful Adventures of Mrs. Seacole in Many Lands*, to show that Capécia's narrative strategies can be situated in a longer tradition of Caribbean women's, first-person, interventionist narrative strategies. Though Capécia was likely not aware of Seacole's text, given her rudimentary education and the fact that the two belong to different linguistic traditions to which neither had access, the focus of each text on first-person narration, subterfuge, mimicry, and evasive identifications serves to demonstrate that what links their works is a shared vision of strategic representations that play with imitation but deny imposed identifications in favor of advancing autochthonomous subjectivities unacknowledged in dominant discourse of the "Other" in which such subjectivities are said not to exist.

I engage the term *(dis)identification* throughout this investigation literally, but I am also loosely borrowing from Teresa De Lauretis's concept of "dis-identification" and from the elaborations upon her idea of its potential for the creation of subject identities not defined principally from dominant culture by Jose Esteban Muñoz, who celebrates the term via linguist Michel Pêchaux's theory of subject construction within ideology (following Althusser), as a countercultural strategy for sexual transgression (particularly in queer, minoritarian cultures via a rerouting of similar ideas put forth by Judith Butler and Žižek). I utilize the term here perhaps more mundanely to mean that Seacole, in her own historical and culturally specific moment, distances herself from the raced and gender-specific discourses that would have been imposed upon her (and that we can see continued in the multiple appropriations of her persona in academic discourses). It seems to me that though De Lauretis and other critics after her leave the plane of race unexplored in their definition of "dis-identification," that the term should be as useful in rethinking racial construction and ethnic (counter) identifications (as defined by Hall). In her 1990 essay, "Eccentric Subjects: Feminist Theory and Historical Consciousness," De Lauretis defines "dis-identification" from the outset as the third component of "a reconceptualization of the subject" that creates "an emerging redefinition of marginality as location, of identity as dis-identification" (116). She locates this subject identity as an "excess" that resists (normed) identification (126) and then comes to understand that any marginalized identity resides in this space of excess, achieving "a constant crossing of the border . . . a remapping of boundaries between bodies and discourses, identities and communities—which may be a reason why it is primarily feminists of color and lesbian feminists who have taken the risk" (138). She speaks here of the risk of dis-identification, of displacement from that space of marginality that dominant discourse confers. While De Lauretis suggests that these "eccentric" or excessive subjects lay beyond the system and can, as such, "displace oneself from the system, to dis-locate, dis-affiliate, or disengage one's attention from it" and thus experience, to echo Marilyn Frye, "a reorientation of attention" (De Lauretis 144), texts like Seacole's offer a representation of an outside that is also an inside. Every "outside," as bell hooks has argued (see her "Homeplace") is also constitutive, at once, because those who inhabit that space and reorient themselves from within it, as opposed to against the conceptual system, perceive it as a center, an inside-space. As such, Pêchaux's third concept of subject construction, one that "neither opts to assimilate within such a structure nor strictly opposes it; rather disidentification is a strategy that works on and against dominant ideology," is particularly useful. Muñoz takes this concept further afield when he strenuously claims the concept for queer disidentification as one that "tries to transform a cultural logic from within, always laboring to enact permanent structural change while at the same time valuing the importance of local or everyday struggles of resistance" (11–12). I do not adopt Muñoz's stance on disidentification but rather Pêchaux's original concept for autochthonomous subjects because it seems to me that the abjection imposed upon raced bodies, particularly African ones, is such that the ways in which such subjects approach disidentification are varied, often subtle, and do not presume the need "to enact permanent structural change" (because they understand all too well that such structural change is unlikely to occur). They are more likely to advocate for completely different kinds of structures or analogous ones that remain located on the outside/inside of "marginality" without yet being marginal (Mignolo and Walsh's "otherwise"); they do not necessarily value "the importance of local or everyday struggles of resistance" (primarily because the arenas of struggles tend to be delocalized, diasporic, or transnational, and the "everyday" does not often figure in the discourse itself; rather, a collective identity is more often than not put forth). Thus, I use the parenthetical term *(dis)identification* to signal the "neither/nor" structuring that Pêchaux describes—an identification that accepts certain aspects of dominant ideology at the same time as it shows sign of weariness, a refusal to assimilate within dominant ideology, even as "Others." Autochthonomous subjects work with(in) dominant ideology while sidestepping the ways in which their identities are conceptually overdetermined. In this sense, at least in the field of discursive representation, the displacement from a "conceptual articulation," as De Lauretis opines, is also, as Butler has stated, "a site of rearticulations" (219). As Medina elucidates, disidentification is for Butler, "an occasion for subversion, for disrupting established relations of similarity and difference and the unifications and divisions they create" (93).

In this sense, then, I argue that autochthonomous subjects (dis)articulate their identities: they rearticulate subjects that are part of and outside of dominant ideology in counter-discursive significations that are also articulations of self; furthermore, they consciously disrupt social relations that have become the bedrock of cultural studies since the late twentieth century, the idea of "articulation theory" through which solidarities across difference are constituted. This is not to say that such subjects seek isolation but that their terms of engagement are much more dispersed or virtual (such as in lakou consciousness) than heretofore conceptualized: they are interested in transforming or transcending social categories, especially racial and class categories, at the same time as they perform a disambiguation from those categories. To (dis)articulate, then, is to consciously utilize available discursive formations to present subject identities not normally or formally recognized by dominant discourse while, through modes of (dis)identification, performing these identities in an "outside/in" space that constitutes both an epistemic center and one of consciousness.

In her work on performativity and autobiography, Sidonie Smith has argued that "[t]here is no essential, original, coherent autobiographical self before the moment of self-narrating" (1998, 108). For Smith, autobiographically derived texts are performances, constructions, that powerfully assert social identifications in historically tethered time (Smith traces the convention back to the Enlightenment). She argues that women, recognizing the potentiality of the form, and because of their placement in "interior" (domestic) spaces in social life, have sought to utilize it to their advantage, to speak "of excess, of unbidden and forbidden performativity" (111). As Smith explains: "The very 'I' of the autobiographer, the apparent sign of a unified 'self' or 'individual,' is always already a phallogocentric fiction of the 'real' and 'true'" and later states: "Distressing the stability and primacy of an uncontested identity by lying about the 'I' challenges, as does mimicry and masquerade, the politics of identity and the aesthetics of autobiographical 'truth' as a gesture toward a 'self-knowledge' always policed by operative regimes of truth" (49). It would stand to reason, then, that Fanon, too, would recognize the form's potential for advancing the "truth" of liminal lives and use it to his advantage. Smith speaks not strictly of autobiographical texts, as her textual examples evidence, but of narratives that make *claims* to autobiography through the use of the "I" voice in order to assume authority over narrative and to speak of an excess of subjectivity denied utterance in social and geopolitical space. By utilizing the "I" narrative, the narrator/author (not necessarily one and the same) disturbs "the contractual obligation of truthtelling," (ibid.) while also relying on the convention to mask its ficticity in order to impose and assert his/her authority as subject and enunciator. Fanon, interestingly, asserts both a phallogocentric fiction of "truth" while utilizing a "feminine," "'I'-lying" to his narrative/political advantage in *Black Skin, White Masks*, after having thoroughly distanced himself from this "feminine" device in his complete and visceral dismissal of Capécia's *Je suis martiniquaise* very early in his own text. He does so not, as others have argued, because he is disturbed by Capécia's narrator's desire for "whitening," but because much of Capécia's narrative and the urges of her narrator are explained by the moral and sociosexual failings and betrayals of Black Caribbean men, which Fanon curiously (as a trained psychologist) refuses to analyze. Capécia makes use of "'I'-lying," in using her character's first-person narrative to explore issues of gender and racial autonomy for a Martinican woman of the working class and in her own masking, utilizing the pen name of "Mayotte Capécia." For Fanon, to recognize this subterfuge would have been to examine, and ultimately indict, phallogocentric (and Freudian) discourse, that is, male privilege in the sociosexual spheres vis-à-vis both women of color and white women as part of the colonial paradigm, but his investments in the former made this indictment impossible. As Chow argues, "The ultimate danger posed by the Negress and the mulatto [*sic*] is hence not their sexual behavior per se, but the fact that their sexual agency carries with it a powerful (re)conceptualization of community—community as based on difference, heterogeneity, creolization; of community as the 'illegitimate' mixings and crossings of color, pigmentation, physiognomy—that threateningly *vies with the male intellectual's*" (48). As Fanon's text became the cornerstone of political organizing during the early years of African/Caribbean decolonization (from the 1950s-1970s) and of critical race and postcolonial theory, Fanon's views on women of color, disseminated via his excoriation of Capécia's text, then became pro forma. Fanon was only the first of many to put Capécia's text to his own use; in so doing, and through his thorough dismissal, he established for readers of decoloniality the idea that Caribbean women, and women of color more widely, were intrinsically incapable of productively participating in ontological or political decolonial discourse, or of articulating a discourse of their own as autonomous Subjects.

Rereading Fanon and Capécia:
Double Jeux and Gendered Misreadings

To date, feminist critiques of Fanon have been limited to the place gender occupies in his work, as defense or denunciation. But, other than a handful of rereadings of Mayotte Capécia, the only Caribbean woman figure Fanon took any pains to discuss liberally in his work, none attempt to argue that women of color, and women of African descent specifically, contribute to the archives as ontologists. For most postcolonial theorists, Fanon alone occupies (or initiates) the space of "black" ontology,[3] a space to which women of color do not appear to have contributed. This incapacity to recognize the contributions of women of color intellectuals and writers has contributed to the accepted, unspoken belief, by omission, that women of color do not philosophize, leading to an internalization of Fanon's pithy phrase, that we "know nothing of her." By grappling first with Fanon's own omission, dismissal, and distortion of women of color's contributions to the field of decolonial ontology, via Capécia's novel, *Je suis Martiniquaise,* while also observing those elements of Capécia's work that appear to have influenced his own (thus the reason for Fanon's dogged pursuit of its acerbic condemnation[4]), I contend that we can begin to unravel this internalization.

Fanon's most explicit pronouncement on the place of women of color in ontology comes in the midst of his analysis not of women of African descent but of the sociosexual relationship of white women to black men. In *Black Skin, White Masks,* he wrote, in what seemed to be an overt refusal to discuss the matter: "Those who grant our findings on the psychosexuality of the white woman may ask what we have to say about the black woman. We know nothing of her" (157). In the original French, Fanon actually wrote, "on pourrait nous demander celles [conclusions] que nous proposerions pour la femme de couleur. Nous n'en savons rien [we could be asked what conclusions we might propose about the woman of color. We know nothing of her]" (Fanon 1952, 145; my translation). Fanon wrote "woman of color," but, in his recent translation, Richard Philcox assumes that Fanon meant to refer to black women specifically, even though other parts of the text dealing with women of African descent conjecture about mixed-raced women (and in the original French text, Fanon continues by referring to "beaucoup d'Antillaises, que nous appellerons les juxta-Blanches [many women of color, that we might call near-Whites" (1952, 145); one must presume from this language that Fanon was referring to mixed-race women of Antillean provenance]. It could be that Fanon's original meaning remains lost in translation, but the ambiguity of the phrasing suggests a general incapacity, even refusal, to "read" the black woman or woman of color of part-African descent successfully within the philosophical or psychoanalytical paradigms then (and now) available.[5] Chow, for one, asserts of the passage, and others like it, that Fanon elides specificity because such passages reveal that he believes that "women of color are *all alike*: in spite of the differences in pigmentation between the Negress and the mulatto, for instance, they share a common, 'nauseating' trait—the desire to become white—that can be generalized in the form of 'every woman'" (38). This "trait," Fanon condemned in mixed-raced women while recognizing it for Black men as a process by which to access equality and end race prejudice (52–53). It is Fanon's incapacity both to recognize women of color's contribution to "black" knowledge and their gendered autonomy that needs to be more fully addressed, and to which I turn later. Fanon's obfuscation, I propose, contributes largely to our lack of awareness of the contributions of women of color's philosophical perspectives.

Feminist scholars have more recently uncovered the fact that Mayotte Capécia's *Je suis martiniquaise* is a work of (autobiographically derived) fiction and that its author utilized a pseudonym to hide her true identity (of Lucette Céranus); both discoveries locate Capécia's narrative act, to repeat Fuss's delineations, in the realm of "mimicry" rather than that of "identification." She ironizes the representation of her main character, whose name is the same as that of the pseudonym but not the same as Lucette, the author. It might also be possible to read Capécia's use of the pseudonym as a signal to readers of the author's own masking and arch-play.[6] More specifically than this, Beatrice Stith Clark, in her critical introduction to her translation of Capécia's novel, conjectures that it would be difficult "to imagine that Frantz Fanon, Capécia's compatriot, was unaware of her true identity, since they were both in Paris during the same period" (x). In fact, it was clear that Fanon chose to excoriate Capécia precisely because their works, at least, circulated in similar circles, and that Capécia, as a fellow Martinican, was receiving a great deal more attention than he at this time. They were not, however, of the same class, as Fanon would have been well aware, since he was of the bourgeois class, and thus would not have frequented the same social circles in Paris, even as Capécia became more popular in the Parisian literary world. In fact, their class difference, as well as gender difference, may go a long way toward explaining Fanon's incapacity, or unwillingness, to better assess the meaning of Capécia's work and its double-edged influence. The editors and translators of *Relire Capécia* [*Rereading Capécia*], Myriam Cottias and

Madeleine Dobie, observe that critics have for decades made the error of misreading the class of each, writing: "To read Fanon, one would imagine that he represents the black proletariat and 'Mayotte Capécia' the bourgeoisie of color, but, in fact, sociologically, it is the reverse. He is the bourgeois, she, the woman of the masses" (36; my translation). Interestingly, in their efforts to recuperate Capécia from Fanon's attack and its lasting stain, Cottias and Dobie go somewhat too far. Capécia was not of the middle or upper classes, but she was also not of the "masses," that is to say, the poor, as her disparaging remarks aimed at those in the lower classes in *Je suis martiniquaise* make abundantly clear. She did, however, belong to the working class, making her way primarily as a *blanchisseuse* or laundress both in Martinique and in Paris, until the success of her book; by birth, she also occupied a precarious social position since she and her twin sister were considered "outside children," that is, born out of wedlock, illegitimate. Especially in the French Caribbean, legitimacy secured land and inheritance rights as well as marriageability and even, at times, employment. It is striking, then, to note that Fanon's analysis focuses exclusively on the second half of the text, which recounts a failed love story between a French soldier and "Mayotte," one that archival research has shown to follow closely the narrative version, in manuscript form, produced by a French soldier with whom Lucette did have an affair and which remains in Capécia's archives. But this, too, is rewritten by the author who, through this pastiche, takes control of her "Mayotte's" representation, removing it from the French man's perspective, or, at least, altering its intent. This half of the novel is one of unrequited love on the part of "Mayotte" and a somewhat perverse tale of love from the point of view of the officer, who, in a letter, entreats "Mayotte" to be faithful, to have their unborn child without him, and to raise him on her own: "You will raise him. You'll speak to him of me. You will tell him: 'He was a great man. You have to work hard to be worthy of him. One day, he left on his boat and, since, he has been as good as dead. But you are here, my big man. You'll become like him and, later, you too will also make a woman happy'" (159; my translation). In response, Mayotte notes her reaction to the latter passage (which critics have discovered is lifted verbatim from the officer's memoir to Lucette): "I had a moment of revolt. Did Andrew believe that he had made me happy forever? Did he believe that I could live solely on memories? Did he think he had no more responsibilities toward this child that he did not know, but was his, by sending me a check?" (ibid.; my translation). In the original, Capécia's first-person narration, exemplifies Wittig's "j/e" cited earlier, a means by which she unifies a first-person subjectivity with a self-awareness of being only an object for André, an object without reality, a memory. The moment of revolt she describes in the passage cited demonstrates the "j/e" by which she unifies "I" and "myself" in realizing that André speaks to her as to another, a social self that she is not, at the same time as she must assume responsibility for a child that André continues to deny. The presence of the child makes "Mayotte" unable to ignore her material self; she has no other choice, then, to create a complete self, a "j/e" that neither assimilates nor denies her liminality but occupies that space as one of (dis)identification that allows her to separate from the "self" created for her by André and white dominant society. Fanon, however, ignores "Mayotte's" unifying gesture. In *direct contradiction to the passages cited earlier*, Fanon writes: "Mayotte loves a white man *from whom she accepts anything. He is God. She makes no demands, requires nothing*, except a bit of whiteness in her life" (Fanon 1952, 34; translation and emphasis mine). In an analysis focused on a Freudian reading of "Mayotte" as having a "lactification" fetish (a pun here on the fact that her occupation was that of a laundress or a *blanchisseuse*—the French term literally meaning, "female whitener"), Fanon overlooks the fact that the essential male figure in the text for "Mayotte" is, in fact, *not* the officer, but her father, a *Black Antillean* father, and that it is her father's actions that push her toward seeking a white partner.

A key passage in the second part of Capécia's novel is worth our extensive analysis given that it seems to retain much of Fanon's attention in his own. To answer the question of whether or not she finds her French lover, André, attractive, "Mayotte" states:

> Was André handsome? All I know is that he had blue eyes, blond hair, pale skin, and that I loved him. Standing, he was a little shorter than I was, and that embarrassed him, but when we were seated, he was pleased to note that he was slightly taller than me. That was because I had incredibly long legs, while he had fairly short ones. (137; translation mine)

The passage is hardly a testament to the lover's beauty, as Fanon claims, especially as it comes to focus on André's *lack* of physical stature and "Mayotte's" embarrassment because of it. It reveals the ways in which "Mayotte" must *compensate* for André's *lack* of attractiveness, even in a bodily sense (having "incredibly long legs") a compensation she finds residing in her love and the distinct advantage of his indisputable "white" features (blue-eyed, blond, pale—also not an entirely positive depiction, though a literal one). Does she love him because of these features? The passage is opaque but conveys in no uncertain terms that, for Mayotte, there is a doubt as to André's attractiveness, which demonstrates that she does not elevate "whiteness" in the manner Fanon claims. In fact, her phrase appears to be a mirror to Fanon's claim, discussed earlier, regarding his lack of knowledge on women of color/ black women. Here, conversely, "Mayotte" asserts "all I know" ("tout ce que je sais")—again calling attention to the authority of the "I" and a Wittigian "j/e"—both a social and bodily identity that (dis)articulates itself in order to assert a subject position all her own. We must recall here Fuss's note that imitation is not the same as identification, noting further the ironizing of André's representation in the passage. He may be white, but he is decidedly not attractive or desirable: he is loved beyond these attributes. What is more important is Mayotte's understanding of the social advantage that André's whiteness brings. As Cottias and Dobie write, Capécia's narrator "does not suffer a phobia with regard to black men, rather, she makes a social calculation" (25; translation mine) and concludes what critics have failed to take into account "that marriage is constantly being related to issues of social status and respectability" (36; my translation). Doubtless, in the period illustrated in *Je suis martiniquaise*, a racial hierarchy dominated societies of the French Caribbean, with "whites" at the top and the darker-hued at the bottom; for a "femme de couleur," ostensibly a mixed-race woman in such a society, color and caste ensured mobility. "Mayotte" thus makes a calculated decision to valorize whiteness as a material entity, in other words, for the social advantages it might bring, not for whiteness in itself. Such a "desire" is not, as Fanon claims, a product of neurosis, though it might be considered an internalization of what Fanon himself termed third-person consciousness, or the internalization of perspective of the dominant gaze upon the subaltern subjectivity. If Fanon focuses excessively on the second half of the text, which we now know consists primarily of reframed writings written by a French officer who abandoned "Mayotte," then we can better grant that some of Fanon's analysis is accurate only in so far as it reflects the mind-set of the "Blanc" who wrote it, rather than that of "Mayotte," who comes to revolt against it.

In his work on black (male) ontology, Fanon seeks to flatten the complexity of the gendered aspect of Capécia's representation of racial discourse from a woman's perspective in the Martinique of the 1930s, a position strikingly similar to the discourse he offers as a "solution" for black males seeking acceptability in the white world (marrying or partnering with white women, which Fanon himself did; 52–53). Quoting only the line from the passage concerning André's whiteness and ignoring "Mayotte's" turning away from her same-age, black, love interest, Horace, when she was still a young woman (due to the public revelation of her father's infidelity, an episode that Fanon altogether ignores but which takes up a large part of the first part of Capécia's text, to which I will return), Fanon comes to a radically dismissive, and vitriolic, conclusion: "it is easy to see, by placing the terms in their proper place, that we obtain approximately the following: 'I loved him because he had blue eyes, blond hair and pale skin'" (Fanon 1952, 34; my translation). The text, however, reveals itself as ambiguous when the passage is read as a whole. One can only wonder if Fanon's sense of the "proper terms" of the text and his rewriting of it is not simply an assertion of his own belief—exemplified in the rhetoric to be found throughout *Black Skin, White Masks*, and echoed in his chapter on the (sexual) rights of access to white women by black men in order to secure sociopolitical mobility—that "white" features are by definition "beautiful."[7] Capécia's text is decidedly unclear as to the intrinsic beauty of such attributes, though it does, at other moments, assume that white features are synonymous with "angelic" qualities and purity. The text literally first questions whether André might be considered handsome and then asserts that her love makes him so and that he is, after all, white, but that he is rather short and ungainly. Furthermore, earlier in the text, "Mayotte" reveals recurring doubts as to the racialized terms of their union. André's speech, explaining why they cannot marry, goes on so long that "Mayotte" reflects: "Was he not going to treat me from now on as a child, like whites conventionally did when they had liaisons with girls of color?" She concludes: "I felt myself becoming another, everything so different with him than it had been with Horace" (133; my translation), her Black Martinican suitor. Incredibly enough, in a text that Fanon (ironically, rather "histrionically") declares to be filled with "idiocies" and incapable of "heart" (Fanon 2008, 35n12), Capécia has managed to have her heroine make a pronouncement on alterity and "othering" not unlike Fanon's own in *Black Skin, White Masks* in which the interpolation of the black man results in his physical and psychological deformity. We must, then, bear in mind what "Mayotte" has to tell us about this Horace, her first love, earlier in the text, that part on which Fanon is utterly silent. If Fanon chooses to focus his reading, and that of his own readers, on "Mayotte's" misguided statements of desire for "whiteness," then he ignores a major thread in the text. That thread, elaborated in the *first* half of the novel, uncovers more accurately Mayotte's attitudes toward race as well as the reason—related to her father, and to her class—why this results in her desperate search for love and acceptance (in the form of marriage) from the "Blanc." It is the first part of the text that establishes the reasons for her "masking" and subterfuge, and which establishes her developing understanding of the workings of racial and gendered power.

In the first part of Capécia's text, of her love for Horace, "Mayotte" declares: "I would marry Horace, keep his house, have his children; we would be happy and learn together beautiful gestures, united for always" (112; my translation). Of *his* beauty, she declares: "Horace was of the most beautiful Martinican type. His very dark skin made the enamel whiteness of his teeth stand out. I never tired of admiring him" (114; my translation). In contrast to her depiction of André, Horace, whom "Mayotte" typifies as "the most beautiful Martinican type," she also extols Horace's "dark skin" and openly confesses her "admiration." In contradistinction to the later description of André, too, she does not need to resort to diminishing her corporeal self in order to compensate for an intrinsic lack in Horace; here, her bodily self disappears and Horace fills the space that she contemplates adoringly. "Blackness" is here valorized in contrast to the utilitarian whiteness André is shown to exemplify. Why, then, does Capécia's protagonist ultimately leave Horace despite the latter's profession of love? After several family trials, including the death of her mother, illness of a beloved aunt to whom her twin sister was given for care, and a long absence of her father from the family home, "Mayotte," presumably in her early twenties, ventures into Fort-de-France on her own, only to discover, when she runs into them both on the street, that her father has set up house with a woman almost her own age.

The meeting is explosive and devastating to "Mayotte," as father and daughter fight openly in public. As a result, "Mayotte" resolves to leave the family home and to strike out on her own, but the effect on her love life is incontrovertible: given her father's behavior and their broken home due to his betrayal, she resolves not to marry a Martinican black man, presuming that all of the same "type" will repeat the devastation she (and her mother) have suffered at the hands of her father. She ultimately rejects Horace for this reason, stating clearly: "The memory of my father made me look down on this physical love that my body demanded." If anything, in psychoanalytic terms, "Mayotte" does not suffer from being "color-struck," as Fanon claims, but from an Electra complex nuanced by race. The character elaborates: "I no longer wanted to touch these men of color who couldn't help themselves from running after all kinds of women and I already knew that white men would not marry a black woman." Having turned Horace away, she goes on to seek financial independence as a laundress, asserting in this same passage as the above that the residents of Fort-de-France came to her because "they were proud to get their clothes cleaned at Mayotte's" (Capécia 2012, 128; my translation). Literally, however, in French the phrase reads: "they were proud to get whitened at Mayotte's." Is Capécia here playing with the reader, providing a coy "*double jeux*," or double entendre, suggesting that her heroine is moving away from "blackness" and seeking to "whiten" herself both figuratively and physically? If so, the conclusion she comes to after the birth of her child, ultimate rejection from her French suitor, and reconciliation with her father is quite the opposite: no matter what she attempts to do, flee Martinique, "marry" white, have a child by a white man, reject her family (as she has felt rejected by them, specifically by her father after her mother's death), she can, in the end, no more change her "race" than she can her paternity. Though "Mayotte" is clearly misguided in her love for the French officer, she comes to recognize this herself, as is evidenced by the fact that, as she raises her child, ostracized by both blacks and whites, it is her father's acceptance of her and of her child that restores her to herself as someone who is mixed, working-class, a hybrid. She notes that her lighter-skinned child does not change her racial allegiance, despite what others in the society may think. "If my child separated me from my race, he did not, in any case, provide me with another," she says (169). When, at the end of the novel, her father accepts her mixed child publicly in order to provide both with a social space in the French-Caribbean community, "Mayotte" observes: "I looked at my Father with tenderness. Never, it seemed to me, had this kind of understanding existed between André and myself" (166).

How, then, do we understand Fanon's inability to grapple with the contradictions inherent in Capécia's text, to understand both its racial and gendered dimensions, as he seems to do so well for the black male, as well as that of subsequent scholars of her text? I would suggest first that it stands to reason that occupying contradictory positions at once, both as a member of the privileged (economic) class and as one meant to occupy a space of liminality by virtue of his "race," Fanon would seek to intervene in the ideological discourse of humanist philosophy through textuality and, second, given that his own important contribution to the field of ontology comes in the form of a first-person address describing the effects of racialism upon the black (male) psyche, he would seek to explore the consciousness of Caribbean women and men through memoirs or autobiographically derived texts. *Je suis martiniquaise* is thus an apt choice for Fanon at the moment of his writing *Black Skin, White Masks*. In his presentation of Capécia's text, Fanon assumed (unconsciously or forcibly) that the text was a memoir and, therefore, autobiographical, even as he ignored or simply did not address its various levels of ironic representation. As already noted, he also strategically ignored the first half of the text, which showed both the protagonist's valorization of black male beauty and the devastating effects of discovering black male misogyny through the betrayal of the father. Scholars' continued insistence at misreading Capécia's novel by reading the text exclusively through Fanon's prism, as a memoir, rather than returning to the original as I have done here, ensures that the text continues to be misread and Capécia mischaracterized. Mayotte's ambiguities and development are misread as the rigid views of a racially confused author rather than as reflecting the arc of a character development (easy to do if one lops off half of the narrative) rendered in a first-person narrative utilizing (proto-feminist) rhetorical strategies directed at (dis)articulating the subjectivity of the main character from imposed gendered and raced categories from which she seeks autonomy. Through the repeated utterance of the "j/e" of the first person address, Capécia instantiates "Mayotte's" growing awareness of her social objectification as a black woman, her bodily consciousness in relationship to both white and black men, and her resistance both to assimilation or objectification in order to reintegrate the body politic of black Martinican life as a black woman whose autonomy is tethered to a sense of community, that is, of kinship with like others (as Chow's comment regarding women of colors' identification as being rooted in community, cited earlier, attests). Fanon's disavowal of the larger fictional terrain of the work as it works out this complex subject position, in favor of misreading the text as a flat, unimaginative memoir is more than ironic given that *Black Skin, White Masks* has, over the years and especially by those not working in race or postcolonial studies, been cited (and misread), as Gwen Bergner has so aptly pointed out, as "a source of autobiographical information on Fanon rather than as an autobiographically informed theory of the psychology of colonial relations" (85–86n1). Why does Fanon, then, insist on the *personal* nature of Capécia's text while playing with his own use of first-person narration in the very same text in which he dismisses Capécia? I contend that Fanon could not have recognized the power of the pronominal "I" as he himself strategically deploys it throughout *Black Skin, White Masks*, a usage that has no more to do with his own personal "being," as subject, than does Capécia's to Lucette Céranus. If, however, we understand Fanon's use of the "I" voice as a form of "'I'-lying," as a means of accessing the authority of the autobiographical "I" to fashion a "whole" self, then we can better understand that Fanon's lambasting of Capécia's fictionalized "I" voice is orchestrated in order to obscure what the latter text achieves: an exploration of the gendered dimension of a racial struggle in a decolonial context and her character's *recognition* that a racial (dis) identification ("whitening") will neither erase racial/cultural belonging or lead to a desirable outcome. "Mayotte" ultimately returns to her island-home and is reintegrated in the (black) community, thereby coming full circle to her place of beginning and belonging, rather than to the absorption into "whiteness" that Fanon mischaracterizes in his reading of the work as being its ultimate objective. The arc of "Mayotte's" story carries the author's message that a return to order necessitates repair from black male "fathers" toward their families of origin, and a return as well, to a community of like others; this is a conclusion that Fanon's text forecloses in denying both the pastiche nature of the second half of the novel and by ignoring in its entirety the first. In other words, Fanon's simultaneous use of the authorial "I" and excoriating of Capécia as a memoirist while ignoring the work's genre and Capécia's real-life identity, as opposed to her fictional creation, are indicative of his need to both literally "master" the use of the first-person address to convince his audience of his own aims, while invalidating the force of an already accepted text by a Martinican woman by that same audience. The fact that Fanon's rendering of the text has, over time, led most readers to never return to Capécia's original text serves to show that he understood this audience well and that his motives were never to examine Capécia's text for what it was but to misrepresent its contents such that Capécia could not occupy a space associated with textual or psychic decolonization. It is in advancing this self-narration in a racialized context of decolonization that Capécia's text sketches a movement toward autochthonomy if one understands this subjectivity as counter-discursive. The return to Martinique also asserts af/filiative kinship connections that the character attempts to preserve rather than sever. Hers is, as Diana Fuss indicates of ironized representation, a "politicized mimicry"; Fanon's error, a side effect of his misogyny, was to mistake (as a colonial power would a subaltern subject) a first-person woman's narrative for an imitation desirous of assimilation rather than a device to counter the forces of gendered and racialized power. In fact, "Mayotte's" character (dis) identifies with the subject positions created for her by both her father and by André, her white suitor; after Pêchaux, hers is a position through which her marginality becomes a location of "resistance and agency" (De Lauretis 139). The *semblance* of autobiography provides the text with its social authority; it also, unfortunately, masks its attempts at (dis)articulation from the social order. Still, Capécia's recognition of the force of personal narrative is one of the ways in which the text "exceeds" its misnaming by Fanon and situates itself as a text of ontology from the perspective of a woman of color.

Of Capécia's critics and adorers, Cottias and Dobie note that (as I will show is also true of assessments of Mary Seacole's earlier *Adventures*) "in reality, each saw what they wished to see in the novels of Mayotte Capécia and it is most likely the reason for her popularity" (55; my translation). It has been my intention to show, conversely, through my brief analysis of some key passages of Capécia's text, that the author herself was very much aware of the race/gender politics of her time. Capécia's strategic use of the "I" narrative is not, of course, unique. A true memoir, Mary Seacole's *Wonderful Adventures of Mrs. Seacole in Many Lands* exemplifies the strategic use of the "'I'-lying" narrative in the assertion of a complex ontology by a Caribbean woman writer at a much earlier time.

Strategic Rationalities: Mary Seacole's (Dis)Articulation of Being

Writing in the late 1850s, Mary Seacole wrote from within a supremely mas-culinist and misogynist society still implicated in imperial colonization, the "darker side of modernity," as Walter Mignolo has recently argued. Seacole's memoir emerges at a time when Africans, enslaved or free, were considered either nonhuman or second-class citizens, while Fanon contributed to the literature that sought to argue for the break of the colonies from European domination, especially in North Africa and in the Caribbean. Both of mixed European and African descent, and from the Caribbean—one Anglophone, the other Francophone—each strove to textually enunciate perspectives on emancipation from within the dictates of their time. By the early twentieth century, the European philosophical tradition of rationality had properly inaugurated universalism with, as Ernesto Laclau has argued, "its own body, but this was still the body of a certain particularity—European culture of the nineteenth century" (24). This body, of course, came to be expressed through its privileged constituents, European white males and their rationalities. This was a world in which modernity coupled with colonialism with facile ease, as Walter Mignolo has discussed, going further than most to assert: "Coloniality names the underlying logic of the foundation and unfolding of Western civilization from the Renaissance to today of which historical colonialism [has] been a constitutive, although downplayed, dimension" (2). By this phrasing, Mignolo is also suggesting that the logic of coloniality/modernity involved other forms of colonialisms, including the subjugation of women, peasant, and working classes, but also alludes to the ideological machinery that made such subjugations and their naturalization possible. Thus, in *Black Skin, White Masks*, Fanon asserts, against the author of *The Psychology of Colonization*, "why does he want to make the inferiority com-plex exist prior to colonization?" (66), and goes on to say, "I sincerely believe that a subjective experience can be understood by all, and I dislike having to say that the black problem is my problem, and mine alone, and then set out to study it" (66–67). Through this text, Fanon appeals to a nonlocalized experience but examines the experience through a number of philosophical strains from Hegel to Sartre to Merleau-Ponty. Here, he clearly points to an anti-Hegelian position, countering Hegel's argument that the servant/slave needs to experience servitude/enslavement—in short, violence and exploita-tion—in order to come to recognize his humanity and to fight for it. Fanon counters such rationalization by exploring the *dislocation* of subjectivity for the "Black man," such that agency is short-circuited and, as he says, (following Merleau-Ponty), "amputated" (to return to a concept covered and redefined in Chapter 1) through the *process* of psychological and physical colonization.

Fanon exposes the "irrationality" of white/colonial ideology through the use of an itinerant first-person singular/plural narrator, "I/we," who should not be conflated with Fanon himself, a first-person subject position he uncovers in Capécia, as I argued earlier. In Fanon, "I/we" is a deliberate construction meant to indicate the instability of Black (male) identification in a white world that imposes what Fanon calls a "third-person consciousness." As Anjali Prabhu has argued, in the fifth chapter of *Black Skin*, Fanon's "narrator assumes a historical-universal 'I' of the black man in tracing out, before the white man's gaze, his many tactics, one of which is, indeed, the 'I' of négritude" (198). Adopting multiple positions in the historical process of decolonization from subjugation to reaction to the recognition of an underlying consciousness moving beneath the imposed "bodily schema" of the white world, Fanon's "I" is a strategic (dis)articulation of black consciousness in which the intent is to reveal the irrationality of structures of domination inherent in philosophical discourse (Hegel, Sartre) as well as psychoanalytical structures (Freud), in the same way that Capécia's "I" was meant to reveal the subject position of a poor, woman of color moving from the Caribbean to Europe and back again as if it were a personal journey. In so doing, he utilizes rhetorical strategies already evident in Capécia that some decades later (as I will show, in my analysis of Seacole), in the theorizing of women's autobiographical writing, would come to be associated with "an ontological and integumentary relationship of interiority to bodily surface and bodily surface to text as well as the identity (synonymity) of the I before the text, the I of the narrator, and of the I of the narrated subject" (Smith 1999 108). Invoking Judith Butler's troubling of gender norms, Sidonie Smith thus argues: "The autobiographical subject finds him/herself on multiple stages simultaneously, called to heterogeneous recitations of identity. These multiple calls never align perfectly. Rather they create spaces or gaps, ruptures, unstable boundaries, incursions, excursions, limits and their transgressions" (1998, 110). Elsewhere, Smith argues that "truth-telling" in such narratives take the form of subversions and inversions, for there is no "real" self to be found, arguing that "there is little access to a 'true self' to be found textually. Splitting of all kinds intervene in direct access to the 'self'" (38). Taking stock of Smith's understanding of feminist reconstructions of selfhood within autobiography, without yet claiming Fanon's work for autobiography but reading within it the rhetorical strategies of autobiography (though it has often been read in this way; for instance, see Alcoff's anthology, *Identities*, which summarizes Fanon's work in *Black Skin* not as a theory of subjectivity and anticolonial critique but as an excerpt from "the diary of a black intellectual recovering from the trauma of the white Western world" [Alcoff and Mendieta ix], while Anne McClintock, in an otherwise insightful reading of Fanon's gender limits, refers to Fanon's writings as hyper-personalized "anguished musings" [285]), I suggest that Fanon consciously makes use of such tropes in order to "subject" the reader to the "lived experience" of the Black consciousness while also demonstrating how the process of subjugation within the white-dominant world in itself ruptures access to a "true self"—a strategy he discovers in Capécia but whose origins he is at pains to reveal, for reasons already enumerated earlier. A passage such as the following can be read through what Smith, via De Lauretis, also terms (dis)identification:

> I had rationalized the world, and the world had rejected me in the name of color prejudice. Since there was no way we could agree on the basis of reason, I resorted to irrationality. It was up to the white man to be more irrational than I. For the sake of the cause, I had adopted the process of regression, but the fact remained that it was an unfamiliar weapon; here I am at home; I am made of the irrational; I wade in the irrational. Irrational up to my neck. (Fanon 102)

If we realize that Fanon's "I" is a rhetorical construction and strategy advanced to examine the violence of the colonial paradigm, we are forced to come to realize, as he writes, not only that "a subjective experience can be understood by all" (114), but that his argument implicitly works to demonstrate that the "I" of the text is not a colonial invention but exists prior to the moment of collision, or of interpellation, and that, even beyond the historical moment(s) of colonization, consistently and persistently reemerges to make itself known as it is always known and present within the subject. This, of course, is not a new reading. Anne McClintock, among others, surmises that the end product of such a journey is to invoke simultaneous identification/(dis)identification and to demonstrate that "white defines itself through a powerful and illusory fantasy of escaping the exclusionary practices of psychical identity formation" (300). If, however, we juxtapose Fanon's narrative, with that of Capécia utilizing similar strategies and of Seacole, writing a hundred years prior, we can better apprehend the role of (Black) women's interventions in facilitating a process of ontological (self) recognition quite similar to, and prescient of, Fanon's.

Though Mary Seacole's text is, on the surface, addressed to an audience to whom she appeals in order to make a living in old age, it reveals itself, in Eze's terms, and those of classic continental philosophy, as a text of a soul in conversation with itself. The transnational journeys she recounts are thus only a mirror of her soul's inner conversation and, in this way, transcends its apparent forum of enunciation, the travel memoir. According to Eze, such experience, translated in language can be formed only from the basis of "freedom . . . to persons of reason" (126)—thereby exemplifying her autochthonomous subjectivity. In situating Seacole as such, I am underscoring that in *exercising* her freedom, both lived and rhetorical, against (what Fanon has termed) the irrationality of the racist pathologies she faced in her efforts to do so (pathologies entwined with sexism as well as xenophobia given her mixed heritage), Seacole is able to narrate her life and her life's perspective in ways that defy the social conventions of her time. In doing so, she transcends not only those conventions but time itself. It is also in this transcendence of time, and thus of history as a fixed form, that her subjectivity presents itself as autochthonomous. Ultimately, Seacole's text demonstrates the ontological and textualized presence of a woman of color's point of view in the colonial period while creating a decolonial discourse in the assertion of an ontological reality that could not be assimilated or understood for the contestation that it was in its own time. As such, it stands as a pre–twentieth-century example of textual racial and gender disarticulation.

I suggest, then, that we move away from reductive readings of Seacole that insist upon a racial bifurcation of her life which appears to have resulted in her effacement from history for almost a hundred years. As Jane Robinson has written in her 2004 biography of Seacole: "Despite the efforts of the Seacole Fund trustees, and those veterans of the Crimean War who loved and admired her, she could never, in the nineteenth and early twentieth centuries, be extolled as a true British heroine: she was too black. And despite the (quiet) pride she had in her homeland and her Afro-Caribbean roots, she couldn't fully identify or be identified with black Jamaicans: she had become too white" (199). Seacole understood herself as transcending such binaries, even if, at times, with accompanying hubris, and composed an alter ego for *Wonderful Adventures* who reflects the belief that social categories could be forcibly reimagined via the manipulation of narrative, and by situating itself in what I have otherwise termed lakou consciousness, that is, within an African Diasporic sensibility.

This final section thus demonstrates that if, as Fanon once wrote, "we know nothing of her," of the woman of color, or, more specifically, of African descent, it is because he/we have willingly relegated her narratives to a space outside of the philosophical just as easily as Hegel was able to dislocate Africa from world history or Fanon was able to dislocate Capécia from an Afro-Caribbean literary trajectory. We know nothing of her not because, as

Gayatri Spivak compellingly argued in her multiply iterated essay, "Can the Subaltern Speak?" the female subaltern has not been speaking, but because we have assumed her speech to be intelligible and not worth a hearing on the basis of antifeminist (and anti-"Black") readings of such works. Further, if Judith Butler is correct in her assertion that "life might be understood as precisely that which exceeds any account we may try to give of it" (43), then I would argue that the gaps I will discuss evident in Seacole's text which reveal its multiple social positionalities and ludic self-mythologizing, also reveal that the genesis of the text resides in this unknowable excess of subjectivity that lay beyond the confines of the narrative frame, an "excess" that I have renamed *autochthonomous* in relation to subjectivities of African descent. In this sense, the text is expressly modern, breaking conventions of Seacole's time inasmuch as she breaks with the gender traditions of the Victorian period applied differently but uniformly to white, Black, and "coloured" women in that women in each category occupied predetermined social categories that defined modes of agency and mobility, but also the ordering and function of narrative. One might say that her transnational subject identity marks her aesthetics: in the same manner as Seacole exercises agency over the movements of her body as an autochthonomous being, the manner in which she orders her text suggests a similar exercise of freedom and authority over her self-representation.

What is of particular interest in Seacole's *Wonderful Adventures*, a memoir and travel narrative, are the similar rhetorical strategies the author employs to defy the colonial, anti-black and antifemale discourse of her time while safeguarding her subjectivity and its autonomy. Seacole's text does not conform to the postcolonial Manichean dialectics to which we have become accustomed and which Fanon exposed utilizing very similar framing devices almost a century later. In reaching back to Seacole's late-nineteenth-century text for evidence of a transcendent African diasporic and gendered subjectivity, which Fanon will later attempt to frame for Black males, I suggest that such agency coexists with her status as a subaltern within English society in much the same way that Fanon's "Black man" is forced to be both a "third-person consciousness" while also knowing himself to be a fully formed subject. Further, I suggest that the confluence of psychic and legal freedom produced in Seacole, as exemplified in her work, constitutes a subjectivity we have only lately recognized as transnational. As a woman, but not only as a woman, Seacole also exercises a prescient feminism that, today, might be termed gender-neutral. More significantly, however, in eschewing gender categories and defying racial type, her text reveals a constitutive identity that escapes the categorizations of race, gender, and nationality to which we have grown accustomed even as the boundaries of each become (or have always been) increasingly mutable. In short, without attempting to counter colonial discourse using the terms for identity that such a discourse would provide a woman of color in her own time, she nonetheless weaves herself back into the "thousand details, anecdotes, and stories" Fanon claims the white man has erected for himself to the exclusion of the presence of *his Other*, the colonized subject (90).

Seacole's *Wonderful Adventures of Mrs. Seacole in Many Lands*[8] has essentially been considered the product of its author's need for self-fashioning for differing ends. Depending on the critic, who one may assume to reflect different communities of readership, Seacole's text is variously read as a narrative of "Englishness" (Gikandi; Poon), of Jamaican creolity (Hawthorne; Frederick), of transatlanticism (Gunning), or, as Cheryl Fish contends, as reflective of a "mobile subjectivity" (6). Though my reading is closest to Fish's, she, like the others and most notably Gikandi, defines Seacole as a "black" woman writer, a label Seacole herself was at pains to decry, not because she was distancing herself from her African roots, but because, as I will show, she disidentified with the racial categorization that such a label imposed upon her. The fact that Seacole's narrative subjectivity can be read so variously is a testament to its bold constructivity. Despite such over-readings, I maintain that the opening lines of the narrative signal Seacole's resistance to over-readings while also serving as a curious imposition upon her reader of a subjectivity not readily identifiable. She writes:

> I was born in the town of Kingston, in the island of Jamaica, sometime in the present century. As a female, and a widow, I may be well excused giving the precise date of this important event. But I do not mind confessing that the century and myself were both young together, and that we have grown side by side into age and consequence. I am a Creole and have good Scotch blood coursing in my veins. My father was a soldier, of an old Scotch family. (1)

Seacole claims her place of birth, Kingston, but not its nationality, Jamaican (which, at the time, did not exist, since Jamaica was still a British Crown colony). She identifies her father as a Scot, not as English (a distinction that no critic to date has pursued), and both herself and her mother as Creole, signifying both mixed-race (African/Indigenous/European) and born outside of the European/British metropole. "It is not my intention," she shortly declares, "to dwell at any length upon the recollections of my childhood" (1). Fish adroitly reads this opening as a rewriting of the slave narrative genre (as does Evelyn Hawthorne) in that Seacole repeats the invocation of birth and location but repeals the possibility of an accurate historical date of birth, thus underscoring a narrative alliance with enslaved African populations while not entirely defining herself as a descendant of slaves (and thus as an offspring of the process of colonization). I would extend this reading to argue that the subjectivity of (African) women has been largely ignored precisely because of an easy conflation with African slave narratives that were often read, at least in the criticism of early- to mid-twentieth-century American literature as meta-texts of the slave experience since the majority were dictated and then rewritten by a white amanuensis. Writing for herself, but through an indeterminate first-person voice, Seacole evades precise racial designation, suggesting at once that she will not be displaced from her own identifications, even as she textually makes her readers aware of her consciousness of how she may be racially codified and spatially located.

In this opening gambit, Seacole attributes to her Scotch blood her decidedly unfeminine desire to travel where men go, as she states: "Many people have traced to my Scotch blood that energy and activity which are not always found in the Creole race, and which have carried me to so many varied scenes" (11). As biographer, Jane Robinson, notes of *Wonderful Adventures*: "It's robust and witty, deftly manipulative of its readers' responses and emotions, and remarkably assured: in fact, more like a professional gentleman's piece of work than a lady's" (172). To her Creole blood Seacole attributes her doctoring skills (12) given her mother's occupation, an occupation related to indigenous (in both the First Nations and African sense of the term) healing practices: this is the foundation for her autochthonomous sensibility to which she returns again and again. She thus attempts to dismantle both racial and gender categories embedded in each: by attributing her "vigor" to her Scotch blood, she effectively neutralizes that vigor one might associate to an "African" sexuality primarily inscribed in the black female body. Concomitantly, by attributing her skills as a doctor to her Creole blood, she effectively neutralizes the idea that her medical prowess can only be attributable to an English (via Jamaica) education. By reversing that which she valorizes in each identity, Seacole destabilizes the notions of a readership that would have invested to either static, binary, or racialized values and advocates for her hybridity, a hybridity that constitutes, as Hall has argued a "new ethnicity," one which is autochthonomous because of its emphasis on her "creole" identity and the skills of healing that have provided her the means by which to cement her identity as a "doctress." The latter is advanced as a valorized identity rooted in African-derived, syncretic healing practices, practices that then ensure her mobility, along with her legal status, in areas where she is otherwise actively shut out. Her audience would have presumably been familiar with her caricatured appearance in *Punch* and other depictions of Seacole made during her lifetime, none of which, it might be said, resemble each other, except in their depiction of Seacole as having a decidedly "of colour" phenotype. What being "of color," means visually, however is really dependent upon those controlling the means of representation. If historian Clare Gittings, in her explanation of how a late 1860s portrait surfacing in a boat sale in the U.K. in the early 2000s could be appropriately identified as depicting Seacole, surmises that compared with other images of Seacole "they all clearly show the same distinctive face" (14), a survey of all existing images of Seacole[9] shows a startling variance in what artists believed they saw. In each portrait, Seacole is mixed, her complexion shown to be darker than "white" by shading, or, if produced in color, typically shown as a sienna brown. Gittings, only, compares a bust of Seacole made in 1971 (existing only in a photographic reproduction) and a carte de visite photograph in which Seacole wears the same three medals she is shown to wear in the 1869 painting. Indeed, these three portrayals depict the same person who could just as well be of African descent as she could be aboriginal, South Asian, or some other ethnic mix "of color." In other depictions, as in the image utilized on the cover of *Wonderful Adventures*, Seacole's facial features are completely different from the plump, rounded visage that her carte de visite confirms to be the "real" Mrs. Seacole; her face is drawn out, oval rather than round, her cheeks shrunken, her gaze severe (another wartime sketch is similar). In the *Punch* caricature, she appears again stout, jovial, the face nondescript, "blackened" so that there is no doubt as to (African) ancestry, so that Seacole is recognized only by her characteristic cape and headdress shown in more realistic drawings of the period, and by the caption accompanying the drawing. In her text, Seacole demonstrates an awareness of at least the *Punch* caricature and its exaggeration of racial phenotype, when she quickly follows her introduction with a recounting of her first impressions of London. In turning to these, she claims that "I am not going to bore the reader with them," but soon elaborates upon them by telling us that "some of the most vivid of [her] recollections are the efforts of the London street-boys to poke fun at my and my companion's complexion." "I am only a little brown," she goes on, "but my companion was very dark, and a fair (if I can apply the term to her) subject for their rude wit." In her punning of the word "fair," at the expense of her companion's description, Seacole is suggesting that despite popular images produced of her, she might herself, unaccompanied by such a marked companion, pass as "fair" (13). Within the first three pages of her text, then, Seacole has made clear that she will neither subscribe to popular definitions of "blackness" or of gender; at the same time, she makes clear throughout the text that she defines England largely through its racism, providing perhaps a partial explanation for her initially overly precise description of her father's ancestry as Scottish (rather than British/English).

Because Seacole and Florence Nightingale, her contemporary, were starkly contrasting contemporaries in a highly racialized historical time and, as women, both transgressed the Victorian codes of their time by being working women, it has been a natural tendency for criticisms to focus on gendered readings of their encounters. For one, Sandra Gunning opines: "Therefore, when we think of Seacole's presentation of herself as a woman in the Crimea, we need to consider as well what limitations and possibilities emerged with the presence of such British white women located completely outside of the traditional domestic sphere" (970). Though Seacole is herself a British subject, Gunning focuses her analysis on how Seacole would have contrasted with Nightingale. She studies, for instance, *Punch*'s portrayal of her in an 1857 caricature in which Seacole is shown selling copies of the magazine to injured soldiers, arguing that "despite her considerable reputation as a healer, Seacole is unrepresentable as a nurse even when imagined in a hospital" (958). The *Punch* depiction is quite similar to one produced of Nightingale some three years earlier whereby Nightingale is shown as a "desexualized and disembodied creature, more spirit than flesh" (Poon 510–511). Neither Poon nor Gunning read these two images side by side, but biographer Jane Robinson notes that Seacole was often "caricatured as a rather ridiculous creature—a surreal hybrid of Mad Sally Mapp (a famously bombastic but successful London quack) and Miss Nightingale—who, beneath the gaudy costumes and substantial brown bosom, possessed a glowing heart of gold" (122). Poon conjectures that Seacole's "race and class effectively bar her from similar representation" (510), but I wonder to what degree readings of the *Punch* sketches rely on post-Victorian readings of gender and race constructions we now understand to have been current at that time. Though race and class are mitigating factors in both Seacole and Nightingale's enterprises and in how both are historically remembered, their portrayals are remarkably similar in that both are rendered desexualized and divorced, within the portrayals, from the arts they practiced. True, Nightingale, is more clearly shown to be "nursing" a soldier, but the disembodied, angelic tone of the image suggests that she is doing nothing more than being present rather than actively healing; though Seacole is depicted rather as a merchant than as "doctoring," it is implied that she too is ministering to the troops. Perhaps more significantly, the Seacole cartoon depicts the British soldier reaching for and holding Seacole's markedly darker hand while Nightingale's cartoon displays no such affective intimacy; though this could be read as a historical conviviality embedded in white male relations to black women, the fact that

Seacole is desexualized in the image as well as decidedly not "mothering" (i.e., in the sense of a "mammy" figure) suggests that the cartoon obliquely grants her the status of nurse in the broadest sense (of "looking after" or "caring for" the ill). While Gunning argues that Seacole's silence regarding Nightingale is in keeping with domesticated images of her persona (960), Poon concludes otherwise that Seacole very deliberately "locat[es] herself geographically closer to the site of the most intense suffering . . . [as] a bid to wield greater moral authority," and thus to grant "her more autonomy . . . to perform the patriotic work only thought possible of an Englishwoman" (512). Though I find Gunning's conclusion debatable given Seacole's almost wholesale neglect of gender issues and Poon's compelling argument in that I agree with her that Seacole seeks to underscore her autonomy, I would like to suggest a more radical reading of Seacole's presentation of her rejection by Nightingale.

In keeping with the humor embedded in the text as well as the self-conscious self-representation Seacole effects in her memoir, it appears, rather, that Seacole attempts to remain neutral regarding Nightingale in order not to alienate their shared readership and, yet, this seeming acquiescence to Nightingale's larger-than-life reputation is clearly undercut by the events Seacole chooses to highlight. I am thus suggesting that we do away with readings of Seacole that seek to situate her primarily as self-promoting, as historian Clare Gittings does when she equivocates in a teacher's guide to the 1869 portrait of Seacole newly identified by London's National Portrait Gallery in 2003 that, in comparison to Nightingale, Seacole was "always an outsider, exhibiting great compassion and courage in the Crimea but not able or apparently wishing to make fundamental changes to how things were organized beyond the scope of her own actions" (25). Though a surface reading of her text would suggest Gittings's conclusion, a very close reading of the text's rhetorical strategies proposes more visceral underlying cultural critiques on behalf of its author. While most critics suggest that Seacole "finds it much more difficult to attribute racism . . . to the English ladies who turn her down as a nurse in the Crimean War" (83), it is also clear that she connects her confrontation with Nightingale with her rejection from the British authorities, a rejection, in turn, based on race. She juxtaposes these events in her chapter entitled, "I Long to Join the British Army before Sebastopol," where she declares with no gender irony: "Now, no sooner had I heard of war somewhere, than I longed to witness it" (Seacole 69). She recounts her rejection from the Medical Department and disingenuously claims: "Now, I am not for a single instant going to blame the authorities who would not listen to the offer of a motherly yellow woman to go to the Crimea and nurse

her 'sons' there, suffering from cholera, diarrhoea, and a host of lesser ills."
Immediately following this refusal to blame, Seacole does just this when she
states, "In my country, where people know our use, it would have been different," thereby distancing herself markedly from the British and claiming
the Caribbean (Jamaica) as her "nation." She therefore makes clear to the
presumed British reader that she wishes to be read as "foreign" and not as a
British subject, though not as "Black" but as Creole-Afro-Jamaican. She thus
practices a nascent autochthonomy that has basis in her understanding of
herself as practicing African-derived knowledge that ensures her capacity to
remain free, and mobile, to practice that knowledge without subordinating it
to Western medicinal practices or to male norms of travel. It expresses itself
as a disarticulation from Western medicinal modes and from the medical
institutions and their representatives that refuse her access in order to practice her healing modes because they come from African-derived modalities;
Seacole, however, undeterred, persists in their use and identification. Immediately following this disconnection from things British, Seacole describes
reaching out to Nightingale's acolytes who "gave me the same reply, and I
read in her face the fact, that had there been a vacancy, I should not have
been chosen to fill it" (75). What Seacole "reads" in the nurse's face is nothing
less than racism. What is particularly striking about Seacole's admission, and
its glossing over by critics, is that Seacole, though the injured party, locates
the wrong in the other party, the party whose gaze she not only returns but
reads. Rather than calling attention to her (physical) difference, Seacole brings
attention to the subject of her gaze thereby underscoring the agency of her
movements and, simultaneously, whatever else might be said of her and of
her hotels, her innocence, thereby continuing to underscore her practice of
autochthonomy.

Within the narrative, at a moment in which she describes her rejection
(in a chapter subtitled "How I Failed"), Seacole uncharacteristically appeals
to a feminized affective response to questions of racial prejudice when she
writes: "Tears streamed down my foolish cheeks, as I stood in the fast thin-
ning streets; tears of grief that any should doubt my motives—that Heaven
should deny me the opportunity that I sought" (74). If Seacole's tears might
be in question, then perhaps her questioning here might also give the reader
pause for contemplation. Is Seacole suddenly asking for a sympathy she
rarely invokes within the pages of her memoir or is she employing the tech-
niques of dissemblance we have seen her utilize elsewhere? I suggest that the
latter is the case. Once Seacole reaches Nightingale's station in the Crimea,
she and her readers are fully aware of the chilly reception that awaits her.
By this time, we have been led, through a previous chapter, to recognize a

subtle yet clear link made by Seacole between American and British racisms; rhetorically, Seacole's stated disbelief regarding British racism is simply a cover for the racism she knows too well and elsewhere uncovers. In fact, her many allusions to American racism and African enslavement would appear to be a means by which to address the racism of the British indirectly. When Seacole turns to her personal experience with racist expulsion within English society, she brings the two cultures in uncomfortably close alliance. Yet, her meeting with the friendly washerwoman in Nightingale's hospital where she is offered a night's lodging in exchange for treating the sick during that night, suggests that Seacole also seeks to demonstrate her lack of racial ill will: "My experience of washerwomen, all the world over, is the same— that they are kind soft-hearted folks" (82). Ironically, Seacole undercuts the scene with her humor when she quickly recounts her experience of the companions who "took the washerwoman's place, and persisted not only in dividing my bed, but my plump person also" so that "in the morning, a breakfast is sent to my mangled remains" (83). What is of interest in this depiction is that Seacole references her corporeal self rather intimately but in such a way that race and gender are evaded. She is, in fact, invaded by fleas who, like the washerwomen, are "ubiquitous" the world over. Strangely yet true to her humorous turn, there is significance to this conflation but not the one we might expect. She is not reducing washerwomen to the state of fleas but suggesting that, washerwomen the world over are the same "kind, soft-hearted folks," fleas attack regardless of race or gender. Both are blind to imposed differences of race and class. To be sure, Seacole's depiction of the washerwoman she encounters in Scutari is romanticized and class-based (in that Seacole reveals herself to be of a different, higher class), but it serves to focus the reader on Seacole's ability to transcend class and race divides while also, otherwise (in the case of fleas) being subject to the liabilities of such transcendence. Because Seacole's references to her own gender are fleeting and, when she takes the time to expound upon it, she never fails to do so in a manner that is ludic and derisive while still recuperating her own definition of her gendered or sexed identity (as I demonstrate later), it would seem important to read her as attempting, insofar as the genre of the Victorian (female) travel narrative allows, to transcend, rather than only subvert, gender categorization. What is important to Seacole is not so much being accepted in the ranks of (white) womanhood (arguing, as did Sojourner Truth, for example, for an alternative definition of womanhood inclusive of Black female reality) but (similarly to Fanon with regard to male supremacy in the process of decolonization) in preserving the *privilege* of her subjectivity and its mobility.

Seacole's insistence on revisiting her disappointing encounters with Florence Nightingale or her surrogates can be read as incidents she reads as
evidence of encroachments upon the privileges she otherwise acquires for
herself during her peregrinations to frontier areas (for instance, in Panama)
or to liminal war zones (such as the Crimea). Because Seacole assumed her
transnational privilege thoroughly in her time, she also assumed its attendant
hubris. Not unexpectedly, this caused friction between the class to which she
was presumed to belong, both because of gender and race. Seacole, however,
appears to situate the blockade against her assumed privileges as a mobile
entrepreneur of a rising middle class in racial disenfranchisement; yet, she
did so indirectly, in keeping with the subterfuges of her self-presentation. At
the same time, the ways in which she reveals racial prejudice as the cause of
her conflict with Nightingale and other official nursing/medical establish-
ments are less about desiring to crusade for racial enfranchisement than they
are about the ways such prejudice impinges upon her sense of self: Seacole
reveals racial prejudice obliquely to her audience to demonstrate that even
for a mobile subjectivity such as herself, it exists. However, the fact that she
also shows, through the *Adventures*, that such interdictions had little to no
effect on the pursuit of her travels continues to reveal that the subjectivity
Seacole posits is one that is not constituted through the race and national
discourses of her time but in spite of them, therefore instituting itself as presciently transnational and rooted in another space, that of African Diasporic
consciousness.

Though Seacole was conscious of the dictates of her time, she lived beyond
their boundaries. She encoded the text to signal an unyoked subjectivity and a
desire to be autonomous from British racial mores. Jane Robinson notes that
modern readers (and critics) are disturbed by Seacole's lack of overt identification with her African heritage and presumes that Seacole did not "thump
the political tub more vigorously and challenge her imperialist Victorian
audience to change their assumptions about illegitimate/unconventional/
lone/female/black travellers/writers-with-attitude, like her . . . because she
shared so many of those assumptions herself" (173). I in no way want to argue
that membership in a minority or marginalized group results in emancipated
thought but I do want to posit that, despite harboring some of her own prejudices, and clinging to her relative privileges, Seacole was *consciously* reduced
to producing a text palatable to contemporaries who had yet to broach the
freedom of thought that her text subtly encodes (akin to Rancière's emancipated subject, which I discuss in the following and final chapter). Many
passages of the text itself signals an unyoked subjectivity,[10] a desire to be free
of British racial mores. While replicating some prejudices within her pages,

Seacole also utilizes rhetoric deftly in order to subtly push her audience into new spaces with regard to social categorizations. In a humorous tale, for instance, she recounts that, when she first arrived in Tchernaya, "very much delighted seemed the Russians to see an English woman. I wonder if they thought they all had my complexion" (160). Though she reverts to her status as "English" and restates her complexion, the story is meant to question how race is "read" cross-culturally; Seacole proceeds to play with the Russians by first pretending to be the Queen of England (instigated by some young men accompanying her), and when this ruse fails, plays along with their declaration that she is "the Queen's first cousin" (162). Though, again, such a story seems to be meant to induce laughter (implied is the sense that Seacole's companions think it ludicrous that a biracial woman could be "noble"), it also encodes a question as to the mutability of race. Seacole's mirth here is aimed at the possibility that, for a moment, she might pass as a noblewoman. It is also an admission of the need to tell her stories and question social mores in such a way that might be acceptable to her readers. She was aware that, "just as a white woman would be prevented because of her colour from sailing off to Cuba or Haiti with a cargo of jam pots and self-confidence to make her fortune, a coloured woman would be prevented from being taken seriously, as a true equal, in anything she did amongst her white peers" (Robinson 28). Seacole thus uses humor in order to convey less acceptable social positions, especially gendered ones, and comes to surreptitiously question the discourse of racial "contagion" rampant, as Anne McClintock has shown, during this historical period.

Though racism is at the center of Seacole's musings throughout *Wonderful Adventures*, it is striking the degree to which gender appears only to disappear. While evading precise racial designation, Seacole foregrounds her gender identity by boldly asserting herself to be both "female and a widow." Readers must presume that she is also childless since Seacole never refers to having had children though she does refer to being accompanied by a child attendant, Mary, in some of her travels. Against some historical evidence that this child is Seacole's own, Sandra Gunning convincingly argues that "it is her widowhood, as well as her presumed childlessness, that makes it possible for Seacole to claim her surrogacy as the mother to English soldiers far from home" (956). It is also a claim she makes in order to distance herself from the sexual innuendo her mixed ethnic and female corporeality signal whatever her movements or true (self-defined) identity. Necessarily, Seacole sublimates any sexualized identity she might have in favor or what appears to be a desexualized "Mammy" figure. When she does take pains to highlight her embodied sex and its attendant gender constructions, it is in a way that comes as a surprise to the reader, who is lulled into accepting Seacole's adventures at face value and also as largely disembodied. In fact, her text reflects the persona of a male explorer so much that it appears that Seacole must pause to interrupt the successful way in which her narrative reads;[11] when she does refer to herself in a gendered fashion, it is in a way that undermines the very effect of calling to the reader's attention to the anomaly of her factual, embodied sex. If Seacole's adventures are, in themselves, a show of arrogance in her defiance of the day's racial norms through her entrepreneurship and medical prowess, then her approach to gender is one of avowed humor. Throughout the narrative, Seacole displays very little affinity and even less empathy for members of the female sex (25; 81). We can thus be sure that when she resorts to describing herself in ways that recall her femaleness, she does so with a clear purpose in mind. On the one hand, she manipulates her readership by conflating two incompatible definitions of womanhood throughout her text; then, on the other, and more importantly, she derides the category of woman, so that "her humor accompanies her hubris" (Hawthorne 315). On more than one occasion, Seacole disingenuously undercuts her clear pride in her prowess as a sutler and medicine woman by referring to herself as an "unprotected female." In one case, referring to her work on battlefields, she exhorts: "And here I may take the opportunity of explaining that it was from a confidence in my own powers, and not at all from necessity, that I remained an unprotected female" (15). She presses on to explain the attentions she received from the opposite sex after the death of her husband, contrary to contemporary readings of Seacole as a "mammy" figure, underscoring that she *chooses* whether or not to be involved with the male sex while also remaining silent on those involvements within the pages of the text. Elsewhere, in reference to the motley characters who took advantage of her table d'hôte at her Cruces hotel, Seacole claims "it was often very difficult for an unprotected female to manage them" (40), as she simultaneously seeks to distance herself from those whom she served who may have been considered disreputable in order to preserve her credibility as a mobile entrepreneur. On two occasions, Seacole suddenly refers to her dress; these recollections are startling in that they interrupt narratives describing scenes of frontier deprivation or war that would have, in her time, been wholly associated with white male witness, thus creating a doubling effect regarding her subjectivity (such as I explored previously via the concept of double-time) and embodied agency: she presents herself as circulating invisibly in a context wholly conflated with white male identity and then disrupts it by rendering her female identity legible, thereby reconstituting her embodied self for her reader and reconstituting the site of white male agency as penetrable and alterable.

In the first instance, as she makes her way through Panama to reach her brother in Cruces, Seacole recounts the difficulties of maneuvering the roads from the railway to the port, describing them as "worse than useless" as she navigates her way. After spending some time describing the base conditions of travel, Seacole interrupts her description of the difficult landscape and turns her reader's attention to her attire:

> And as with that due regard to personal appearance, which I have always deemed a duty as well as a pleasure to study, I had, before leaving Navy Bay, attired myself in a delicate light blue dress, a white bonnet prettily trimmed, and an equally chaste shawl, the reader can sympathize with my distress. However, I gained the summit, and after an arduous descent, of a few minutes duration, reached the riverside; in a most piteous plight, however, for my pretty dress from its contact with the Gatun clay, looked as red as if, in the pursuit of science, I had passed it through a strong solution of muriatic acid. (20)

By using adjectives like "delicate," "prettily," and "chaste," to describe her attire, Seacole draws a pious portrait of herself; yet, contrasted to the adjectives utilized to typify her ordeal, "arduous," "piteous," and the ultimate desecration of her blue dress as having been subject to "muriatic acid," she violently does away with the previous effect. This dissemblance is meant to be preposterous and ludic. She undercuts her appeal to be accepted into the realms of white womanhood while also denying her interest in those ranks. Eventually, without describing her habitual attire, she will admit to having done away with her respectable gowns, lending them out to soldiers entertaining themselves in the Crimea by cross-dressing. "I lent them plenty of dresses," she says, "Indeed, it was the only airing which a great many gay-coloured muslins had in the Crimea. How was I to know when I brought them what camp-life was?" (155).

In the second instance, and in the midst of war, after having been roundly rejected by the English Medical Department (72) and as a nurse in Nightingale's hospital (79–82), Seacole finds herself assisting the wounded. Faced with human suffering, Seacole says, "so strong was the old impulse within me, that I *waited for no permission*, but seeing a poor artilleryman stretched upon a pallet, groaning heavily, I ran up to him at once, and eased the stiff dressings" (87; emphasis mine). After having described the myriad ways in which she was turned away from public service as a nurse in the war effort, Seacole here makes clear her ability to assume responsibility for her own actions. She also assumes mastery over white male bodies in defiance of the colonial premise that "the white body is expected not to be looked at by black bodies" (Gordon 1995, 102). Blinded by his wounds, the soldier described in this incident proclaims, according to Seacole, his repeated thanks for "a woman's hand" (88); thus she not only looks upon the white male body but touches that body against colonial interdictions that would preclude a "black" female from having access to and, indeed, power over, a white male body. Seacole underscores that the man thanks her for her *woman's* touch, italicizing the word in one of the repetitions, and then muses that she is not sure why the surgeons had yet failed to notice her though she "had not neglected [her] personal appearance, and wore [her] favourite yellow dress, and blue bonnet, with the red ribbons" (88). In this passage, Seacole clearly reveals that gender is of some importance but not in the ways we might at first surmise. *Despite* her feminine attire and *despite* her raced visibility, she wanders unnoticed amid the wounded. When she is approached by a doctor who takes note of her nursing the artilleryman, she curiously states, after describing her attire, that he "would have laughed very merrily had it not been for the poor fellow at my feet" (ibid.), thus causing us to reflect on the cause of such merriment. The causality Seacole draws between the nursing story, her invisibility, her attire, and being discovered leaves no doubt that only her attire is to be laughed at, thereby evading what Fanon later calls the "grinning *Y a bon Banania*" (92)—that is, the "black" individual who can respond to the pain of racism only with a grin or laugh that will be misconstrued as acquiescence at best, joy and infantilism at worse. She thus escapes both the deformation of her identity as a raced subject through a racist bodily schema that would misread her humor as well as her agency as conformity but defies the notion that "white" and "black" bodies, especially of the opposite sex, cannot touch and be touched. Seacole underscores this notion, again against the prescriptive notions of racial "contagion" of her time, in the description of an autopsy she performs on a "brown-faced orphan infant" who dies of cholera in her arms in Cruces, New Granada.

Though we are given no explanation for how the child finds its way into Seacole's arms, she recounts the child's death as silent after having described the suffering of grown men: "They screamed and groaned, not like women, for few would have been so craven-hearted, but like children." The child, less than a year old, dies without a sound. Seacole seizes upon the occasion of the child's death to "learn more of the terrible disease which was sparing neither young nor old, and should know better how do to battle with it" (33). Fish reads this scene as Seacole's assertion of her skills as a doctor, transgressing gender mores, but Seacole clearly states that this was "my first and last post mortem examination." Moreover, she ends the narration of the scene by refusing her readers access to the results of her findings: "I need not linger on this scene, nor give the readers the results of my operation; although novel to me, and decidedly useful, they were what every medical man well knows" (34). Seacole's first-person narration asserts her right over the dead child's body and invokes her skills as a physician (again underscoring her West Indian heritage and the inheritance of her mother's "creole" healing knowledge) against race and gender types, but her comment that the results of the operation were both "novel" and "well-known" embed the story in a contradiction that suggests another reading: that the object of the story is to allegorize the body of the child as that of the body politic of both African Diasporic subjects and of Seacole herself as one of its representatives.

Autopsied, the child's body reveals "what every medical man well knows," thus situating the body of the "brown child" in the field of shared humanity across geographies and racial or ethnic types: the child's cholera is the same as everyone else's (just as the fleas attacking the flesh of washerwomen indiscriminately, discussed earlier). Bent over the child's body, assisted by a local man, Seacole performs a postmortem on medical and ideological discourses that situate the brown body outside of the bounds of normalcy. That she does so in a context of contagion, herself falling ill to cholera by the chapter's end, deflects notions of miscegenation as a form of contagion, since the scenes of illness she recounts in Panama, New Grenada, and the Crimea result from mobilities instigated by European and Euro-American imperial and capitalist expansion ("scattered hegemonies" of expanding empires to which she is a mobile witness). Her critique, then, falls not on the brown body, the "poor little body [she buries] beneath a piece of luxuriant turf" (ibid.), but on the forces and agents that have visited upon that body its own disease and ultimate death. Seacole, newfound knowledge in hand, defeats the contagion of racialist discourse and defeats her subjection as a raced subject, a marginalized subject in the economy of the imperial gaze, anticipating the critiques of her works a century later, and affirms the modernity of her subject position through her experience, self-directed mobility, and manipulated account of self.

In fact, Seacole pointedly brings attention to the pastiche nature of her text and to the performativity of its narration when she explains near the end of the *Adventures*:

> In the last three chapters, I have attempted, without any consideration of dates, to give my readers some idea of my life in the Crimea. I am fully aware that I have jumbled up events strangely, talking in the same page, and even sentence, of events which occurred at different times; but I have three excuses to offer for my unhistorical inexactness. In the first place, my memory is far from trustworthy, and I kept no written diary; in the second place, the reader must have had more than enough of journals and chronicles of Crimean life, and I am only the historian of Spring Hill; and in the third place, unless I am allowed to tell the story of my life in my own way, I cannot tell it at all.

In this manner, Seacole appropriates for herself control over her narrative—disarticulating herself from chronology—as well as over the reader's expectation of what a travel narrative or Crimean memoir should be. In effect, she is reminding her readers of her intent, that is, to give an accurate portrait not so much of war and travel but of herself. In fact, she chides disappointed readers by calling to attention her tremendous responsibilities: "and if the reader should be surprised at my leaving any memorable action of the army unnoticed, he may be sure that it is because I was mixing medicines or making good things in the kitchen of the British Hotel" (128). Several of the preceding chapters, those leading up to her time in the Crimea and those detailing life in the Crimea itself, focus on highlighting Seacole's actions for the war effort as indispensable and, in some sense, without equal. Though she often mitigates in a "ladylike" manner against being thought vain, it is clear that most of the text here is meant to foreground her adventures as the text of a heroine. In order to convince her readers of both her heroic actions and her indispensability, she incorporates into the text the testimony of a number of soldiers, usually quoting at length from those with some standing in rank. Thus, as she makes her way through Bacalava toward the Crimea, she interrupts her text with a letter from "Major R" who confirms her work for "poor sick and wounded soldiers." She prefaces the letter by clarifying its purpose in the narrative. "I must have recourse," she says, "to a plan which I shall frequently adopt in the following pages, and let another voice speak for me" (89). Almost the whole of her chapter entitled "My Work in the Crimea" is devoted to such letters confirming her "intention in seeking the army . . . to help the kind-hearted doctors" (110). Breaking again with the linearity of her text, Seacole asks her readers at the end of this chapter to return to an earlier chapter, Chapter VIII, to "see how hard the right woman had to struggle to convey herself to the right place" (118). Chapter VIII, is, of course, the chapter that contains the disingenuous subtitle "How I Failed" and describes her rejection by both the British Medical department and by Nightingale and her nurses. By forcing her readers to return to the earlier chapter, Seacole twice circumvents the protocols of linearity and insists upon her version of the facts of her life. Tantamount to her recollection is the desire to have her role in assisting troops on the war front celebrated while putting to shame those who attempted to prevent her from fulfilling what she designs as her destiny.

This is why, in her chapter focusing on the "the last bombardment of Sebastopol," she paints an image of herself as *sovereign over her domain*, having accomplished what she set out to do: "And here, with refreshments for the anxious lookers-on, I spent most of my time, right glad of any excuse to witness the last scene of the siege. It was from this spot that I saw fire after fire break out in Sebastopol, and watched all night the beautiful yet terrible effect of a great ship blazing in the harbour, and lighting up the adjoining country for miles." She then sets out on mule-back to provide her provisions of "bandages and refreshments" (146) but protects the reader from "many scenes of woe, that I am lo[a]th to dwell much on these" (151). What she intends to leave in the mind of the reader, having demonstrated her ability to survive in white male domains and doctor as well as any white woman, even Nightingale, while defying both raced and sexed discrimination, is her self-directed agency despite any obstacles thrown her way, and the means she takes to secure and maintain it even in the most extreme of conditions; also clear is that, by abandoning the rules of chronology to underscore her volition, her triumph is her heroism. Speaking of the abandoned Russian hospital she comes upon after the bombing of Sebastopol, Seacole confides to the reader: "I would give much if I had never seen that harrowing sight. I believe some Englishmen were found in it alive; but it was as well that they did not live to tell their fearful experience" (ibid.). She, on the other hand, survives to tell her tale, outwitting death, prejudice, and the limits of her gendered form, to achieve witness for the benefit of her multiple audiences. Her tale provides us with every indication that more than the attempt to be counted in the ranks of the privileged, Seacole seeks to be remembered in the annals of history as a fully operating subject-agent, that is, as autochthonomous. Seacole does not need to prove her agency: she assumes it. Relaying that reality to others in a time when her identity would have been overdetermined from without, however, is another matter. The occasion for her textual self-representation is thus her attempt to fill the gap between her known identity and that imposed upon her, whether raced or gendered.

In all these ways, then, Seacole's text might be understood as attempting to break with understandings of her persona as a liminal figure or one defined only by its alterity. Homi Bhabha reminds us that "as a signifier of authority, the English book acquires its meaning after the traumatic scenario of colonial difference, cultural or racial, returns the eye of power to some prior, archaic image or identity" (2007, 34). Taken as a sign, the "book" relies on its construction of authority to wield it; like the words printed upon its pages, it too relies on an effacement of the gap between signifier and signified to find its natural articulation. This process itself produces an opportunity for disruption, which Bhabha takes to be most salient in the idea, concept, or reality of "hybridity" which he terms "the sign of the productivity of colonial power, its shifting forces and fixities . . . the name for the strategic reversal of the process of domination through disavowal" (2007, 42). Hybridity, for Bhabha, "enables a form of subversion, founded on that uncertainty, that turns the discursive conditions of dominance into the grounds of intervention" (34). In this way, then, we might read Seacole's text as performing a contestatory intervention some hundred years *prior* to both Capécia's and Fanon's entangled confrontation in the terrain of narrative decoloniality. Ultimately, Seacole's text demonstrates the ontological and textualized presence of a woman of color's (first-person) point of view in the colonial period while creating a decolonial discourse in the assertion of an ontological reality that could not be assimilated or understood for the contestation that it was in its own time. It stands as a pre–twentieth-century example of textual racial and gender (dis)articulation. In "real life," that is, off the page, as Robinson notes, Seacole did not distance herself from her Jamaican family, whom she treated "with loyalty and generosity" while also choosing "for her early travels the new republics of Haiti and New Granada" and embracing traditional healing arts (173–174). Only when we understand Seacole's text as a self-conscious fabrication, a representation of a persona meant to elicit the compassion (and funds) of its readership, can we better apprehend the arch-play on race, gender, and nationalities it performs. We cannot presume that because it is an autobiographically derived text its words are "truthful" as such or a play-by-play of actual thoughts and events. Like Capécia's narrator, and Fanon's rhetorical "I," Seacole's memoir/travelogue utilizes "'I'-lying" to get at underlying truths with the full force of authority invested in the first-person mode of address.

Conclusion

To think the terms *African Diasporic, woman of color, feminist,* and *philosophy* simultaneously within the context of the Euro-American philosophical academic tradition is to think largely in terms of misnomer and impossibility. My analysis in this chapter necessarily, then, began with a reconsideration of Frantz Fanon's role in the removal of Caribbean women from the ontological terrain as decolonial discourse first began to emerge. I also argued that Fanon ingests and reproduces Caribbean women's narrative strategies, especially those that arise from the "memoir" form, because they produce voices of authority through first-person address. I revisited his reading of Mayotte Capécia's novel and the novel itself to show that Capécia's narrative ultimately demonstrates, through the manipulation of first-person narration and its conferral of authority, the need to escape the limitations of raced/gendered class in order to assert an Afro-Caribbean identification. Finally, I posited through an analysis of Mary Seacole's nineteenth-century memoir that Caribbean women's early, ambiguous, yet deliberate narrative strategies of dis/identification and (dis)articulation, already sought to expose an understanding of the ontological complexities of subjects whose identities are impinged upon by historical, material reality resituating it within an Afro-Caribbean sensibility. Recognizing these African Diasporic women's wrestlings with identity effects transhistorically serves to reveal a more profound subjectivity, one I argue resides in lakou consciousness given divides of geography, time, and language. Fanon himself recognized the power of this subjectivity through the very lens of his opposition.

I have posited that Seacole's narrative strategies reveal a refutation of the liminal identity to which African Diasporic/women of color are relegated in Western ontological and social discourse in function of their gender, race/ nationality, and representation. I have argued that Seacole's "first-person" narrative strategies, in contesting Victorian definitions of gendered propriety, overdetermined racial categories, and in the pains she takes to fashion her self-representation to appeal to a white, British, upper-class, readership while simultaneously speaking to traveling "others" like herself, points to an "excessive" subjectivity, which is not circumscribed by her narrative or by her social position. This excess, in the Sartrean existentialist phenomenological sense (as well as through the tenets of psychoanalysis), is that which "escapes all representation" and which is "fundamentally, one's real self, one's capacity to negate, and the seat of purposeful action and choice" (Alcoff 69). It transcends those aspects of identity that Seacole demonstrates, through their refutation/ (dis)articulation, are socially inscribed on her gendered and racialized body. As I have shown, her self-composition which articulates affirmations of an African Diasporic subjectivity, and of its agency, gives us clues as to how she navigates her interiority within the strictures of an external world that would seek to define her only through her material body as well as deny her capacity for an intelligible self, or being-in-itself, not predicated by patriarchal/ white colonial social hierarchies. In this sense, her late-nineteenth-century transnationalism is a vehicle for advancing a subjectivity unmoored from both the racialized and gendered definitions of identity current in her time (and still in effect in ours). Further, the ambiguities inherent in her self-fashioning reveal the complexities of a subject whose identity is impinged upon by historical material reality: Seacole wrestles with a desire to be of the colonial class while being subject to a colonial gaze. She seeks to escape the limitations of her (raced) class while also exercising her legal freedom as a British subject. Yet, it is this very wrestling that reveals a more profound, resonant autochthonomous subjectivity that I hope to have uncovered. My aim has been not so much to demonstrate that Seacole's text can be read as transnational and feminist but that *in the exercise of what could be defined as transnational agency, she reveals a subjectivity that exceeds colonial tropes and which realigns itself with African gnosis.*

As a self-defined, Jamaican-Creole-Scott, Mary Seacole's text can be read as profoundly anti-Hegelian in refuting claims of Africa's (and African's) ahistorical presence but, more than this, refutes claims, much like Fanon will at a later date, to subaltern *irrationality*. Her text affirms philosopher Emmanuel Eze's claim that "there is neither in the purest conceptions of human rationality nor in the language of any cultures evidence that reason or language escapes time and sociality" (125). Experience, Eze argues, is "an essential attribute of humanity" and "[by] way of language, it is memory and history that, dialectically, constitute the subjectivity of an individual . . . the conversation of the soul with itself" (126). Though Seacole's text is, on the surface, addressed to an audience to whom she appeals in order to make a living in old age, it is also a text of a soul in conversation with itself. According to Eze, such experience, translated in language can be formed only from the basis of "freedom . . . to persons of reason" (ibid.). In situating Seacole as such a subject, I am not seeking to argue that I am intent on demonstrating Seacole's rationality: it is a given. What I am underscoring is that in *exercising* her freedom, both lived and rhetorical, against what Fanon has termed the irrationality of the racist pathologies she faced in her efforts to do so (pathologies entwined with sexism as well as xenophobia, given her mixed heritage), within an African Diasporic understanding of herself (a lakou consciousness) Seacole is able to narrate her life and her life's perspective in ways that defy the social conventions of her time. In doing so, she transcends not only those conventions but time itself and establishes her autochthonomy, that is, her subjectivity as autochthonous to a transnational space of mobility for a woman of African descent, belonging to a hybrid expression of cultures and traditions and exercising her will/agency fully during a time in which such an identity was forcibly invigilated. Seacole's courageous peregrinations through liminal terrains of colonial expansion and the pastiche account of self she offers in her nonlinear travel narrative, satisfy multiple readerships without ever situating the author in a stable discourse of self/other. The mobility and modernity reflected in her recollection and composition of self demand that we rethink and at last abandon Manichean dialectics in favor of discovering the "unknowable" subjects residing in us all beyond the discursive strategies employed to support outdated and always mythic notions of subjects and subalterns that have served only to obliterate our common humanity.

From the work of self-fashioning we have discovered in the writings of Mary Seacole, Mayotte Capécia, and, after them, Frantz Fanon, I turn, next, to African Diasporic travel writings, to investigate the actualization of lakou consciousness and of autochthonomy, as represented in works by two African American writers in the early part of the twenty-first century. I extend the present analysis into a consideration of how early-twentieth-century writers of the Harlem Renaissance attempted to establish autochthonomous, African Diasporic, transnational identities, that is, identities braced in subject identities tethered to concepts of emancipated/lakou consciousness, autonomy, and mobility. The autochthonomous legacy of Harlem Renaissance predecessors demonstrates that they discerned the importance of intradiasporic af/filiations anchored in cultural tropes that could be put to the service of decolonial epistemes and also serving as affirming sustenance.

4 Autochthonomous Ambiguities

Travel, Memoir, and Transnational African Diasporic Subjects in (Post)colonial Contexts

The itinerary displaces the foundation; the background of my identity, and what it incessantly unfolds is the very encounter of self with the other—other than myself and, my other self.
—Trinh T. Minh-ha, *elsewhere, within here: immigration, refugeeism and the boundary event*

There are years that ask questions and years that answer.
—Zora Neale Hurston, *Their Eyes Were Watching God*

Inter-Nations: African Diasporic (Self)Representation, Mobility and the Nation

To this point, I have discussed the ways in which race, in the context of the United States, has become an overdetermined category by which individuals are circumscribed in order to delimit their circulation, their political and economic reach. I have endeavored to demonstrate that beyond racial typing, individuals conform or are coerced into performing raced identities and that some so-defined persons consciously exercise a practice of foregrounding their "excessive" identities as beings belonging to specific ethnicities with long histories and traditions in which they participate via cultural and historical af/filiations and continuities beyond the borders of their nation-states or sites of citizenship. I have examined the ways in which overlooking cultural filiation in favor of overdetermined racial categories can lead to the continued enracination of narratives of dispossession that position Africa and people of African descent within the Hegelian construct of world history, therefore out of history and, outside or on the cusp of modernity. Such narratives have the consequence of tethering people of African descent to a unilinear historical construct derived from Europe and positioning people of African descent as ultimate "others," forever lost to themselves as a consequence of the violent upheaval of colonization and enslavement; they necessarily topple into the ahistorical in vain attempts to recover what the Hegelian trope situates as nonexistent. Consequently, I have examined how the refusal of such overarching claims of dispossession, or lack of origins, by artists of African descent spanning from the late nineteenth century to the twentieth, have pushed against the boundaries of the nation-state, of ethnic designation, of "racial" type, in order to produce what I have been terming *autochthonomous* texts reflecting African Diasporic subjectivities. In this chapter, I extend this notion further by examining exchanges between African American and Afro-Caribbean contexts, as expressed in Harlem Renaissance texts that reproduce, for readers, contexts of intradiasporic exchange in order to create a new foundation for African-descended realities. I suggest that Jacques Rancière's reformulated concepts of engaged spectatorship and of subject emancipation might serve as useful guides when thinking through intra–African Diasporic exchanges in postcolonial contexts to which colonial vestiges cling or inflect alternative notions of identity and autonomy. Here, I turn to works by writers of the Harlem Renaissance with specific attention to their apprehension of Haitian indigenous realities as an expression of what could presently be apprehended as autochthonomous realities. I suggest that, in these earlier texts, lakou/yard consciousness unfolds, not without ambivalence for national allegiance but with an understanding of the ways in which cultures of African descent in the Americas speak to one another and form increasingly autochthonous modes of expression in the early decades of the twentieth century. This latter reality has increasingly been lost in contemporary writings, wherein writers of African descent seem to take for granted that the sole basis for exchange with others of African descent are histories of suffering and expulsion (as they have become more "integrated" into the nation), misrecognizing opportunities for af/filiation that reach beyond mere surface appearance to the level of language, ritual, and identities derived from African syncretic foundations.[1]

One could argue, as I will later, that what made it possible for Harlem Renaissance writers to identify with other cultures and aesthetics produced by other writers and cultures of the African Diaspora was the movement's professed search and advocacy for an African American sensibility that would birth a "New Negro" not defined by the state or by a history of subjugation but through a valorization of the roots of African American culture within the United States and in relationship with African folkways retained transhistorically. The movement also overlapped and was fed by similar movements, literary and artistic, in other parts of the world, especially via négritude and Pan-Africanism. Assertions of Pan-African sensibilities dominated the mid-twentieth century but died down by the late 1980s and 1990s, replaced then by other, more discrete movements within cultures and geographical locales (for example, the rise of Black Feminist writings/thoughts in the 1980s in the United States—the rise of Caribbean Literature as a "national" literature across nation-states of the Caribbean, of Anglophone African Literature, and so forth). Harlem Renaissance writers, in part, wrote more about cultures of African descent beyond the United States, because incursions into spaces beyond the U.S. borders as a part of the U.S. policy of manifest destiny made such travel possible. But, at that time, the impulse to write about those spaces within the travel genre was more or less nonexistent. As we shall soon see, writers like Claude McKay and Zora Neale Hurston, wrote about (or through) their travels, within other genres—McKay in memoir and fiction, Hurston through anthropology and (masked) in fiction. People of African descent, by virtue of their subjugation through colonization were simply not in a position to assume the authority of the travel writer, very much a classed (white and bourgeois) identity. When mobility became more accessible to such writers emanating from the United States,[2] the impulse was not one of domination, such as we see reflected in traditional travel texts, but one of *af/filiation* (as defined in previous chapters). We must, before continuing, then, understand clearly the role of the travel text in colonial and postcolonial societies.

Traveling Subjectivities and African Diasporic Translations

In postcolonial scholarship of a revisionist nature of the last decades, scholars have endeavored to relieve the "black body" from the weight of its history, most expressly in investigations of constructions of race in the eighteenth and nineteenth centuries as these turn upon the imperial projects of Europe in what was once called, and perhaps still is, the New World.[3] At all cost, miscegenation, *métissage*, and other forms of racial mixing had to be avoided. This avoidance would consequently assure the "purity," and dominance, of the European, the white. The colonies were desired sites to deposit "contagion" as they were already determined to be degenerate. "Degenerate" whites could thus be deposited there and Europe purified; at the same time, however, those deposited could differentiate themselves from the African and Indigenous populations and reorder the body politic, projecting their own degenerate status onto these newly encountered others. It is within the context of this composed universe that travel narratives came to function as texts of the (imperial) nation.

More than works of entertainment, though they were that as well, travel narratives were meant to control that which seemed beyond policing: the abject, the colonized. They also served as a way to comfort the reader that the "new world" beyond the known was only an extension of themselves and that whatever contagion was pushed off into these exotic lands could remain contained through an imaginary that translated the "other" as a *manageable* force of nature. James Clifford, for one, has defined travel itself, as "an inextinguishable taint of location by class, gender, race, and a certain literariness" (1992, 110). In his influential revisioning of the fields of ethnography and anthropology, "Traveling Cultures," Clifford struggles with the terminology of the field, that which determines that the interlocutor of culture is almost always a white European, male, while the "informants" are always "natives." As he investigates these divisions further, he questions the position of the "native" in such exchanges, surmising that they might be termed "cosmopolitan intermediaries" (100). Clifford edges toward accessing the possibility of a non-European, nonwhite traveler with his or her own agency and subjectivity but doesn't ever quite get there, admitting: "I struggle, never quite successfully, to free the related term 'travel' from a history of European, literary, male, bourgeois, scientific, heroic, recreational, meanings and practices" (106). Although I am proposing to investigate the content of narratives written by Harlem Renaissance writers, rather than Victorian "cosmopolitan intermediaries" of color, the premise of this chapter is to investigate Clifford's suspended interrogation, that is, what texts written by those situated as contemporary subalterns by virtue of ethnic filiation might yield. When read, rather, as expressions of autochthonomous subjectivities and af/filiation, other interpretive possibilities for understanding the texts emerge. Though contemporary or modern writers of color ought not to be facilely deemed "subalterns" as genealogical descendants of formerly colonized people, in that a "subaltern" is normatively defined as "a person without lines of social mobility" (Spivak 28), my investigation here will show the degree to which consciousness of oneself as a Subject, despite being categorized otherwise, might indeed, free the term "travel" from Clifford's etymological claim for the term. Furthermore, I am interested in how shifts in social class, through mobility, for such descendants, would occasion concomitant shifts in the understanding of space, landscape, and those who inhabit sites of (physical) exchange. Such an investigation might yield a compelling discursive reassessment of how we might rethink the role of "native informants" as cosmopolitans who, despite a fixed identity within a minority group denied social (i.e., class) mobility, can speak a consciousness freed from marginalization that remains, to varying degrees, part of communities of origin (i.e., an autochthonomous group with af/filiative connections), even as the border crossings they effect provide them with purchase within the economy of a society that largely frustrates the possibilities of movement for the constituents of the larger community that such urbane travelers represent.

In this sense, my analysis here is related to that of Patrick Holland and Graham Huggan who, in their *Tourists with Typewriters: Critical Reflections on Contemporary Travel Writing*, make room for an analysis of postcolonial travel writing (citing, for example, the work of Caryl Phillips and Jamaica Kincaid) in the following manner: "A postcolonial approach to contemporary travel writing . . . might therefore seek to examine the continuing complicity between travel writing and cultural imperialism; to analyze new forms of travel narrative that resist these earlier models and that explore the possibilities inherent in travel writing as cultural critique; and, finally, to assess the extent to which these various revisionist or counter-narratives are themselves bound up in an ideology of exoticist consumption" (48). To a large extent, I am interested to see how narratives of travel produced by writers of African descent in the late twentieth century negotiate the double bind of responding to or critiquing European norms while also working in a genre defined traditionally by its Eurocentricity, and, beyond this, whether the texts follow in the example of their predecessors (of African descent) or respond to and reveal intradiasporic affinities.

Here, a useful link may be forged to the opening essay of Jacques Rancière's recent work on spectatorship, *Le spectateur engagé*. As foregrounded earlier, Rancière's concept of the emancipated intelligence/spectator provides a framework by which to think through the avenues open for the Subject emanating from postcolonial geographies, that is, for the Subject who was previously positioned as a passive recipient of the colonial structure and positioned as a subaltern within it, who emerges in the postcolonial period as an emancipated subaltern and, possibly, as one with privilege. Here I mean also to suggest that there is a double entendre in my analysis, that is, that I want to suggest that we hinge together the two definitions of "emancipation": emancipation in the sense of the free Subject as articulated by Rancière, and emancipation in the historical sense of the freedom of formerly enslaved Africans and the identities that African-descended writers have constructed in its wake. Rancière has argued for the equality of intelligences, positing that the "ignorant teacher," "disassociates his mastery from his knowledge" (17) in order to guide the pupils through their own process of acquiring that which they do not know, which is not necessarily the knowledge of the master but the means to fill the pupil's own lacunae. Rancière's attempt to close the gap between a pedagogy of liberation and the emancipation of the viewing Subject is instructive in considering the positionality of a viewing subject normally situated as outside of the possibility of action in societal discourse. "Emancipation," writes Rancière, "begins when we interrogate the opposition between looking and acting, when we understand that the traces that structure the relations of speaking, seeing, and acting all belong to the structure of domination and of subjection" (19; my translation). Once that interrogation begins, then it follows that we must work to efface Manichean distinctions and entertain interchangeability on a new plane, that of presumed equality. Though the translation/transformation aspect of the exchange between audiences and performances they view, might be equitable, and thereby signal the formation of a "communal" or "shared" experience of spectatorship, the Subject becomes emancipated, even from a sense of community, and acquires an equality with the capacity to transcend the hegemonic structuring of translational exchanges (theatrical or social).

Rancière thus moves from a discussion of theatrical spectatorship to social performances, positing that his concept of the "equality of intelligences" creates a space in which each individual has the power to translate her/his perceptions in order to affirm her/his equality to all others in the theater of lived existence. He elaborates: "Ce que nos performances vérifient—qu'il s'agisse d'enseigner ou de jouer, de parler, d'écrire, de faire de l'art ou de le regarder—n'est pas notre participation à un pouvoir incarné dans la communauté. C'est la capacité des anonymes, la capacité qui fait chacun(e) égale(e) à tout(e) autre. Cette capacité s'exerce à travers des distances irréductibles, elle s'exerce par un jeu imprévisible d'associations et de dissociations. . . . Être spectateur n'est pas la condition passive qu'il nous faudrait changer en activité. C'est notre situation normale" (23).[4] For Rancière, all spectatorships have embedded in them this potentiality for liberation; privilege, from such a vantage point of diminished hierarchy, exists only as a node of possibility; it need not permeate the whole of one's existence or perceived place in the order of things. Liberated from a static notion of the authority of the stage and the passivity of the viewer, and informed by the concept of equal intelligences, Rancière's Subject is granted an emancipation from discourses in which the Subject is already formed as a passive recipient who is acted upon or who can perform only a certain range of sanctioned responses within the structures that compose her/him. Rancière's emancipated spectator is a new Subject who already walks among us, who finds her/himself articulated through the versatility of idiom, and who, as such, can appropriate and create history.[5] Is it possible in today's postcolonial age to be both an emancipated *being* and an African Diasporic one? I suggest, in the following exploration of McKay's and Hurston's deployment of autochthonomy in their respective texts, that it is.

Kreyolization as Lakou Consciousness

Harlem Renaissance writers, I argue, were foundational, in the North American context, in establishing the circuitry for a modern African Diasporic subjectivity situated in the United States. I suggest, however, that they did so not in isolation or even as the precursors to other movements but in awareness of, and in conversation with, writers of African descent elsewhere, as occasioned by contact with other nations through the world wars and, in particular, U.S. gun boat diplomacy in the Caribbean Basin, which resulted in the occupations of Panama, the Dominican Republic, and Haiti, respectively. Harlem Renaissance writers circulated with some amount of ease, owing partly to the fact that a number were either themselves from elsewhere or only one or two generations removed from the Caribbean (as was the case for McKay, W. E. B. Du Bois, and James Weldon Johnson, among others), and to their increased visibility in the domestic and international literary scenes. Among these in particular, Claude McKay and Zora Neale Hurston escaped the disciplining (imperial) gaze of their own time and deployed a subjectivity that was not subaltern in its constitution but fully humanistic, even as they struggled against the confines of a nation state (the United States of America) that relegated people of African descent to second-class status legally, socially, and politically through practices of de facto apartheid (segregation).

In positing new reading practices for African Diasporic texts, I am particularly interested in how we might read Hurston's *Their Eyes Were Watching God* as an encoded, *kreyolized* text marked by her passage in Haiti, a period during which time she researched her anthropological text, *Tell My Horse*, in Port-au-Prince while writing the novel, in its entirety, in a feverish six-to-eight-week sprint. In doing so, I explore how the text could have escaped the author's geographical resettlement, however brief, in an African-derived culture saturated with storytelling and a rich folkloric history. Further, I am interested in how McKay's memoir, *A Long Way from Home*, published in the same year as *Their Eyes*, and the earlier text, his first novel, the picaresque "plot-less" novel *Home to Harlem*, provide a glimpse of a thoroughly cosmopolitan figure able to move easily between worlds as he does continents (the Americas, Europe) and nations (Russia, Germany, France, England, Morocco) yet singularly focused on the intradiasporic experience in the Americas, highlighting Haiti in his works for both cultural and political reasons, as I will show. Born a British subject in Jamaica, McKay presents a perplexing case of an artist of African descent in the early part of the twentieth century who has lately been reconsidered as a key figure both in the African American literary tradition and in modernism as transnationalism and globalization have become the key terms for exploration. Without such critical developments, McKay could well continue to shadow other figures of the Harlem Renaissance, remembered only for his sonnet "If We Must Die" of 1919. While Hurston defied convention as an African American writer/ethnographer/anthropologist, McKay defied convention as a Jamaican/American poet and world traveler at a time when males of African descent were still considered subject to the disciplining of the (European) nation. Both have left behind valuable records of a subjectivity we are still at pains to assess and accept, a subjectivity that I argue was foundational for subsequent generations of African-descended writers in the Americas. The increasing refusal to perceive of African-descended people as having autochthonomous identities, that is, as having cultures rooted in both physical and af/filiative networks of sustenance and exchange, rather than only in Manichean dualities and as defined only by modes of resistance to anti-Blackness has resulted in the loss of understanding of these preexisting intradiasporic exchanges. As such, what I argue marks the two texts I consider here is their investment in the representation and assimilation of cultural codes borrowed or integrated from an African Diasporic culture other than their own as a process of advancing the autonomy of a speaking subject who, though subject to the tides of history, is not submerged by or subordinated to them.

Their Eyes Were Watching God and *A Long Way from Home*, then, do not "speak back" to empires nor do they correspond to what would later be termed "resistance literature" (to invoke Barbara Harlow's text of the same name). They do not resist: they participate. But to what discourse do these texts belong if not to the traditions of resistance and uplift that has come to define the Black American experience? I posit that they participate in a preexisting tradition of embodied subjectivity that neither denies the fact of slavery and the marking history of the Middle Passage nor glories in them, that is, in autochthonomous subjectivity. This subjectivity participates within the parameters of dominant discourse at the same time as it encodes competing philosophical perspectives derived from the lakou/yard, which diasporic Africans transplanted into non-African ground to create new, African Diasporic ethnicities. In reconciling opposing epistemologies, McKay and Hurston sought to demonstrate a nascent erasure of dualistic hegemonic binaries enshrining the artistic production of said-subalterns to a subordinate discourse of resistance; they thus provided, in parallel development with African Diasporic writers located elsewhere, the blueprint for how to write the "Black" self.

Claude McKay's Haitianism

The recent surge of interest in McKay by literary and queer theorists has begun to provide a space in which to read McKay not simply as a liminal or disaffected player in the Harlem Renaissance movement but as an intellectual poet whose political engagement has been misunderstood by virtue of past inabilities to situate the author as an expatriate *Caribbean* exile. McKay has tended to be read only as an (African) American expat, by virtue of an inability to think of McKay in global and pluralistic national contexts that were perceived to be inconsistent within the literary tradition of Black uplift and socialist/communist agitation to which he was witness and in which he participated. Thus Ramesh and Rani assert in their recent text, *Claude McKay: Literary Identity from Jamaica to Harlem* that McKay's *A Long Way from Home* "records his ideological evolution from being a British colonial writer in exile to being a black writer in search of identity" (177), concluding that McKay, as a Caribbean exile "embarked on a long and torturous search for viable *native* roots" (178; emphasis mine). Though Ramesh and Rani's attempt to situate McKay in a broader African Diasporic context is refreshing, they nonetheless continue to understand McKay in African American terms as they suggest that what has been called McKay's "autobiography," and to which I will refer as a "memoir," participates in an African American literary tradition. They write: "African American scholars trace the roots of African American autobiography to the slave narratives, which were primarily produced to prove their humanity and to claim a historically denied voice" (7). Though the authors suggest that there is more to McKay's memoir than just this, they are hesitant to situate the memoir in that space of "otherness," whether that space be defined as Caribbean or, in our present-day lexicon, as global or as transnational (Ramesh and Rani). Why not read McKay's text as having resonance with texts by other Jamaican (though these may have been sparse) and Caribbean writers with whom he would have been familiar, such as the late-nineteenth-century memoir by fellow Jamaican, Mary Seacole, discussed in Chapter 3, or the writings of contemporary authors from Haiti such as Jacques Stephen Alexis or Jacques Roumain, whose first essays and books would have been emerging within the same decades as McKay's own oeuvre?[6]

To define *A Long Way from Home* not as "autobiography," that is, as a "true" account of McKay's life but as a "memoir," I believe, facilitates a broader assessment of the work as a creative achievement that seeks to consciously frame and reframe both personal and historical moments lived and witnessed by the author already alive in the contemporary imagination. Unlike autobiography, the memoir, as genre, does not attempt to be factual; it renders a representation of lived experience that readers recognize as fallible, as accurately *impressionistic,* as opposed to accurate in its details. As McKay himself notes at the end of the memoir, "all I offer . . . is the distilled poetry of my experience" (270), a phrase that denotes poetic license in choosing and shaping the retelling of key episodes (from McKay's perspective) from the author's traveling and most productive writing years in the late 1920s and early 1930s. For instance, much of the memoir grapples with McKay's attempts to develop as an artist, to find publishing outlets for his work as well as reaching a wider readership in the face of implicitly racist assessments of his writing, a particularly postcolonial narrative. As McKay noted: "In most of the reviews of my poems there was a flippant note, either open or veiled, at the idea of a Negro writing poetry. After reading them I could understand better why Bernard Shaw had asked me why I did not go in for pugilism instead of poetry" (72). "Why should a Negro's love poetry be offensive to the white man," questions McKay, "who prides himself on being modern and civilized? Now it seems to me that if the white man is really more civilized than the colored . . . then the white man should take Negro poetry and pugilism in his stride, just as he takes Negro labor in Africa and fattens on it" (73). McKay connects the reduction of Black artistry to mimicry or entertainment as a distortion produced *through* imperialist history that purposely deflects critical gazes on the African continent away from the exploitation of Africans for human labor and native resources in the project of "civilizing" Africa. To counter this discourse, following the discussion of his reviewers, McKay launches into a lengthy appreciation of a first-century (500 BCE) pre-Islamic poet, Antara Ibn Shaddād al-'Absi, the son of an Arabian and of an African slave woman whose poetry apparently "produced the model for the earliest of the romances of chivalry" (Clouston qtd. by McKay 73). McKay expounds on the irony that a precursor of European chivalric poetry should be an African Arabian, thereby upsetting notions of "modernity" and "civility" ascribed only to Europeans. He concludes that the miseducation of both Euro-white and African-black children has obscured this pre-European history, owing to the invention of Africa as an uncivilized terrain in need of disciplining and an imperialist nostalgia that must reimagine Africa (much like America) as either un-peopled or inhabited by "savages" without gnosis or epistemologies. Writes McKay:

> In the universal white system of education the white schoolboy learns about Homer and Virgil and their works, even if he does not read Greek and Latin. He learns nothing of Antar, although it is possible that European poetry derives more from Antar than from Homer.

Note here McKay's careful diction, a hesitance to be too strident and yet make his point. He continues:

> The Negro child, born into an inferior position in the overwhelming white world, is in a different category. He should know something of the Antar who was born a slave, who fought for his liberation, who loved so profoundly passionately and chastely that his love inspired and uplifted him to be one of the poets of the Arabian Pleiades. (74)

He ends on a point of irony to say: "Perhaps if black and mulatto children knew more of the story and the poetry of Antar, we might have better Negro poets. But in our Negro schools and colleges we learn a lot of Homer and nothing of Antar" (75). Such "miseducation" stems from what Mudimbe has termed the violent, "missionary language of derision" as a "cultural position, the expression of an ethnocentric outlook" (52). McKay continues to pursue the thread of miseducation in the subtext of the memoir; that thread eventually asserting itself as a subversion of the proposed or perhaps obvious short-changing of African-descended children in the educational markets of Europe and America. It also, in pointing out the achievements of writers of African descent in various geographical spaces underscores their affiliation in a shared cultural continuity, and thus McKay's own participation in lakou consciousness, that is, his awareness of his affinities for and with other writers of African descent.

In the Russian context, where McKay is pressed to speak out on the "Negro" question, a position he claims not to occupy while visiting Russia, McKay advocates a rallying propagandist infiltration of the "Negroes of the South" so that they might be spurred out of stasis and into insurrection. When pressed on this issue, McKay defers to the director of the Eastern Bureau, a Japanese American educated in Negro colleges named Sen Katayama. McKay relates:

> Sen Katayama had no regard for the feelings of the white American comrades, when the Negro question came up, and boldly told them so. He said that though they called themselves Communists, many of them were unconsciously prejudiced against Negroes because of their background. He told them that really to understand Negroes they needed to be educated and among Negroes as he had been. (141)

McKay does not elaborate on this point but expounds on the racism of some leading communist figures from Britain and the United States. Still, his lack of comment is a comment in itself: it suggests that the truly miseducated are the former imperialists and their progeny and suggests implicitly that the "Negro" has an alternative epistemological reality from which something can be learned. His admiration for Katayama demonstrates McKay's desire to see a shared intellectual intercourse between ethnicities that would acknowledge and valorize African intellect, much like Achebe will advocate some twenty years into McKay's future. Hidden here is also an indication of what will become more explicit in other writings, as I show in my examination, later, of McKay's *Home to Harlem*, that is, for an anti-imperial, anticapitalist politic that speaks to and through an African Diasporic, autochthonomous sensibility. Though McKay's reach and outlook are global and international, it also reveals itself, in the criticism leveled against Euro-American communism, in search of a communism that can bespeak the needs of African-descended people, a communism he will find evinced in the writings of fellow Caribbean authors not of the Anglophone region initially, but that of Haitian writers. Here, at least, we see McKay deploy an anti-imperialist nostalgia[7] grounded in a dismissed history of precolonial African civilization posited in service of a hopeful future. This is why, in his assessment of his meeting with Bernard Shaw, McKay makes two wry observations, the first being that all he clearly remembers is Shaw's discussion of cathedrals and the second is a belated response to Shaw's entreaty that he forgo poetry in order to take up boxing. Of the latter, McKay concludes: "Perhaps the black poet has more potential scope than the pugilist. The literary censors of London have not yet decreed that no book by a Negro should be published in Britain—not yet" (60). Here, as he does elsewhere, McKay speaks to the future, of the importance of leaving literary traces that will survive the present and take up residence in the future. Of Shaw's expounding upon the grandeur of cathedrals, McKay retains the following: "I have spent hours upon hours meditating about modern movements of life in the sublime grandeur of cathedral silence" (55).[8] It seems that McKay is searching for a transcendent language and he finds it in the metaphor of cathedrals, "miracles of the medieval movement of belief and faith" (55); later, "Cathedral" reveals itself to be the history of African Diasporics, especially as reflected in the annals of the Haitian Revolution.

Though I have focused primarily on the racial issues raised in McKay's memoir to this point, it would be inaccurate to summarize it as a treatise on the "Negro problem" of the time; indeed, when the discussion emerges in the text it is largely a by-product of summarizing the anxiety around racial issues to which McKay, like others, was subject. The memoir, however, is compelling because it posits itself as the memoir of an artist in search of dialogue with other artists and with readers. It is the text of a cosmopolite invested in the larger questions of his time, from questions of aesthetics to political discussions of a changing world in the midst of world war and competing models for modern progress. How the memoir has escaped consideration as an archive of its time is a larger question I pose. In reassessments of McKay, most notably in Gary Edward Holcomb's *Claude McKay, Code Name Sasha: Queer Black Marxism and the Harlem Renaissance*, efforts have been made to reclaim McKay as a queer predecessor. As Holcomb writes of past assessments of the author's oeuvre, "The problem that the nomadic McKay and his transnational, aesthetically itinerant writing inevitably posed was where to locate him" (1). Holcomb chooses to situate McKay as a creolized subject, in Edouard Glissant's terms, and his writing as "pioneering the queer critique of gender performativity" (11). Though these claims have resonance when one looks to McKay's early novels (as Holcomb does), they seem less pertinent to this particular memoir. In an effort to "reconstruct the body of black modernity," Holcomb posits "a new grammar must be brought to an understanding of McKay's . . . earlier writing and rewriting" (9). That "grammar" is evidenced in the spirit of politicized blackness as posited in McKay's narratives. Holcomb thus situates McKay's work in "what Deleuze and Guattari call a 'minor literature' . . . laboring from the margins" (17). Yet, it is clear from reading McKay's memoir that he did not see himself as operating from the margins; indeed, in reproducing his encounters with figures from Shaw, to Trotsky, to Alain Locke, among many others, McKay presents himself as a figure circulating freely, autonomously, even expansively, from one country to another, crossing open seas, and having the doors to elite literary and political figures open to him not by magic but by virtue of his own recognized status as a literary figure of significance—as an expatriate American author, a communist propagandist, a modernist, or all three. Perhaps McKay constructs within the pages of the text a myth of himself. Mythic or not, it creates an alternative sign system by which we are meant to read McKay as an actor in his own life rather than as a subaltern fighting his way through a marginal existence.

In compelling analysis, Holcomb argues for reading McKay's work against that of T. S. Eliot and Whitman but, even as he does so, he claims for McKay an oppositional Black Atlantic voice. Does the reality of McKay's raced existence necessarily mean that his art would be marked by different literary choices, choices that relegate him on the margins of modernity, or is it possible that these might situate him in an*other* modernity derived from an African Diasporic sensibility? When McKay produces the Shakespearean sonnet "America" (1921) in advance of T. S. Eliot's "The Waste Land" (1922), is it possible to read the poem, as Holcomb does, as more than a racial allegory by which "the poem undoes the racist sexual certitude by making the white female the antagonist . . . identifiable in the shape of the Statue of Liberty" (28)? Though from a black nationalist perspective Holcomb's analysis is compelling, McKay's invocation of the Statue of Liberty suggests an alternative reading worth exploring.

There has, for some time, been a debate as to whether or not the Statue of Liberty was originally figured as an African slave freeing herself from chains of bondage, a debate which has been put to rest by scholars over time in such a way that suggests that such a possibility was not out of the question historically; historical records do confirm that the motivation for France's gift of the statue to the United States, was more than partly due to the emancipation of African and African-descended slaves on U.S. soil, though plaques to be found in the Statue's "series of wayside exhibits" are devoid of such mention.[9] This is something McKay would certainly have known from his peregrinations to France given the fact that an early model created by Bartholdi on the occasion of the Exposition Universelle of 1900 was bequeathed by its maker to the Musée du Luxembourg where it was exhibited in the museum gardens from 1905 (until 2014); this early mock-up of the statue was modeled with broken chains at her feet, peeking out from beneath her robes, presumably attached to her ankles. Thus, when, in the poem, McKay writes: "I love this cultured hell that test my youth," he speaks as an American subject critiquing the nation from within, wherein the Statue of Liberty reflects the dual history of enslavement and emancipation; the form of the poem invokes this Janus-face. He utilizes a conventional form to make an unconventional commentary derived from both European and Black Atlantic traditions and histories.

If for Holcomb, the New Negro of the Harlem Renaissance is the "photo-negative unintended issue of modernity . . . a being who has risen from the ashes of blackface minstrels" (30), then I posit that in McKay's disavowal of the New Negro and Harlem Renaissance projects he emerges as a true modern whose racialized experience of America is made complex by his shifting and mobile self but is also quintessentially modern in refusing to be made to conform uniformly to a bygone era. In *A Long Way from Home*, McKay attempts to transcend his time and to view a future in which the "Negro" might participate in the world economy (269). In this, he presciently engages notions of globalization and transnationalism that are as optimistic as they are humanist but he ultimately does so by attempting to underscore the contributions of African Diasporic cultures to humanity as he himself composes his own literary oeuvre. This is best evidenced in his "novel without a plot," the picaresque "buddy" story of Home to Harlem in which two male characters of African descent with radically different national identities—Jake, the African American working-class protagonist and Ray, the Haitian agonist—confront their differences in ways that illuminate the role that transnational mobility plays in shaping the trajectory of their lives. Through such exchanges, McKay comes to reveal his questioning of European modernity by positing the presence of an African modernity born through the Haitian Revolution; further, he seeks to awaken, through Ray, an awareness in his readers of the presence of a Black communist ethos in neighboring Haiti and of Haiti's struggles against American imperialism. In this, the novel is produced to reflect contemporary realities and to serve as a meditation on forgotten historical traces of Black subjectivity—what I have been terming "lakou" consciousness as the ground for advancing an autochthonomous subjectivity—long before late-twentieth-century reconsiderations of the role of the Haitian revolutionary thought on Enlightenment thinkers such as Hegel, or on the evolution of Latin American nation-states, or of the American South in resistance to what was then seen as the "horrors of St. Domingue"[10] were widely engaged.

Home to Haiti': Modernity in the Wings

In 1888, William Wordsworth published a poem entitled "To Toussaint L'Ouverture," which reads in part:

> Thou hast left behind
> Powers that will work for thee, air, earth, and skies;
> There's not a breathing of the common wind
> That will forget thee; thou hast great allies;
> Thy friends are exultations, agonies,
> And love, and Man's unconquerable Mind. (206)

Reproduced in whole in the body of Claude McKay's 1928 novel, Home to Harlem, yet not often taught or analyzed, William Wordsworth's ode to Haitian "Jacobin" leader Toussaint L'Ouverture stands as a testament to the impact of the Haitian Revolution not only for the followers of L'Ouverture, and others, who found, through him, their liberation, but of the impact of the decade-long struggle for freedom gotten by force (rather than through the legal apparatus of emancipation) on the powers of the imagination. McKay's invocation of the Haitian Revolution within the novel is not a flight of fancy: it is a manifestation of an autochthonomous subjectivity. Little remarked upon or understood, the inclusion of the Wordsworth poem alone should have, over the years, given critics pause. I suggest that this inclusion, by a poet well accustomed to modernizing the sonnet form to make political statements, is indicative of the importance that McKay gives to its content: by including the poem in whole, McKay emphasizes the importance of the Haitian Revolution on European scribes and, thus, of the importance of Haitian history and actualization in transforming twentieth-century understandings of modernity. He also emphasizes the cultural importance of Haitian *epistemes* formulated through the Haitian Revolution that gave rise to important philosophical and literary movements in the early part of the twentieth century during the dawn of U.S.-based neocolonialism.

After decades of interfering in Haitian affairs from the mid-to-late 1800s through "gunboat diplomacy," the United States occupied Haiti for nineteen years, from 1915–1934, years that coincide and encompass that of the Harlem Renaissance, typically situated as beginning in 1925 with the publication of Alain Locke's *New Negro* anthology and ending around 1937 (largely to encompass the work of writer/anthropologist, Zora Neale Hurston, and her signal work, *Their Eyes Were Watching God*, discussed below; otherwise, the period closes in 1929 with the stock market crash and subsequent decline of middle-class Harlemites and Harlem's arts scene). While many scholars of the Harlem Renaissance believe that African American writers of the period had an undue influence on Haitian letters, which also began to take flight in earnest during these overlapping decades, in doing so, they expunge both a discrete Haitian intellectual history reaching back to the 1880s, and a flourishing literary tradition anchored both in preexisting French literary canons and new aesthetics developing in local space both syncretically and in reaction to political events such as the occupation within what was then known as Saint Domingue. Jeff Karem opines that this may be the result of W. E. B. Du Bois's self-positioning as "father" of Pan-Africanism in the 1920s while simultaneously effacing his collaboration with the antiracist and Haitian anthropologist, Antenor Firmin and Haitian journalist/activist Benito Sylvain. This collaboration began as far back as 1900 when they each were brought together by Trinidadian Henry Sylvester Williams to attend the first Pan-African Conference organized by Williams in London in 1900 (77–78). In an otherwise insightful essay, which culminates in an examination of the influences of Garveyism on the Harlem Renaissance (and thus on West Indian/Caribbean participation in shaping the politics of the period), and taking for evidence the work of Lilyan Kesteloot who argues that the passage of Locke, Cullen, Toomer, and Hughes in the literary salons of (Martinican) writer/journalist, Paulette Nardal, demonstrates that they, rather than West Indian, surrealists, or French novelists were the "fathers of the Negro cultural renaissance in France," Robert Philipson boldly asserts: "In order to help them formulate their inchoate ideology during the 1930s, the founders of negritude, Lópold Senghor (Senegal), Aimé Césaire (Martinique), and Léon Damas (French Guiana), looked to the writings of the Harlem Renaissance as examples of literary expression of a positive Black consciousness" (153). Both ignore Nardal's French-Caribbean origins and the fact that she founded through her salon, along with her sister, Jane Nardal, the "Revue du Monde Noir" in collaboration with Leo Sajou (who was Haitian) and the fact that the salons gathered all intellectuals of African descent in passage in the city of lights without care for linguistic or national differences, a true Pan-African space—in short, a lakou. Damas, Senghor, and Césaire were also guests, as were less prominent, since-forgotten figures of Black intellectual life in Paris emanating from Africa, the West Indies, and the United States. What the salon did was to put the principal actors of these movements in contact with one another, but to say that the appearance once or twice yearly of Harlemites on the Parisian scene gave birth to Négritude is to practice a narrow, nationalistic chauvinism that limits our understanding of literary history across geographical divides. The proof of the flow of influence is in the writings themselves; as I will show, Haiti, its history and its people, proves to be a signal theme in works by Harlem Renaissance writers McKay and Hurston,[11] but the concerns of African Americans only becomes more present thematically in the work of Haitians after the end of the U.S. occupation with the rise of civil rights activism and with poems such as Roumain's "Alabama" of 1945 addressing themes of violence, heritage, and desegregation in the American South. This, to my mind, demonstrates, partially, that Harlem writers were heavily marked by their confrontation with Haitian culture and history, especially as occasioned through the occupation, but they, in turn, encountered, in Haitians, a well-developed cultural ethos, which, though embattled, had a far longer history of autonomy in autochthonous space than their own.

U.S.-based literary scholars have, without question, taken Du Bois's narrative of this period for fact and, as the Pan-African and Négritude movements moved further apart in aim and methods (and were divided somewhat by language difference), completely vacated the contributions of West Indians and, specifically, of Francophone Antilleans and Haitians as well as the import of exchanges between the groups with one another in historical time. Further, this glossing over belies the rich history of interaction between intellectuals of African descent in Europe and in the Americas who had begun to dialogue, through their work, and in person, on the necessity and means of decolonization for individuals of African descent residing in European territories and (former) colonies in and out of the African continent *prior* to the advent of the rise of Négritude and a narrowing of movements before their ultimate splintering into proto-national factions.

At this point, all evidence suggests that if there can be a designated "father" of what we've come to understand as a Pan-African consciousness, a truly transnational union of people of African descent based on both their shared cultural heritage and experience of colonialism, then the seed of that vision rests with Trinidadian Henry Sylvester Williams, who convened the first Pan-African Conference in London in 1900[12] after periods of studying and living in Canada and the United States where he confronted racial prejudice he had not known in his native Trinidad. But it is a seed that was nurtured in conversation with both Haitians and African Americans and with particular attention to the decolonizing thrust of early Haitian intellectuals, Antenor Firmin and Benito Sylvain. In 1885, Firmin had published and defended his rebuttal of Comte de Gobineau's racist 1853 *Essai sur l'inegalité des races humaines* (*Essay on the Inequality of the Races*), in his study appropriately entitled *De l'égalité des races humaines* (*Of the Equality of Human Races*), the first such work of this kind. In 1901, Sylvain published a work on the legacy of slavery by European colonials (French, British, and German) in their colonies and the complex legacies of race and color prejudice they engendered, respectively entitled *Du sort des indigènes dans les colonies d'exploitations* (*Of the outcome of indigenous peoples in colonies of exploitation*) (note here the language of the title). According to Karem, via the work of Marika Sherwood, Sylvain's work, as evidenced in personal correspondence between the two, had a profound effect on Williams's ultimate articulation of an inclusive Pan-African vision. Via the work of anthropologist Jean Price-Mars (*Ainsi parla l'oncle* 1928; translated as *So Spoke the Uncle*), we also know of Firmin's extensive influence on native Haitian thought. In his own time, Price-Mars crossed paths not only with Williams but corresponded with Booker T. Washington, met with José Martí, collaborated with Frederick Douglass while minister of foreign affairs for Haiti when the latter served as U.S. minister of foreign affairs, and collaborated further with W. E. B. Du Bois, whose views, expressed earlier in *The Souls of Black Folk* (1902), both he and Sylvain would heavily influence (77–80).

By the time of the U.S. occupation, then, an intellectual position and perspective that was both anti-imperialist and self-affirming had been articulated by Haitians through what Price-Mars termed an "indigenous" sensibility, proper to Haiti, and then expanded in collaborations and exchanges with black intellectuals from other regions, especially from the United States, searching for allies and to form a global movement of decolonization, thus forming what we can conceive of as an intellectual lakou. In this, Haiti and

Haitians had a singular role in that, of those participating in the emerging discussion, they were the only *former* colony, if imperfect, participating in the discussions. As such, they provided what some are now referring to as a "postcolonial" outlook since the Haitian Revolution had already made of them a postcolony; intellectuals such as Firmin and Sylvain, by virtue of their educations and mobility both within Haiti and in the space of their former colonial powers, could advance, with some foresight, possible outcomes and pitfalls of liberation from those powers. The relationship to the United States was already vexed, as the U.S. government sought to manage its own affairs vis-à-vis its exploitation and unequal treatment of African Americans in the face of a neighboring country who had not only defied this exploitation but reversed the hierarchy of power staunchly established in the United States since its founding. Those intellectuals of African descent who crossed paths during the turn of the century recognized that they were headed in a similar direction—liberation not only from slavery and colonial ties but political and ideological autonomy as well. I would suggest, then, that the U.S. Occupation of Haiti created a crisis of identification and of affiliation. On the one hand, as Price-Mars argued in *So Spoke the Uncle*, it forced Haitians away from "collective bovarysme"—by which Haitian (upper-class) society conceived of itself as "French" and denied its African and Indigenous (Arawak or Taino) heritage (8). Price-Mars would go on to articulate the position of *indigénisme*, a precursor to the Pan-African concept of *négritude*, through which he and other Haitian intellectuals countered the devaluation of Haitian life and customs through the military American presence and imposition of U.S. norms, including segregation and color stigmatization.[13]

Indigénisme called for a return to indigenous forms of cultural expression, that is, expressions born on the soil, residing in folk traditions and focalized in the practices and being of the peasant, the quintessential Haitian, derived in large part from African folk customs. In so doing, Price-Mars thus called for a valorization of African retentions on Haitian soil but also for the valorization of new forms of creative life that found their expression in Haiti as a result of the commingling of diverse cultures. Simultaneous to a decolonizing project of autochthonomy, then, socialist and communist perspectives were awakened by the brutality of the Occupation and its racist implications. Through the 1920s and early 1930s, novelist and activist Jacques-Stephen Aléxis, influenced by philosophers such as existentialist Jean-Paul Sartre (who was to become deeply involved in his support of the *négritude* movement) advocated for an engaged Caribbean literature he would call "social real" in that it would reflect the deep structures of spiritual thought practiced by Haitians while also advocating for their sovereignty. He wrote:

> Creating realism meant that the Haitian artists were setting about speaking the same language as their people. The Marvellous Realism of the Haitians is thus an integral part of Social Realism, and in its Haitian form it follows the same preoccupations. The treasure of tales and legends, all the musical, choreographic and plastic symbolism, all the forms of Haitian popular art are there to help the nation in solving its problems and in accomplishing the tasks which lie before it. (Aléxis, in Ashcroft, Griffiths and Tiffin 197)

Aléxis thus advocated for an indigenous form of artistic expression reflecting the beliefs and sovereignty of the people who produced it, an interpretive community whose sensibility came from an amalgamation of cultures and ethnicities while having created its own autochthonomous reality. By 1937, another activist/writer, Jacques Roumain, would create Haiti's first communist party.

All this, then, sets the stage to galvanize the interests and spark the imagination of Claude McKay, a Jamaican expatriate navigating the social waters between his native, rural Jamaica, urban Kingston, African American life in Harlem, and, ultimately, in France, Russia, and Northern Africa. According to Michel Fabre, although McKay was very influential on Harlem writers, he wrote very few of the works appearing during the period of the Harlem Renaissance while in the United States. Of particular interest is the fact that McKay wrote *Home to Harlem* (the focus of my ensuing discussion here) while in France and published in the States in 1928 (101). McKay was thus composing the text in the early to mid-1920s while the activities, exchanges, and formulations I described earlier were taking place. Though there is little archival evidence of McKay's knowledge of Haitian literature, the passages referring to his Haitian character's origins in this work suggest that though he may not have been intimately steeped in Haiti's literature, he knew of it, and certainly understood Haiti's symbolic importance, recognizing the significance of both as the product of the first Black Republic in the Western hemisphere. He was also in touch with James Weldon Johnson (103), who had spent a great deal of the early 1920s as an envoy of the NAACP, documenting violation of human rights by U.S. Marines in Haiti during the Occupation. Perhaps coincidentally, McKay returned to the United States in 1934, also the year in which the occupation ended, fifteen years after having expatriated himself to Europe (112).

In the novel, when recounting Ray's discomfort with African Americans, and, particularly, with the protagonist, Jake, with whom he creates a close affinity as the two get to know each other, rooted partly in class difference, McKay also explains Ray's displacement as the product of linguistic and literary history: "He possesses another language and literature that they knew not of" (155). In this brief reference, McKay signals his own awareness of that literature and of the barrier that language and lack of translation creates regarding opportunity of exchange. Consequently, he embarks on "translating" Ray to Jake and, in so doing, to the reader, to impart some knowledge as to the importance Haiti/Haitians *should* hold in African American life, at a time when Caribbean people were summarily dismissed in the United States by the derogatory phrase, "monkey-chasers." Indeed, faced with Ray's Haitian heritage, Jake is taken aback and unable to, at first, assimilate Ray's difference; despite their class difference (Ray is educated while Jake is not), Jake assumes a position of superiority with regard to Ray. This shifts upon his hearing the history of Haiti and, indeed, its place in the history of the world. McKay is deliberate as he writes: "Jake was very American in spirit and shared a little of that comfortable Yankee contempt for poor foreigners. . . . And West Indians were monkey-chasers. But now he felt like a boy who stands with the maps of the world in colors before him, and feels the wonder of the world" (134). At first, Jake exhibits American provincialism upon learning that Ray's first language is French. Only pages before his conversion, McKay writes of Jake: "He learned that the universal spirit of the French Revolution had reached and lifted up the slaves far away in that remote island; that Black Hayti's [*sic*] independence was more dramatic and picturesque than the United States' independence and that it was a strange, almost unimaginable eruption of the beautiful ideas of the 'Liberté, Egalité, Fraternité' of Mankind, that shook the foundations of that romantic era" (131). Indeed, McKay belabors the importance of the Revolution and the impact it should have on African American consciousness through the initial exchange between Ray and Jake. McKay writes of Jake's tutelage by Ray on this topic:

> For the first time he heard the name Toussaint L'Ouverture, the black slave and leader of the Haytian slaves. Heard how he fought and conquered the slave-owners and then protected them; decreed laws for Hayti that held more of human wisdom and nobility than the Code Napoleon; defended his baby revolution against the Spanish and the English vultures; defeated Napoleon's punitive expedition; and how tragically he was captured by a civilized trick, taken to France, and sent by Napoleon to die broken-hearted in a cold dungeon.

Of Jake's response to this information, McKay writes: "it was incredible to Jake that a little island of freed slaves had withstood the three leading European powers" (132). This revelation of an African Diasporic presence in the Americas was "beautiful in his mind. That brief account of an island of 'savage black people,' who fought for collective liberty and was struggling to create a culture of their own. A romance of his race, just down there by Panama" (134). Ray goes on to situate this "romance" of a "black people," as something that until this point had been beyond Jake's imaginings, in world history:

The waiter told him that Africa was not jungle as he dreamed of it, nor slavery the peculiar rôle [*sic*] of black folk. The Jews were the slaves of the Egyptians, the Greeks made slaves of their conquered, the Gauls and Saxons were slaves of the Romans. He told Jake of the old destroyed cultures of West Africa and of their vestiges, of black kings who struggled stoutly for the independence of their kingdoms: Prempreh of Ashanti, Tofa of Dahomey, Gbehanzin of Benin, Cetawayo of Zulu-land, Menlik of Abyssinia. . . . Had Jake ever heard of the little Republic of Liberia, founded by American Negroes? (135)

The interlude between Ray and Jake regarding the Haitian Revolution and world history goes on for a good five pages of text in this novel-without-a-plot. It is also an interlude at the *center* of the novel, suggesting that McKay is attempting to centralize readers' attention on this point of exchange, in the process indicting both French and American imperialism, and focalizing Haiti as the nexus of interpretive departure. By altering the point of view by which to apprehend history from an African Diasporic perspective rather than from a Eurocentric one, Ray teaches Jake (the stand-in both for African Americans and for the presumed reader) to situate himself in lakou space, making him conscious of an African-centered world beyond European views. Later on, we are privy to Ray's inner thoughts as he continues partway with Jake, working in the kitchen on the train on which Jake is a laborer. Ray is in the United States during the period of the U.S. Occupation of Haiti, it must be remembered, and shares the following, again, from an African-centered point of view: "Ray felt that as he was conscious of being black and impotent, so, correspondingly, each marine down in Hayti [*sic*] must be conscious of being white and powerful" (154). He comes to this understanding through a *loss* of identity: "He remembered when little Hayti [*sic*] was floundering uncontrolled, how proud he was to be the son of a free nation. He used to feel condescendingly sorry for those poor African natives; superior to ten millions of suppressed Yankee 'coons.' Now he was just one of them and he hated them for being one of them. . . . But he was not entirely of them, he reflected. He possessed another language and literature that they knew not of" (155). Ray exits the text after falling ill from an apparent breakdown, relayed in coded language as suppressed emotions for Jake, as when he dreams that "[a] thousand pins were pricking Ray's flesh and he was shouting for Jake, but his voice was so faint he could not hear himself. Jake had him in his arms and tried to stand him upon his feet." Prior to this moment in the dream, Ray, however, is experiencing a return "home," to a place where being of African descent is not a taint or mark of denigration. He describes such a world as follows:

And the world was a blue paradise. Everything was in gorgeous blue of heaven. Woods and streams were blue, and men and women and animals, and beautiful to see and love. And he was a blue bird in flight and a blue lizard in love. And life was all blue happiness. Taboos and terrors and penalties were transformed into new pagan delights, orgies of Orient-blue carnival, of rare flowers and red fruits, cherubs and seraphs and fetishes and phalli and all the most-high gods. (158)

For Ray, autochthonomy is as much a state of existing in indigenous space as sovereign and autonomous as it is a state of being able to freely love. If McKay equates racial freedom with that of sexual freedom, this is because, in keeping with over determinations of black sexuality, he perceives that freedom from such stereotypes necessarily entails freedom from heteronormativity. Such freedom is simply a natural extension, in McKay's view, from the autonomy derived from an emancipated subjectivity. He assumes, then, that if people of African descent can exercise their autonomy as free subjects, even more so than other groups whose sexuality is not tethered to their subjugation, this, too, should be given subject to the same liberties.

By and large, scholars of McKay have ignored or by-passed the importance of Ray's ethnic/national identity in the novel and focused only on his encoded gay sexuality. There are several reasons for this. The first and perhaps most discussed emanates from the fact that McKay's first novel was a runaway bestseller, often read as a riposte to Carl Van Vechten's exotic and stereotype-ridden 1926 novel, *Nigger Heaven*, which detailed the underbelly of Harlem Black life in its heyday. If a redress of Van Vechten's themes, for some, *Home to Harlem* fell woefully short as it, too, engaged the Harlem demimonde, discussing activities such as gambling, drug-taking, prostitution, speakeasies, and, as has become more and more evident through queer analyses of the text, gay/lesbian life in Harlem. In his June 1928 review of the novel for *The Crisis*, W. E. B. Du Bois infamously denounced the novel, calling it "filth," expressing that he had felt that he had to take a bath after completing its reading (ironically indicating that he had read it to its end despite its "objectionable" content). Critics who, in hindsight, have found the novel with merit, typically have defined Ray as "West Indian" (normally defined as Anglophone Caribbean) and collapsed him with the identity of his maker, suggesting that he acts in *Home to Harlem*, as well as in its sequel, *Banjo*, as McKay's doppelganger. Melvin Dixon, thus writes: "The West Indian Ray, an aspiring poet, parallels McKay's life and wanderlust" (32).[14] By way of a dismissal of identification with Jake in *A Long Way from Home*, Gary Holcomb extends Dixon's, and others, assumption, to claim: "The gesture is revealing. On one level McKay is suggesting that his actual autobiographical semblance is Ray, not Jake, the closeted homosexual in *Home to Harlem*" (736). Holcomb, both in his essay, "Queer Black Proletarianism in McKay's *A Long Way from Home*," which precedes the more developed chapter of the same name in his book-length treatment of queer representations in McKay's work, *Code Name Sasha*, underplays Ray's Haitian identity in order to foreground a narrow queer identification between character and author, given that both Jake and the reader's introduction to Ray on the train-line on which they will both work is to Ray reading a short story by Alphonse Daudet entitled "Sapho" (128). What ensues is a discussion of the real-life poet, Sapho, and the Greek tragedy of her life and passion for a boy named Phaon, followed by how Sapho's poetic passions fueled woman-loving identifications. To Jake's lesbophobia ("That's what we calls bulldyker in Harlem. . . . Them's all ugly women" [129]), Ray counters, "Not *all*. And that's a damned ugly name. . . . Harlem is too savage about some things," (ibid.). The conversation then quickly moves on to the issue of Jake's native language and homeland, as recounted earlier. Of this, critics like Holcomb, though utterly impassioned and convincing about their queer readings of the text, which the text makes richly available, have little useful or insightful to say. In fact, their approach to Ray's ethnicity is to dismiss or underplay it, in stark contrast to McKay's bold foregrounding of its importance in the novel. This is simply a result of dismissing the importance of African Diasporic consciousness in the text, as evidenced by McKay's centralizing of Haiti's importance in hemispheric and world history. For McKay, African Diasporic autochthonomy is as important, if not more so, as queer identification. Indeed, he participates here in Seacole's form of (dis)identification by obscuring queer context in favor of highlighting the lakou consciousness by which he hopes to have transformed Jake's vision of himself, and, in turn, the reader's capacity to place characters like Jake and Ray in a wider field of vision that centers African Diasporic subjectivities. In this way, McKay has *kreyolized* his text while at the same time suggesting, through Ray's breakdown, the incompatibility of autochthonomous identification within a U.S. identification that centralizes white/European history and identity at the cost of the wholesale erasure of African history, epistemes, and consciousness. Ray can do nothing more than "go crazy," after having dispensed his information, or disappear from the text, in other words, since he has no context in which to exist fully. When Ray reappears much later in a chapter called "Relapse," McKay conveys to readers how the Occupation of Haiti, and living in the United States under segregation, has affected Ray's mind and spirit: "The sudden upset of affairs in his home country had landed him into the quivering heart of a naked world whose reality was hitherto unimaginable. It was what they called in print and polite conversation 'the underworld'" (224). In that underworld, Ray comes to understand all of humanity. If he, like Jake, once looked down upon African Americans as they did upon him (and other Antilleans), he realizes their common plight: "I have been forced down to the level of pimps and found some of them more than human" (244). Thus, McKay is advocating for an intradiasporic exchange where subjugation does not come to define African Americans, any more than African retention serves to undermine African-centered cultures. Ray is thus key to unlocking the novel's symbolic use of two overlapping strands of African Diasporic cultures; he serves as the reader's means of apprehending an African Diasporic "interpretive community" centered in the Caribbean while utilizing this refocusing to *decenter* African American stories in the novel from a Euro-American narrative of subjugation and deprivation. While not glossing over U.S. segregation, Ray's role is to provide alternate and intradiasporic ways of reading the text.

The titles of the two texts by McKay I discussed earlier are worth signaling here as they indicate a desire on McKay's part to disavow overdetermined racial and national identifications; they signal, like Seacole's narrative strategies (and Capécia's), an active *(dis)identification* with such categories. His memoir/autobiography, expresses a longing and search for home ground reflected in the title's bittersweet assertion of a longing for that ground, *A Long Way from Home*. In it, as I demonstrated earlier, McKay sketches his af/filiation with lakou consciousness in redrawing the parameters of his known self within the histories and cultures of people of African descent and his own experience in European spaces as a member of the African Diaspora. He searches for and seeks his likeness and finds it. Similarly, in Jake's peregrinations across the United States and abroad, the return to Harlem invoked by the novel's title, *Home to Harlem* is only achieved once Jake has encountered and been transformed by Ray, his Haitian counterpart, and comes to understand himself not in terms of segregationist, American-style apartheid, but in such a way as to understand that history as part of a larger, global African Diasporic context in which his subjectivity need not be defined solely by his subjugation and dispossession within the United States. Armed with the lakou consciousness imparted by Ray, Jake can then "return home" to Harlem an autochthonomous being, an emancipated consciousness.

"Harvesting" Port-au-Prince: Zora Neale Hurston's Literary (Dis)Articulation of Being

If McKay engages the modern on its own ground, by refusing to be marginal in a Eurocentric discourse, and by foregrounding the modernity of African Diasporics that can reveal themselves only through imagined or real lakou/yard exchanges via Haiti/Jamaica, even as he travels through both America and Europe (West and East), Zora Neale Hurston similarly but differently engages notions of autochthonomy through such spaces of intradiasporic meeting. Interestingly, more so than McKay, she does so by pursuing the collection of African gnosis in the Americas both as an anthropologist and as a storyteller; yet, unlike McKay, she is often challenged to forgo her nationalist (American) impulse, withdrawing into what McKay wrote of Jake, her "American spirit" and "Yankee contempt for poor foreigners" (134). Inasmuch as Hurston encounters Haitian culture primarily through folklore, and thus through the peasant class rather than through its intelligentsia, she is quick both to dismiss Haitian intellectual contributions while otherwise embracing the folk culture she recognizes as being consonant with her own gnosis as an African American seeking to valorize local (Southern United States) knowledge.[15]

In the following analysis, I argue specifically that Zora Neale Hurston challenged the disciplining (imperial) gaze of her own time in order to deploy a humanistic subjectivity but not without experiencing and deploying subjugations of her own in her (mis)representations of others. For instance, in *Tell My Horse*, she utilized seemingly unreflexive commentary in the nature of a travelogue in which, in the chapters preceding those on vodou Hurston reveals herself to have become a *vodouisant* initiate, yet damns the Haitian elite as well as its peasants in ways more consonant with Wilsonian politics of the time than with those of W. E. B. Du Bois (whom she heavily criticized). To be sure, there was no issue on which Hurston did not speak out, and often in contradictory ways, but it is in the juxtaposition of two of her texts I might term "Haitian" that we might find an *informed* reason for her duplicity, which itself is consonant more so with Haitian women's tradition of *dédoublement* within Haitian culture[16] than with that of double consciousness within a polarized white/black hegemonic one (reflecting, to some degree, Bhabha's notion of "double-time" within hegemonic national identifications, previously discussed). She was simultaneously developing her voice as a fiction writer while rethinking the disciplinary methods of anthropology and ethnography, fields which, as a folklorist, she never felt entirely at home with, and which she reworked textually.

Some scholars have contended that *Tell My Horse* bears more resemblance with William Seabrook's *The Magic Island* than to the works of Herskovits or, that of her mentor, Franz Boas, in its imperialist overtones; in *Tell My Horse*, Hurston reveals her surprise at encountering a culture, in some ways, completely unknown to her, which relegates her to its margins, and from which margins she can emerge only through the use of American entitlement. As Gwendolyn Mykell notes in an early essay: "Zora Neale Hurston's Haitian notes embody the unresolved conflict between her value judgments and the insider's perspectives which accept the logic of god's behavior and their subjects' responses. She becomes what the people are, experiencing what they experience, then stands back and says, "The Haitian people are gentle and lovable, except for their enormous and unconscious cruelty" (220). Mykell suggests that it is Hurston's training at Columbia at the time, that is, training within a white-dominated institution within a hegemonic American educational system, which colored her perspective. I would like to suggest further, that read with or against *Their Eyes Were Watching God*, a cross-reading that few in her own time would have bothered to do, as these were texts intended for very different audiences, and because it was to be decades before anyone would make the link between Haiti and *Their Eyes*, that Hurston was profoundly aware of what she was doing in *both* texts and dissimulated her profound understanding of Haitian folklore, culture, and language, in each.

Given the entrenched anti-Haiti, anti-vodou sentiment, which fully emerged under the U.S. occupation, and given that anthropology was largely a field which undertook, then, to uncover the ways of "others" for white audiences, Hurston understood that it would not serve her well, as an African American woman, to tell the truth of the situation in *Tell My Horse*, and she thus issues occasional scathing indictments of Caribbean, Jamaican, or Haitian cultures. Take, for instance, the opening passages of the chapter entitled "Women in the Caribbean," in which Hurston writes: "It is a curious thing to be a woman in the Caribbean after you have been a woman in these United States. . . . The majority of men in all the states are pretty much agreed that just for being born a girl-baby you ought to have laws and privileges and pay and perquisites. . . . But now Miss America, World's champion woman, you take your promenading self down into the cobalt blue waters of the Caribbean and see what happens. You meet a lot of darkish men who make vociferous love to you, but otherwise pay you no mind" (57); of course, while seemingly chastising Caribbean culture for its chauvinism, Hurston also self-mockingly reveals her reciprocal involvement in making "vociferous love" to the "darkish men" she comes across. A little further in the same chapter, she makes a series of declarations regarding class, color, and caste in the Caribbean that would seem to elevate the American woman by comparison: "if a woman is wealthy, of good family and mulatto, she can overcome some of her drawbacks. But if she is of no particular family, poor and black, she is in a bad way indeed in that man's world. She had better pray to the Lord to turn her into a donkey and be done with the thing. It is assumed that God made poor black females for beasts of burden, and nobody is going to interfere with providence" (58). Remember again, then, that Hurston was researching

Tell My Horse while in Haiti, and wrote *Their Eyes Were Watching God* in a seven-week stretch alternately reported to take place in Port-au-Prince, La Gonâve, and other sites not far from the capital; recall too that one of the novel's most famous lines is the phrase that states that black women are the mules of the world. Though *Tell My Horse* was published in 1939, it was formulated alongside *Their Eyes*, published in 1937, and the observation related about women to the Caribbean space in the former is expressed in the latter in the American landscape and about the social state of African American women specifically, across color and class, as is exemplified by Janie's journey from her grandmother's house down to the muck of the Everglades. Surely the author of both texts was aware of her transposition and even deliberate in its performance. Why, then, the subterfuge?

It must be remembered that most of Hurston's folkloric texts were produced under patronage, and, as I have already stated, that the Occupation was one of brutal anti-Haitian sentiment from which various African American personalities benefited in that they were free to travel to Haiti under the auspices of the U.S. government as American citizens rather than as African American subjects, though they could not escape the one for being the other. At the same time, as they circulated as Americans and benefited from American tutelage, most understood that there was a relationship between U.S. foreign policy, the Occupation, French colonization, and their own history of enslavement. Let me make my point another way. In a chapter entitled "The Next Hundred Years," detailing Haiti's relationship to the United States, Hurston appears to perversely emphasize Haitians purported "habit of lying"—could it be that she meant to say that Haitians, like the "folk" elsewhere, "tell tales" as modes of survival and knowledge-keeping?[17] If this might be so, then the following passages take on a different hue. In a dialogue Hurston re-creates for the benefit of her readers, recounting the Haitian perspective of a U.S. Occupation, Hurston takes up the tone of a skeptic, interrogating the easily, carried-to-exaggerate, Haitian everyman. She writes:

> "You evidently were very slow to wrath because they stayed here nineteen years, I believe," I said.
>
> "Yes, and we would have let them stay here longer but the Americans have no politeness so we drove them out. They knew that they had no right to come here in the beginning."
>
> "But didn't you have some sort of disturbance here, and were you not in embarrassing debt to some European nations? It seems that I heard something of the sort."
>
> "We never owed any debts. We had plenty of gold in our bank which the Americans took away and never returned to us. They claimed that we owed

debts so that they could have an excuse to rob us. When they had impoverished the country they left, and now our streets are full of beggars and the
whole country is very poor. But what can a weak country like Haiti do when
a powerful nation like your own forces its military upon us, kills our citizens
and steals our money?"

"No doubt you are correct in what you say. However, an official of your own
government told me that Haiti borrowed $40,000,000 to pay off these same
foreign debts which you tell never existed at all."

"Mlle., I swear on the head of my mother that we had no debts. The Americans did force us to borrow the money so that they could steal it from us. That
is the truth. Poor Haiti has suffered much." (85)

Within this dialogue, Hurston has explicitly spoken about the Occupation as
an invasion, referenced Haiti's sizable indemnity to France, the $40 million
of debt the United States forced Haiti to incur, as well as the killings that
occurred during the Occupation, that of Charlemagne Péralte and the *cacos*
revolutionaries she otherwise appears to disparage being the most notorious.
She has managed here, in half a page, to summarize a litany of wrongs during
a time period when the United States was represented as being unable to do
wrong, and in which travelogues depicted Haiti and Haitians as the subservi-
ent recipients of U.S. beneficence. Presented as "exaggerations," each assertion
is archived, thereby providing textual evidence of historical wrongs that, as
time has shown, are, in fact, the truth of Haiti's neocolonial suppression at the
hands of American forces. In other words, as Françoise Lionnet has written,
Hurston recognizes here that, "It is the contextual frame of reference, the
situation of the telling, that determines how a tale is reinterpreted by each
new teller; hence, for the anthropologist there is no 'essential' quality to be
isolated in the content of those tales, but there is a formal structure that can
and must be characterized if she is to make sense of, and do justice to, the
data gathered" (101). The dialogue format, the assertion and reassertion of
U.S. wrongdoing by the Haitian everyman is a "formal structure" by which
the "folk" tells his tale and through which Hurston reveals the realities of U.S.
incursion upon Haitian soil without appearing to "believe" or sympathize
with the storyteller even as she recounts and thus affirms the import (and
veracity) of the data collected.

Because of its lack of referencing in historical texts, these "lies" (i.e., truths)
have long been forgotten, as has been evidenced in post–2010 earthquake
discourse in which Haitian and Haitianist scholars have had to quickly reconstruct Haitian history in order to fend off old prejudices against the nation and its inhabitants that have sought to define both as depraved and
ungodly. Since the 1800s, the United States has operated to "misrecognize"

Haiti in ways useful to the tenets of Jeffersonian racial fears—to keep Haiti "black," and the United States "white"—even as neither nation could uphold such codes of "purity" in an increasingly mobile and hybrid world. Indeed, the Occupation of 1915–1934, as many have noted, and as Tracy Kidder and Colin Dayan both underscore in their recent writings, left the country further crippled. Noting the brutality of the Occupation, Dayan writes of 1919: "more than 3,000 peasants had been killed. Another 5,000 died in labor camps that the *garde* supervised for the occupying forces. When the United States left, she saddled the country with another foreign debt—a massive $40 million—which destroyed any possibility that Haiti might enjoy a stable financial regime" (2010, 2). Note here that Dayan's numbers coincide with Hurston's. I would suggest, then, that some of the scathing notes of Hurston's "travelogue" reflect deep-held ambivalences toward the nation-state, questions of racial democracy, and confusion yet parodies white/European travel writings of the time. By cryptically, even negatively, framing Haitian history and Haitians through stereotypes of her (and our) day, Hurston manages a small feat, that is of telling the truth at a slant as she embeds facts and figures from the Haitian massacre, to U.S. Marine killings of Haitians, to the huge financial pit created by the Occupation for the Haitian state (from which it has not recovered) as products of the imperial venture she otherwise, on the surface, appears to defend. I would agree here with Lionnet's assertion that Hurston's strategy is to "[involve] herself and her reader in a transformative process; she transforms and is transformed by her autobiographical performance. To look at life from an aesthetic point of view and to celebrate her ethnic heritage are thus two complementary projects for her" (104). If Lionnet makes this argument with respect to Hurston's autobiography, *Dust Tracks on a Road*, I extend this argument to her fictional works as well, and to *Their Eyes Were Watching God*, in particular.

I suggest that we read the novel as a *kreyolized* (with a "k") text marked by her passage in Haiti, and as a memoir or travelogue of a different nature. If we are to read the novel as an encoded travel narrative of Hurston's confrontation with the Haitian landscape and geography in which the text was written, as I will sketch in the remaining portion of this analysis, then we can understand the text as engaging in a dialectic relationship not between "white" and "black" but "black" *to* "black"—not in resistance but in acknowledgment of the store of knowledge embedded in the African Diasporic experience. Interestingly, Hurston does so in opposition to the anti-Haitian sentiment she herself invokes in *Tell My Horse*, which, as I have already briefly argued, masks her reverence for and appreciation of both the epistemes and folklore of Haitian culture.

Though Hurston commonly acknowledged the site in which she wrote the novel, it has been of less interest to critics of her writings until more recently. Critics and writers such as Leigh Anne Duck and Edwidge Danticat have recognized, for instance, Hurston's retelling of Haitian history in the representation of Matt Bonner's yellow mule, recognizing its allusion to President Antoine Simon's elaborate funeral for his pet goat, Simalo (Danticat xv). Of Bonner's yellow mule, Hurston writes in *Their Eyes Were Watching God*: "They had him up for conversation every day the Lord sent" (51). Bonner, unlike President Antoine Simon, is a poor African American male in the Black township Joe Starks has consolidated. Like Matt, the yellow mule, is emaciated, underfed, and impoverished. Their destitute state proves to be fodder for the "porch talk" Hurston is famous for having recorded here as in her other folkloric tales. In an attempt to humiliate Matt, the porch men tell emasculating tales about the mule, such as, "De womenfolks got yo' mule. When Ah come round de lake 'bout noontime mah wife and some others had 'im flat on de ground usin' his sides fuh uh wash board" (52). As other critics have observed, Matt Bonner's yellow mule is a stand-in for Janie, herself, and other women of her ilk, "high yella'" women seeking a better life for themselves and resisting patriarchal as well as racialized norms that suppress the trajectory of their lives; when the mule is left hitched to the porch and subsequently taunted by the porch men, Janie is the only one who refuses to participate. Says Hurston of Janie: "She snatched her head away from the spectacle and began muttering to herself. 'They oughta be shamed uh theyselves! Teasin' dat poor brute beast lak they is!" (56). When the mule, spent, finally dies, the carcass is taken off by the townspeople and a great ceremony takes place; unlike the case of Simon's presidential ceremony for his pet goat, Hurston makes use of the incident to impugn Jody Starks's character. Starks's pomp and insensitivity are remarkable and they assist the reader in understanding Janie's position, as a "yellow mule," in the marriage. At the same time, by obliquely making use of the Haitian Simon story under a new guise, Hurston comments on the tragic turns of Haitian emancipation whereby an officiating president can drain state coffers of funds intended for the indigenous population in order to celebrate a pet. That Hurston may have transposed incidences of life from the Haitian landscape to the black South of Florida is suggestive of further "Haitianisms" in the text, and, thus, of her conscious participation, as such, in lakou consciousness. The lyricism of the language and its lexical difference from other of Hurston's collected (U.S.) folk tales offers a different register of black English; it suggests to me that the language of the text, and perhaps even its imaginary, is *kreyolized*. This is to say that though, undoubtedly, the text remains an important repository of

Hurston's black southern folklore, it is simultaneously an encoded text. The text encodes traces of Haitian sayings and sensibilities, transposed by Hurston into her imagined black Southern landscape. This kreyolization speaks to Hurston's compelling desire to know "the ways of Black folk," and the great means she took, through her travels, to explore cultures of African descent with geographical proximity to the South she knew so well and sought to preserve.

Hurston makes use of evocative phrases peppered through the text that describe the emotional states of her character; some of these are not derived from black English; a number, in fact, are translations of Kreyol proverbs or sayings. The ease with which these phrases fit into the text testify both to Hurston's creative genius and her apprehension of the narrow filaments of expression, whether through dance, ritual, or language, tying together communities originating in part or in whole from Africa. For instance, early on in her story, Hurston makes use of a striking phrase in describing Janie's grandmother's state as Nanny explains her reasons for marrying Janie off to an elderly African American man, Logan Killicks. Afraid that her granddaughter will suffer the fate of two previous generations of women, that is, rape, abandonment, pregnancy by rape, and alcoholism (in Janie's mother's case) in the face of her destroyed life, Nanny marries Janie off to a man she perceives to be economically stable and sound of mind. Ignoring the fact that she is simultaneously co-opting Janie's agency and making her subject to a man's will through the marriage, Nanny expounds: "Ah don't want yo' feathers always crumpled by folks throwin' up things in you' face. And Ah can't die easy thinkin' maybe de menfolks white or black is makin' a spit cup outa you: Have some sympathy fuh me. Put me down easy, Janie, Ah'm a cracked plate" (20). Nanny attempts to force Janie to go along with her plan, and Janie does, by appealing to her own physical fragility, as summarized by the phrase, "Ah'm a cracked plate." Nanny's entreaty, "Put me down easy, Janie, Ah'm a cracked plate" (ibid.), is, in fact, a quasi-literal translation of two common Haitian proverbs; the first is: "*metem atè tou dousman*" [put me down easy[18]]; the second, "*m'se ze fele*" [I'm a cracked egg]. In the Kreyol, either phrase can be used to the same effect, that is, to mean, "be careful with me as I am feeling fragile." However, used independently, the phrases have slightly different meanings. "*Metem atè tou dousman*," can mean "leave me out of the argument" or "please don't involve me" while "*m'se ze fele*" connotes more readily the sentiment of fragility as in "I can't take it anymore." A variation on the latter phrase, "*li se ze fele*" is often used to mean "they are vulnerable or they get sick easily."[19] The phrases, though uncommon, can be combined for emphasis: "put me down easy; I'm a cracked egg." Hurston's creative addition, then, is to combine the two proverbs and her translation of the phrases to amplify her character's psychological state. She also feminizes the meaning of the phrase in pursuing her novel's theme, that is, of the emancipation of an African American woman in the early part of the twentieth century. Indeed, this phrase has an interesting corollary in Janie's assertion, broken by her second husband's will, when she states "she stood there until something fell off the shelf inside her" (72). The image of women as fragile china that can be broken by a harsh life (as in Nanny's case), physical abuse (in the case of Janie's mother) or by emotional abuse (as in Janie's case with Joe), is evocative; in the context of 1937, Hurston's means to demonstrate that, though African American women may be treated as the mules of the world (14), and thus as beasts of burden who can bear the weight of exploitation and denigration, they are, in fact, sentient, sensitive beings whose humanity is also feminine, deserving of care. The domestic imagery points to the inclusion of African American women to the private sphere at the time maintained as the arena of proper white American women (similar in fashion to Seacole's intervention in the genre of the travelogue in the late nineteenth century). Janie accesses this private sphere, at the time, and formerly, associated with white womanhood and virtue, but she is not satisfied with it. Her search for an emancipated life is haunted by Nanny and her mother's rapes and, in her marriage to Joe, which she once thought liberatory, she experiences Nanny's feeling of being "a cracked plate" or "*ze fele*," a cracked egg. Hurston's imaginative interpretation of the Kreyol phrases also points to the fact that her own text is actively syncretic, as is the native language of Haitians. In this, she performs the pivoting axis proper to cultures of the circum-Caribbean geographical region.

In other instances, Hurston's borrowing from Haitian Kreyol is more explicit and more literal, yet Hurston continues to adapt the phrases for her purposes, testifying both to her creativity and the transmutability of African Diasporic experience. Take, for example, the following Kreyol phrase: "*m'grangou; ti trip ap vale gwo trip tounen*," which literally translates as, "I'm hungry: my small intestine has swallowed my large intestine." An exaggerated image proper to Haitian *Kreyol*, the proverb voices hunger by claiming that the small intestine is so hungry that it is swallowing the large intestine. Another Haitian phrase also voices a similar sentiment with the stomach/intestine entwined: "*lestomak mwen ap kòde*" [my stomach is tied in knots; my intestines are knotting up]. In the novel, Hurston borrows and inverses the phrase when Janie attempts to voice her discontent in her second marriage to Jody Starks: "Ah might take and find somebody dat did trust me and leave yuh." Jody responds:

Shucks! 'Tain't no mo' fools lak me. A whole lot of mens will grin in you' Face, but dey ain't gwine tuh work and feed yuh. You won't git far and You won't be long, *when dat big gut reach over and grab dat little one*, You'll be too glad to come back here. (30; emphasis mine)

Interestingly, Hurston inverses the original proverb phrase by imagining that the big intestine will gobble up the small one; physiologically, the image does not quite work; perhaps Hurston simply misunderstood the original phrase. Whether the result of mistranslation, transcodage, or a desire, again, to camouflage the source of a striking image, the phrase is clearly a kreyolism.[20]

Yet, the most compelling example of the translexical influence I have been sketching can be found in a key phrase of the text—what Danticat refers to as the "intimate storytelling" of the text but simply reads as an effect of call and response. I return here, then, to the ground of the story's framing. As Janie tells her story to Phoeby, her "kissing" friend, the text does not participate in a process of call and response. Phoeby is not given an opportunity to "talk back" the story: she recounts it for Janie who does not have the courage to tell the story repeatedly to various community members curious to understand Janie's two marriages and ultimate "*plaçage*"[21] with her much junior and final lover, Tea Cake, with whom she descends from the parlor of a mayor's house in a Black township, to the "muck" of the Floridian Everglades. That phrase, "Dat's just de same as me 'cause mah tongue is in mah friend's mouf" (6), has previously been read as a lesbian subtext between Janie and Phoeby (despite Janie's two marriages and passionate relationship with Tea Cake) (Kaplan 133). Indeed, the lesbian reading of the text, produced in the early 1990s hinged upon the "queer" reading of this phrase. Carla Kaplan, for one, contends, within the opening line of her provocative 1995 essay, "The Erotics of Talk," that: "Reduced to its basic narrative components, Zora Neale Hurston's *Their Eyes Were Watching God* is the story of a young woman in search of an orgasm" (115); she elaborates: "Telling her story to Phoeby supplies the erotic fulfillment Janie misunderstands as 'marriage,' and in this sense Phoeby, whose 'hungry listening helped Janie to tell her story,' is the 'bee' to Janie's 'blossom'" (116). So, Kaplan claims, "Janie's tongue isn't in Tea Cake's mouth" (132), and thus argues that, Janie and Phoeby, as "kissing bees" offer a "figuration [that] goes beyond 'female bonding' to suggest not only the intimate familiarity of their friendship and its erotic tracings, but also both the intimacy and eros necessary for a successful discursive 'self revelation'" (120). The implications of Janie's placing her tongue in Phoeby's mouth as a means to tell her story is thus erotically charged; in its larger sociocultural context, it is also read as evidence of Hurston's search for voice through her character. The phrase itself does not appear to have resonance in American black English. It does, however, have a corollary in Haitian Kreyol in the folk phrase: "*Bouch an bouch; youn di lòt*"—which translates to mean: "(from) mouth to mouth; one tells (the) others."[22] In *Kreyol*, the phrase has no erotic overtones whatsoever; it is simply a phrase by which speakers invoke the need to have someone else tell their story,[23] whether out of solidarity or in search of a witness to their own grief. In the context of the novel, Janie figuratively places her tongue in Phoeby's mouth not in an erotic gesture but as a means to expediently disseminate her story to others within her community who refuse her their listening ears. In fact, she prefaces the phrase by saying, "Ah don't mean to bother wid tellin' 'em nothin'. . . . 'Tain't worth de trouble. You can tell 'im what Ah say if you wants to" (6). In locating the phrase in the commonspeak of Haitian Kreyol, I do not mean to suggest that the phrase *cannot* be read as a possible lesbian encoding nor that, within the context of the novel (though I do find it interesting that queer readings of both *Their Eyes Were Watching God* and *Home to Harlem* have resulted in the obfuscation of more complex readings of African Diasporic effects or crossovers in both texts), the phrase does not perform an erotics of communication that may or not be read as lesbian but as a discursive strategy, as Kaplan has argued, for self-realization both for the author and her character. What I do mean to say is that the linguistic gesture points implicitly to further corroboration between Hurston and her writing locale. As in the other examples cited, Hurston makes use of kreyolism as a means of expanding her artistic vision; the borrowed phrase enables the emergence of a (African American) feminist assertion of voice within a larger, lakou context, both African Diasporic and transnational.

To conclude, Hurston's travels through the Haitian landscape were ostensibly designed to harvest the lore of the culture, to capture in movement, song, worship, and words, the ways of a people. In Port-au-Prince, Hurston found more than this, she found a reflection of her own self, actualized, of a culture that was no longer what it had been but still aspired to be more than it had become. She recognized, in the *hounfort* the fortitude of Haitian women, what *fanm vayant* Haitian women are, modeled Janie after them, and sought to become one as she apprenticed to become a mambo/vodou priestess. What would she say of Port-au-Prince today, postearthquake, of which she once wrote: "There shall come a voice in the night. A new and bloody river shall pour from a man-made rock in your chief city. Then shall be a cry from the heart of Haiti—a great cry, a crescendo cry. There shall be survivors, and they shall have a look and a message" (1990,65)? Under unsuspecting postcolonial eyes, her texts perform the service of affirming autochthonomous subjectivity in the early years of a twenty-first century that still dared to question its existence, as it dared to question the temerity of the formerly enslaved to have freed themselves some two hundred years prior. Hurston found her freedom through Haiti and the novel that speaks of this most clearly was written in the cradle of her rebirth, in Port-au-Prince, Haiti.

Hurston's Haitian texts caution us to understand that any gaze can be hegemonic when trapped in national discourses that would make the citizens of other nations subalterns even as their cultures are exalted for their difference. Had Hurston not died as early as she did, in penury and isolation, broken from the cosmopolitan life of liberty and inquiry she had tried to fashion for herself, she might have come to produce less ambivalent representations of Haiti. Still, Hurston was able to extract from Haitian culture lessons of folklore that allowed her to recontextualize aspects of African American culture that she wished to pursue. In the same way that McKay found in the promise of Haitian autochthonomy, the possibility for sexual emancipation, so, too, did Hurston pursue through the kreyolizations of her texts ways to convey the pursuit of gender (and sexual) freedom for her African American heroine. Both authors resisted demonifications of the Haitian culture, which U.S. schooling and culture had taught them to despise, and entered into an intradiasporic conversation giving rise to a lakou space within the texts themselves. This allowed both, within the texts I have explored here, to harness the flight of their creative spirits in the service of af/filiation so that the contents of their texts were enriched, and so too the genre of the texts themselves. McKay's novel-without-a-plot reflects the sensibility of a memoir, thinking through home space to realize the intradiasporic conversations between Jake and Ray, while Hurston's encoding of kreyolizations in *Their Eyes Were Watching God* allows us to retrace her passage through Port-au-Prince, Haiti, so that the text is as much memoir/travel narrative as it is a novel. Altering our reading practices to encompass that of the embedded African Diasporic interpretive communities within the texts allows us to understand these, and their contexts, in new ways.[24]

Conclusion

Masquerading as narratives of travel, the texts I discussed in this chapter retrace African Diasporic memory as a space of contest at the crossroads of Euro-American privilege and historic dispossession that seek to centralize African Diasporic subjectivities. Earlier in the twentieth century, texts produced during the Harlem Renaissance against the friction of marginalization within the United States nonetheless provide evidence of participating in a larger epistemic cultural perspective anchored in lakou consciousness. Despite pulls away from such consciousness through American national identification (Americanization, or, in McKay's case, through the process of assimilation), the texts reveal a compulsion to retain and recover defining features of cultures rooted in African folk traditions. In both McKay's and Hurston's works, Haiti stands as the locus for such African Diasporic recognition and collectivity. Both delved further into this Afro-centered neighboring culture of historical significance as a source of inspiration and innovation. This is a worldview that is fast being lost in the North American context, for reasons owing to the assimilationist nature of U.S. culture, the age-old practice of consolidating African American identity through the building of the United States empire rather than as a continuation of a world history in which Africa and African-descended people are centralized. It is an identity also consolidated through an adoption, via upward mobility (class enfranchisement), of both these views as constitutive of subjectivity, at the expense of any sense of autochthonomy, a subject identity that exceeds purchase in the nation-state.

Conclusion

In Chapter 2, I moved abreast of the main concepts in this study, *autoch-thonomy* and *lakou consciousness*, to add to these the concept of the *(in)imaginable*. In reading Raoul Peck's work through the latter concept in explicitly gendered ways, I have wanted to suggest that the most forward-looking works of African Diasporic autochthonomy pay attention to women's place in history, both in the ways that they have been subjected to colonial violence and in the ways that they have preserved cultural memory for themselves and for their communities. Although specific to my discussion of the genocide that took place in Rwanda in 1994, it would be applicable to similar, ongoing situations in the African context such as the civil war in the Democratic Republic of the Congo. At the same time, it is a concept that need not be limited to such contexts, as my final two chapters returning us to earlier stages of literary production make clear. In the work of Mary Seacole, Mayotte Capécia, and Zora Neale Hurston, in the encoding of their texts with an African Diasporic subtext, each makes use of methods of dissimulation akin to the *(in)imaginable*: that which appears to be absent (because of the time period in which they were [mis]read for various reasons, or because of the genre they chose for their works) is actually encoded in the text and discernible only for those who employ tools particular to the African Diasporic, transnational interpretive communities in which each situates itself. I demonstrated how Seacole and Capécia both utilize forms of the pseudo-memoir and the authorial "I" to present authoritative narrations from the point of view of women of the African Diaspora, utilizing strategies of (dis)identification as a constitutive element of autochthonomy (the refusal to identify with social racial and gender categorizations in Seacole; "'I'-lying"

in Capécia), to assert autochthonomous subjectivities. These were successful enough that male writers resorted to similar rhetorical strategies while
refusing to acknowledge that these were shared across the genders intradiasporically so that women's texts produced from the same communities would
diminish in influence; some of these male writers, as we have seen in the case
of Fanon, were then themselves misread by readers whose point of view was
not their own (usually, white) so that their autochthonomous assertions were
by-passed in the interest of producing reductive readings of their works to
avoid/ignore their incisive sociopolitical and racial critiques. This need for
subterfuge (in the case of Seacole/Capécia) was necessary in order to transmit
autochthonomous ways of seeing at times and in cultures in which African
Diasporic or female/feminist points of view were discounted or ignored;
this is why they remain dissimulated but why I argue that we must develop
the skills to unearth this nonetheless present reality beneath the obvious or
overarching readings that limit understanding of African Diasporics as only
appendages to dominant Euro-American (read "white" structures of being
and subjugation). We see such strategies continue in the works of a writer
like Zora Neale Hurston whose anthropological writings, when they had to
do with African Diasporic cultures other than her own, were steeped in the
American chauvinism of her time. Yet, for those conversant in the subjectivities of the interpretive communities in which she participated—in her
case, African American, Jamaican and Haitian—it is clear that she created
"intertexts" that are also intensely intradiasporic, in conversation with communities of the African Diaspora beyond her own. Consistent with Stuart
Hall's contention that "new ethnicities" (and, indeed, all ethnicities) are the
product of discursive formations, I have shown, in *Their Eyes Were Watching
God*, that it is language itself that provides Hurston with a bridge between
African American and Haitian cultures; Hurston's note-taking of folk phrases,
including Kreyol phrases, is documented by her niece, Lucy Anne Hurston,
in the 2004 collection *Speak: so you can speak again* which provides replicas
from Hurston's notes throughout her writing life and provides evidence of
Hurston's interest in the living language itself, in addition to folk and spiritual
practices she wrote of in her not unproblematic *Tell My Horse*. Knowledge
of Haitian history and of Kreyol proverbs is necessary, however, to be able
to decode Hurston's imaginative transliterations; they, too, are a form of the
(in)imaginable of autochthonomous realities—residing hidden in full view
within the imagined, fictional text. So, rather than delineate "indigenous"
forms of African realities from ritual to cultural practices that compose
various societies, this project has proposed that the real issues are reading
incapacities, curtailed by a Hegelian point of view through which people of

African descent are seen as constituted by European disruption rather than part of a long history of human exchange anchored in a particular place (the African continent) and then dispersed from it, as have been other cultures and ethnicities, transhistorically and across geographies. For years now, I have been bemused by the ways in which my students (if they believe themselves to be "white") consistently and actively misread texts by writers of African descent as if the concerns of people of African descent can only be white dominance/subjugation or as if they, as readers, do not have "permission" to enter the text on its own terms. For instance, students have actively avoided the ways in which *Sometimes in April* engages memory of the genocide of Rwanda from the perspectives of Rwandan's interethnically and across gendered experience, opting to focus on the few scenes in the film that footnote Rwanda's colonial history with Belgium or the lack of intervention as details of the carnage became known; the latter scenes comprise less than twelve minutes of the long duration film. What Rwandans struggle with together or what Peck brings to the film as a Haitian-Congolese-French filmmaker are sidelined when they should be, as I have argued, foregrounded for the difference in perspective and interpretive conclusions these aspects of the film and filmmaker bring out that is quite different from other representations produced from outside of an African Diasporic point of view.[1] Resolving such incapacities begins by situating communities of African descent within their own interpretive grounds and understanding these within the context of autochthonomous subjectivities that have their own complex histories and politics of representation.

In a certain sense, the narrative strategies I have focused on in these analyses are performances in themselves; but, differently from those performative acts I discussed in Chapter 1 that focus solely on racial habitus, those that reveal the wholesale and historical construction of racial categories, they perform and give life to an African Diasporic sensibility that is too often denied. In my chapter on representations of the genocide of Rwanda, in contrasting visual texts that have sought to represent the genocide of Rwanda from cross-cultural points of view, I have shown that when an artist from the African Diaspora utilizes autochthonomous subjectivity as a framing device (much as did Gien in her one-woman play concerning apartheid in South Africa), the result not only produces an af/filiative text, it provides the possible fabric for empathetic responses from its viewership, which is then forced, whether African Diasporic or not, to view history and culture from an (in)imaginable standpoint—one that is said not to exist or that is said to reside beyond the imaginable. We are compelled to enter that (in)imaginable space and to understand reality from a point of view in which the West (white/European) viewpoint is no longer authoritative. A larger world reveals itself, one in which African Diasporic points of view are centralized. We are no longer dealing in false universals or false notions of enlightenment principles. In fact, we accept the failure of European continental enlightenment philosophers in their willful inability to recognize autochthonomous subjectivities and their willful creation of hierarchies of being within humanity. There is no need for us to romanticize these worlds in order to be "recognized" under Western Eyes. Inhumanity occurs everywhere, no more and no less because of the cultures affected by power differentials and violence. *How* they depict the effects of that violence, however, is deeply reverential of the humanity affected by it. In Peck's work, a traditional cinematic narrative that appears to be linear and focused on male heroes is subverted from within, such that women's place in the genocide and (in)imaginable acts of sexual violence are framed by real testimony provided in international court so that the fulcrum of the film rests almost entirely on the one scene in which such testimony is provided. That the film work in the scene visualizes the effects of the testimony on our male protagonist is also instructive: he is altered by the testimony, even sees his reflection differently, seeing in himself the violence that men are capable of, but that he will not repeat. In an interesting way, the scene reverses, in the Rwandan context, the dynamic between a Fanon and a Capécia, discussed in the following chapter.

Whereas Fanon was inspired by Capécia but found it necessary as a consequence to destroy her work through a public misreading in order to obscure the fact that he found her textual and authorial strategies convincing and put such strategies to use for Black male advancement in his text at the cost of equal advancement for Black women, Peck's text, in the end, argues that there is no advancement if men of African descent do not integrate women of African descent's testimony, experience, memory, as their compass. The work of lakou consciousness and of autochthonomous subjectivity, then, is not simply the work of asserting intradiasporic exchanges within the African Diaspora; it is also the work of making salient the importance of women's experience within them. Additionally, as we have seen in the work of Claude McKay, and of Seacole, it is a space that opens itself to assertions of other denied identities, such as queer or un-gendered perspectives; this is largely due to the (dis)affiliative nature of autochthonomous subjectivities. In the work of Claude McKay, the possibility of autonomous queer, or non-gendered identity, is presented as analogous to African Diasporic autonomies in terms of preexisting subjectivities that demand their autonomy despite disapprobation from dominant society, or, in other words, it is autochthonomy that allows McKay to make such a claim, as the Haitian example, for him, demonstrates that social, and even legal, interdictions have little to do with the integrity of the subject that knows itself prior to its entry into sociality. It is my hope, then, that my analysis of each of the African Diasporic texts discussed earlier has demonstrated the utility of acknowledging and analyzing intra–African Diasporic content and exchanges in the works of African Diasporic cultural producers who define themselves within the parameters of African Diasporic af/filiations. Such readings open up a world, one that we have for far too long neglected and yet breathes, exists, persists—and continues—in spite of recognition, acknowledgment, analysis, or lack thereof.

In this project, then, I have challenged, through readings of carefully chosen texts that participate in cross-cultural, African Diasporic dialogues, such received ideas on race, identity, and subjectivity. As discussed in my introduction, I have chosen texts that have long circulated in American, African American, Caribbean, and cultural studies but that have continued to be misread or have had their African Diasporic intra-textualities elided in favor of fixing the texts solely in Manichean dialectics of a postcolonial nature. I have argued that such fixing not only limits the terrain of interpretation but the insistence on such limited or reductive readings actually leads to the persistence of hierarchical models of power relations based on fictional constructions of race (as well as of gender, class, and nationality), that have, over time, made themselves real. As such, they guarantee the persistence of racist constructions and consequences upon lived lives and they guarantee the erasure of the cultures from which racialized others emanate. One of the consequences of such misreadings and categorizations also means that the fields of analyses in which these texts circulate replicate interpretive incompetencies in that they replicate ignorance of the communities that have created the texts, the cultures, and the epistemes, and thus, the interests, that animate them. The willful neglect, denial, or outright dismissal of African Diasporic contexts embedded in the texts surveyed here (and others not considered) has led to misreadings (in particular of McKay, Hurston, Capécia, Seacole) that invariably eliminate the possibility of reading the texts in any other way than in the Western/Euro/American–white fashion. I hope that this study has demonstrated that there are other means of reading texts, and of being responsive to interpretive communities that do not define themselves as the latter.

That we continue to ignore (or pretend) that race is *not* a construction, *not* performed, and is somehow innate or natural, even with much evidence to the contrary, means that such misreadings and overreadings will persist. As such, Chapter 1 considered texts by African Diasporics intent on going beyond the performative nature of racial categorization to demonstrate how we might engage one another in terms of other variables (culture, language, ethnicity, and age, for example, as we saw in Gien) and how social categorizations, especially in contexts of state suppression affect, not only the marginalized but those who benefit (legally and socially) from such constructions. In the work of Gien and Butler, trauma revealed itself as a conduit toward willfully recognizing, shedding, and reshaping racial categorizations such that cultural considerations could form the basis for identity formation. Following in the work of Oliver, these texts revealed how taking as a departure point the subjectivity of those marginalized could alter social and political relations to create a more equitable world and to reconsider the effects of history upon the present. Those currently privileged by histories of colonization could provide witness to the traumas such history engendered as a means of joining the testimony of those who survived the most extreme forms of violent subjugation. Kinship, then, is formed through af/filiation of a dual nature—forged in the recognition of the harm wrought through hierarchies of power that disenfranchise some while empowering others through fictive constructions of the human but also through the recognition of the saliency of African culture, its modes of being, and of survival.

Chapters 3 and 4, informed by Jacques Rancière's concept of the "equality of intelligences," grouped texts that lend themselves to intradiasporic readings in order to demonstrate their deliberate exercise of autochthonomy. These present deliberate efforts to participate in, and transmit, lakou consciousness where it is said not to exist, by speaking to and across cultures of the African Diaspora to recognize kinship across national, geographic, or even historical borders. Thus, we saw the ways in which Capécia, Seacole, McKay, and Hurston, each sought to create narrative strategies within the genres of the memoir, novel, and travelogue in order to relate intradiasporic realities. Such efforts are not always successful; they fail when the author is unable to transcend the limits of nation or, because of national identification, is intent on demonstrating or proving her/his belonging to the dominant class. Strategies of dis/identification and dis/affiliation in the work of Capécia, Seacole, and Hurston reveal the necessity of not only resisting such assimilations but the necessity of preserving that which connects African Diasporics: culture, language, and a memory of the past not defined by dominating powers, postcolonial or neocolonial.

Lakou consciousness is both a virtual space for such exchanges and defined by an acknowledgment of autochthonomous subjectivities, which makes such preservation possible: it is the understanding of sovereign subjectivities anchored in preexisting cultures and geographies that even the process of colonization cannot ultimately extinguish. Writers like Capécia and Seacole in particular provide texts that are instructive in that their use of the authorial

"I" voice in their texts provides a means to "disarticulate" from the authority of the contexts in which they produced their works; it allows them to reshape their readers' perspectives and impose upon them their own points of view, displacing gender and racial norms to new ground. By reading all of these texts across genres—fiction as memoir, memoir as autobiography—and applying critical theories across disciplines—in ways that reveal the author's border-crossings also allows the interpretive communities of their makers to become apparent. In the same manner that the authors of the texts included in this study have creatively found ways to alter forms and narrative strategies associated with Euro-American texts, my innovations in this study have been my own effort to transmit to readers potential reading strategies—both analytical and theoretical—that participate *with* these cultural producers in their efforts to provide political and cultural commentary from African Diasporic points of view. Such viewpoints are necessarily expansive, looking further than the narrow avenue of the fact of historical colonization to reflect the global, transnational, and transhistorical nature of African Diasporic realities. This is most explicitly explored in my second chapter, in which taking a look at a local event through global eyes reveals the extent to which interpretive community af/filiations *do* matter.

It is my hope that this work of cross-cultural, interdisciplinary analyses of texts, paying attention to folk, cultural, and historical details (such as reflected in parallel historical trajectories, as in the case of Hispaniola/Rwanda, or that reflected in proverbial wisdom between African American and Haitian folk cultures), subject autonomy, sovereignty of the subject and of African Diasporic cultural groups—some forming recognized nation-states, some not, can impact understandings of contemporary racial dynamics by relying not on spectral racial difference and the constructions that have been spawned from them, but on intradiasporic relations and exchanges, for interpretation, whether such interpretations take place on the interpersonal level or are applied to the reading of texts for academic or scholarly purposes. In doing so, another, complex world is made intelligible, which has the force of tipping the racialized Eurocentric world off its axis.

If I have stressed the use of interpretive neologisms throughout this study, it has been to suggest their possibility rather than their authority. Though I hope the terms I have deployed here will be found useful to others, it is less important that they be put into use than that the ways in which I have sought to explain their viability as tools by which to further apprehend and centralize African Diasporic perspectives be understood in themselves. If they encourage others to use the same, or similar, terms in order to provide cultural studies and literary studies scholars with more accurate terms to describe such texts, then they will have done their work. More importantly, if they have caused readers to rethink the notion of "interpretive communities" (as coined by Stanley Fish) and how African Diasporic communities might reflect their own concerns, epistemes, histories, modes of thinking, and chief concerns, then the project, as a whole, will have contributed to a reconsideration of how to read, interpret, analyze, and teach African Diasporic texts from starting points emanating from the free subjectivities of their creators.

I acknowledge that not all African Diasporic texts will lend themselves to such readings. Part of the postcolonial production of African Diasporics is constituted by projects of resistance, of speaking back to colonial powers and speaking out against white supremacy. As already stated in my introduction, this project does not deny the importance of such works, nor their existence, nor that some of the texts under discussion here also otherwise participate in this discourse. Although some of my discussion privileges Haiti as a centering African Diasporic nexus in the Americas and my concept of lakou emanates from its Haitian definition (originating in African cultures), and I do believe that there are political reasons for doing so—as I have discussed in previous works with regard to Haiti's place in world history as the first African/Black identified nation in its hemisphere—this is only one of a number of starting points that one could take to center discussion for African Diasporic readings. Given this, I could have also privileged Francophone texts from the French Caribbean and various former colonies of France in the African continent; I chose, instead, to focus on texts that readers based in the Americas and working in English/American literature could easily access in order to create cross-cultural and intradisciplinary accessibility. In either case, certain approaches and texts are privileged while others remain absent or unaddressed; this will occur with any study. I hope that other scholars will reveal other concepts and approaches of similar kind emanating from other cultures of the African Diaspora and add to the lexicon of virtual lakous as they continue to proliferate between cultural workers of African descent invested in such exchanges. Lakou consciousness, after all, begins in African continental contexts while autochthonous subjectivities exist wherever African-centered cultures have shaped local culture and persisted alongside, in spite of, or beyond colonial intervention/interruption. The current study was initially inspired by investigating further Haitian/Congolese filmmaker Raoul Peck's cultural investments as revealed in *Sometimes in April*, a film that has been distinguished from more mainstream films on the genocide, such as *Hotel Rwanda*, by experts in the field for being more faithful to the sentiments and realities of Rwandans themselves.[2] I then mapped these findings further onto texts that I had always read as being af/filiated with various parts of the African Diaspora, but which had been under-investigated in this respect. This study, I hope, contributes to alleviating such under-investigations while providing tools for their undertaking. In the end, doing so will make readers of all backgrounds more culturally competent such that, when faced with difference in the African body, there will be a greater sensitivity and sensibility drawing from African Diasporic structures of knowing, rather than from theories of subjugation or racial animus, as Alcoff has suggested, to alter responses to difference in ways that may be not only productive, but life-saving.

Notes

Introduction

1. Mignolo includes the Anglophone Caribbean via C. L. R. James but James's magnum opus concerns the Haitian Revolution; as such, it is more accurate to understand the intellectuals Mignolo cites (James, Césaire and Fanon) as belonging to the French Caribbean tradition. For a primer on the concepts and history of decoloniality, see Mignolo and Walsh, *On Decoloniality*.

2. For the sake of ease of reading, however, I will continue to use the term *postcolonial* to refer to literature produced by individuals situated in formerly colonized sites; this does not mean that I do not regard the works as "decolonial," as per Mignolo's definition, but that I believe that the term is more elastic than Mignolo warrants. Also, given that I am working with postcolonial theory as a part of my main methodological apparatus, it would become confusing to redefine the term further here.

3. I am not speaking here of a *minor transnationalism*, to invoke the very useful term coined by scholars Françoise Lionnet and Shu-mei Shih in their book of the same name. There, the scholars define *minor transnationalism* specifically as a consideration of the status of "minority" individuals in the United States and Western Europe and their shifting identities as they negotiate a variety of national contexts, but also as an attempt to bridge the "vertical" chasm between disciplinary boundaries within ethnic studies to a horizontal dialogue exploring minoritarian politics and minority cultures' relationship to one another within "white"-dominated societies. In their introduction, the editors explain: "More often than not, minority subjects identify themselves in opposition to a dominant discourse rather than vis-à-vis each other and other minority groups. We study the center and the margin but rarely examine the relationships among different margins" (x). As much as I admire and sympathize with the project, agreeing with Lionnet and Shih as to the necessity of cross-cultural dialogue between and within minority groups rather than only in an

oppositional dialectic with dominant discourse, this project forks away from the latter in its refusal to identify individuals of African descent solely as minorities, even within Euro-American dominated contexts.

4. I am here referring to the term, not its appellation (spelled *autochtone*—without a second "h"—in French). Since I am writing in English, I am using the Anglophone spelling of the term and the root of my neologism resides in the Greek (as a blind reviewer for this manuscript has usefully pointed out); what I am stating here is that the term is common usage in French/Francophone studies for what Anglophones would normally term *indigenous*. From the Greek, *autochthon*, meaning "sprung from the earth" [autos (self) + khton (earth, soil)], the term *autochthone* evolved to mean "an original or indigenous inhabitant of a place; an aborigine"—in ancient Greece, this distinguished original inhabitants of a place from settlers and those of mixed heritage. https://en.wikipedia.org/wiki/Autochthon_(ancient_Greece) accessed 3/7/19). From the end of the twenty-first century through today, the term has come to be attached to any group with longstanding, historical ties to a place, a "continuous habitation" reflected in the development of customs and practices particular to a land or nation such that, even if not properly speaking, "indigenous," the people now residing in that place are perceived as "autochthonous." This is particularly the case for island people, particularly of the Caribbean, but similar arguments can be made for peoples of other islands, territories, and nation-states. The importance of the use of the term *autochthone*, then, is located in its root, the concept of the earth/ground, which need no longer be a place of origin but one of continuous habitation such that the local inhabitants have come to be (and, at times, also by admixture and acceptance by preexisting indigenous groups, should they remain) the locally recognized indigenous society. Anthropologist, Michaela Pelican advances the following, useful summation of the linguistic (French/British) divide as to the usage of these terms: "Whereas the English version of the UN declaration refers to 'indigenous peoples,' the French version—because of the negative connotations of the colonial term *indigène*—uses *peuples autochtones*. The English idiom (and also the Spanish) is derived from the Latin *indigenae*, whereas the French *autochtone* has Greek roots; both terms entail the idea of priority in time (Daes 1996). The reason for the terminological variation in the declaration is the terms' different historical and value connotations in the respective languages (Bowen 2000:14)" (54). Pelican's article focuses on the case of the Mororo, an ethnic group crossing many national lines in both West and East Africa, but particularly their situation in Cameroon, because this group is classified as "indigenous" by the UN but is, in many instances, considered "foreign" in local jurisdictions because of their traditional nomadism; through this example, Pelican demonstrates that the state of "indigeneity" is largely a political construction in need of constant invigilation and, that, in particular, in the African context, the term *indigenous* cannot mean what it has come to mean in other geopolitical spaces.

5. Definitions taken from http://en.wiktionary.org/wiki/autochtone, accessed June 28, 2013.

6. Self-governance or sovereignty, in the cases in which it has been granted, is, at best, provisional or partial, limited to policing on reservations created by colonial powers, or, as in the case of Inuit territory, subordinated to the laws of Canada.

7. Indigeneity, then, on both sides of the Atlantic, whether attached to First Nations peoples in the Americas, or to those on the African continent, became synonymous with the "uncivilized," the illiterate, the sub-modern. Those perceived to have "fit in" with the model of modernity imposed by Europe were thus seen as having escaped this categorization. This is implied, it would seem, by the political definition of indigeneity currently provided via the UN recognized World Council of Indigenous People (WCIP) which, in its meeting in Guyana of 1974, defined indigenous people as follows: "The term indigenous people refers to people living in countries which have a population composed of differing ethnic or racial groups who are descendants of the earliest populations living in the area *and who do not as a group control the national government of the countries within which they live*" (qtd in Rÿser 213; emphasis mine). This definition would, consequently, exclude the vast majority of populations in Africa.

8. Writes Pelican: "The English equivalents to *autochtone* are *native* and *son* or *daughter of the soil*, coupled with the negative opposites, *stranger* and *migrant*. Both *autochtone* and *native* are terms originally introduced by the French and British colonial authorities that have entered local parlance in francophone and anglophone Cameroon, respectively" (54).

9. I am conscious here of the problematic ways in which *autochthony* is deployed in African contexts to deny migrant or nomadic groups political rights or access to land; it is not my purpose here to contribute to such divisions. My use of the root here does not reflect a desire to negate the rights of oppressed minority groups in African contexts; I use it more generally to reflect a positionality denied Africans in global contexts by which both dominant and minority African groups are perceived as rootless and "without a home," especially in that they exist in sectors of the African Diaspora produced by colonialism (either through the slave-trade or partitioning of the continent among European powers). In other words, I am arguing that African/Diasporic groups can be understood as autochthonous—whether or not they are nomadic or displaced—because what matters is their continuity in time and maintenance of cultural traditions within local spaces and ethnic groups. Oppression or marginalization as the defining trait for self-definition as an autochthone is problematic in that it continues the idea that local groups or specific ethnic non-European groups that have undergone colonization cannot be defined outside of the colonial impasse. It also means that there can be no points of origin prior to colonization; I refuse this impasse.

10. This is essentially a problem of nomenclature and etymology. Nonetheless, what I argue here, for a narrowing of association between First Nations groups in the Americas and African/Diasporic groups is not anomalous. Mignolo and Catherine Walsh make a similar assertion, using standard terminology, when they align both groups while speaking of decolonial praxis. In *On Decoloniality*, Catherine Walsh writes explicitly: "The struggles for and on territory and land as the base and

place of identity, knowledge, being, spirituality, cosmo-vision-existence, and life, have long organized the collective insurgent praxis of ancestral peoples, identified as indigenous, Afro-descendant, or Black, and sometimes as peasant or *campesino*" (35). The two groups are here encapsulated in the phrase "ancestral peoples" while "indigenous," made lowercase, does not necessarily refer only to First Nations groups but to a variety of groups who belong to a particular place that has undergone colonization. My approach differs from Mignolo and Walsh's in that I am not as convinced, as they are, that there is no "outside" to coloniality, that it defines all relations of power. In the same text, when describing second wave decolonization in African and Asian contexts, Mignolo specifically refers to populations in both enacting resistance against European nation-states as "activated by the Indigenous population and not by Creoles and Mestizos of European descent as was the case in the Americas" (124). Here, Mignolo capitalizes *Indigenous* and applies the term to both African and Asian populations of resistance, having defined *the indigenous* as reflecting the vocabulary of populations situating themselves as "originating in specific countries or regions outside of Europe" (121); the slippage in terminology, then, between Walsh and Mignolo in their own text is instructive as it demonstrates that even like-minded intellectuals can be reflecting similar concepts differently and that nomenclature has a historical afterlife that is difficult to undo.

11. See Sylvia Wynter, "No Humans Involved" (1994); see Weheliye, *Habeas Viscus* (2014).

12. I am indebted to an anonymous reader of this manuscript for this insight and connection. I also thank Susan Z. Andrade for raising questions that have pushed me to elucidate the connection between transnationalism and indigeneity between First Nations and African societies.

13. James Clifford notes that Pan-Africanism had two movements, one originating in the Americas from the 19th century on, articulated by figures such as Marcus Garvey and W. E. B. Du Bois, while the continental movement emerged postwar (from the 1940s forward) with the rise of African nationalists such as Nkrumah and Padmore. Clifford gleans from this that Gilroy's "Black Atlantic" revives and revises the Pan-Africanist model, "with a postcolonial twist," explaining that "Gilroy returns the black cultural tradition to a historically decentered, or multiply centered, Atlantic space. In the process, he breaks the primary connection of black America with Africa, introducing a third paradigmatic experience: the migrations and resettlings of black British populations in the period of European colonial decline" (*Routes* 261–262). Clifford's accounting of Pan-Africanism holds, however, only if one assumes it to be an endeavor situated primarily in the Anglophone world. In this sense, Gilroy's project is an extension of Anglophone projects that compellingly center the conversation in (black) Britain (albeit via the discourse of African Americans such as Du Bois). However, there are many Pan-Africanisms with overlapping linguistic traditions and actors. Keeping this plurality in mind, Zeleza thus contends that there were not two but six articulations of Pan-Africanism: 1) "linking continental African and its diaspora in the Americas"; 2) confining "itself to the African Diasporic communi-

ties in the Americas and Europe, excluding continental Africa" (ex. Gilroy's *Black Atlantic*); 3) "focused primarily on the unification of continental Africa"; 4) "restricted themselves to the peoples of the continent north and south of the Saraha; and 5) Pan-Arabism, which "extended itself to western Asia or the so-called Middle East; and 6) "[seeking] to reclaim connections of African peoples dispersed to all corners of the globe" (36). My project situates itself, then, within the seeds of the first movement and is propelled by the last, or sixth, the global. However one defines Pan-Africanism and its variations, what unites these is their transnational feature and entanglements with notions of mobility and migration, in short, of diaspora.

14. See Hall via Appiah, *The Fateful Triangle*, 33.

15. Anderson also elaborates on the necessary separation of "Indios from "Blacks" by the Spanish Crown for purposes having everything to do with governance and control of lands (15).

16. Shona Jackson advances the idea of a "creole indigeneity" premised on the disappearance of Indigenous peoples in the Caribbean: "native displacement and either real or figurative disappearance serves as the *necessary* or enabling condition of black being in the Caribbean, both epistemological and ontological, and is essential for constitution of that being through the rise of national consciousness and class consolidation" concluding, thus, that "we see the rerouting of indigeneity or instituting of new natives, Creoles, in both of the region's dominant critical or philosophical traditions" (28). Jackson's perspective is consonant with Hall's concept of "new ethnicities," as such, though Hall's breaks with the idea of a necessary institution of a national ethnicity. Though my own perspective aligns, in some respect, with Jackson's in terms of the rooting of African culture where Native identity once flourished, my own term is not premised on native displacement, but on the ways in which both Native and African identity have been formed within colonial paradigms and often pitted against one another at the service of Empire building, as my next section delimits within new approaches to Indigenous Studies.

17. Native scholar, Lynn Gehl, recounts and theorizes in her memoir/scholarly work, *Claiming Anishinaabe*, the ways in which she contested land claims and Indian Act provisions for being reinstated as a registered member of the Anishinaabe, a designation denied her through land ownership and blood quanta as delineated in the Indian Act. In the process of defying these provisions legally, she lays out other ways in which tribal and cultural affiliation can be reclaimed through Indigenous knowledge and philosophy.

18. Huhndorf also points out that since nationalism is bound up in patriarchal hegemony, traditional nationalist Indigenous agendas have neglected Native women's roles historically and contemporaneously, politically and culturally (5).

19. For example, Simpson refers to the Mohawk/Iroquois as Kahnawà:ke throughout her work.

20. For those skeptical of the connection between Indigenous and critical race/postcolonial studies, it may be important to note that Huhndorf, for instance, clearly states that she takes inspiration for placing Native Studies at the center of American

studies from an African American trailblazer, "Mary Helen Washington's 1997 presidential address to the American Studies Association, 'Disturbing the Peace: What Happens to American Studies if You Put African American Studies at the Center?'" (3n2), following in her footsteps by similarly putting Indigenous studies at the center of American Studies; the final chapter of Huhndorf's *Mapping the Americas* focuses on Leslie Marmon Silko's *Almanac of the Dead* in which Silko goes even further, to reconfigure alliances *transnationally*, "that share a history of genocide, slavery, and dispossession." From this, Huhndorf remarkably (for my purposes) concludes: "Even Africa is included. The map conjoins colonialism and slavery, as it foreshadows revolt, by labeling Haiti the home of the first black Indians" (142). For Silko, and thus also for Huhndorf, "native" identity does not exclude cultures of African descent, especially not in the Americas—it includes them. This is an intellectual move that most scholars, even within Indigenous Studies, are not yet prepared to make, but which, when engaged, will, as I hope this project demonstrates, redirect and extend engagements across fields and across decolonial projects.

21. Since the Caribbean is an agglomeration of differing nation-states, this perspective cannot be said to be anchored in any particular nation. A regional or disciplinary perspective does, however, inform this project.

22. Here, Beaubrun cites an unattributed source, presumably one of her sources for the book itself.

23. There is an obvious indebtedness to feminist standpoint theory as articulated by thinkers such as Sandra Harding and Donna Haraway. The reader is referred to Harding's *The Feminist Standpoint Theory Reader: Intellectual and Political Controversies*, London: Routledge, 2003, and Haraway's essay, "Situated Knowledges: The Science Question in Feminism and the Privilege of Partial Perspective," *Feminist Studies* No. 3 (Fall 1988), 575–599.

Chapter 1. (Re)Presenting Racial Permeability, (Dis)Ability, and Racial (Dis)Affiliations

1. In fact, though Alexander Weheliye has made a convincing argument for the racializing of the Deleuzian term, *assemblages*, one might argue that since race pervades every facet of Western social organization, they are always already raced even if that racialization, in its original construction, results in the complete erasure of people/bodies of color, especially if they are of African descent.

2. Recall here Moten: "The coalition emerges out of your recognition that it's fucked up for us. I don't need your help. I just need you to recognize that this shit is killing you, too, however much more softly" (Harney and Moten 10).

3. The physical "calling cards" were initially produced as part of a performance series Piper called "guerrilla performances," designed to intervene in situations of political/cultural cooptation; the physical calling cards and their texts are the remains of these performances and continue to be exhibited in various venues. To read a synopsis of the performance, see a previously unpublished text by Adrian Piper, written in 1990, explaining the performance, "27. My Calling (Cards) #1 and #2" in her *Out*

of Order, Out of Sight. Vol I: Selected Writings in Meta-Art, 1968–1992. Cambridge: MIT Press, 1996 (219–221).

4. Harvey Young similarly discusses racial habitus as "embodied social expectations that influence and inform behavior" (14) and, similarly to Alcoff, concludes that "[t]he existence of multiple habiti demonstrates that racial identity and projection exist in different forms" (15).

5. Source incomplete; this source was provided by the Jeff Koons Archive (2014), without complete bibliographic notation; the author is listed as "JCB" but the catalogue copy source is unlisted.

6. Yet, the pairing of the chimp, "Bubbles," with Jackson, often read as in keeping with classical, sculptural representations of consorts retains the disturbing racialized conflation of black subjects with animals, especially chimps.

7. Sutton. "Jeff Koons' Controversial Michael Jackson."

8. As Bansel writes: "As superman, in this assemblage, Pistorius is above judgments of good and evil, above the law" (43).

9. For a fuller accounting of how mental health professionals were deployed during the trial in ways that mobilized a "pre-existing and powerful medical model of disability," see Harvey 301.

10. This is not unlike the "settler" logic found in Canadian culture in which (white) settlers are perceived as being vulnerable to the land/nature and depicted as valiantly overcoming the forces of nature while indigenous peoples are perceived as an extension of the perceived perils of confronting nature. For more on the perceived settler/nature conflict, see Margaret Atwood's, *Survival/La Survivance.*

11. See here Kafer, "The Cyborg and the Crip: Critical Encounters."

12. It strikes me as ironic how often the death of Western Man is invoked in poststructuralist and feminist manifestos—from Foucault to Deleuze, to Agamben, even to Fanon and, more recently, Weheliye—and yet what this "death" leads to is seldom articulated, as if being subject to Western logos—which all acknowledge to be the product of ideological constructions, means that we cannot imagine anything outside of this logos at the same time as there exists unexplored terrains of non-Western and syncretic models (for example, in postcolonial worlds—Caribbean and elsewhere, including North America).

13. As the work of Alondra Nelson, Jenny Reardon, and Dorothy Roberts has shown, genetic testing has assisted members of the African Diaspora to retrace their roots back to a ground of origin in the African continent as a means to repair the wrenching from such roots caused by the slave trade; genomics has by and large demonstrated that it is nearly impossible to continue to categorize human beings through racial categories. Since the Human Genome Project was created in 1990, it has continued to reveal "race" as a fiction. Roberts writes, in *Fatal Invention,* "[t]the Human Genome Project confirmed what many leading biologists and anthropologists had concluded several decades earlier: race is a social and not a biological category. The project validated a shared humanity that many people had long known without the need for genetic evidence" (51). The project has revealed that human beings "are

99.9 percent genetically alike" (Roberts 26) and, that "[w]hile it is true that the 0.1 percent of human genetic difference is meaningful, it does not mean that human genetic difference is organized by race" (51). Roberts also underscores an aspect of the findings that remains understudied and undervalued, that "the greatest amount of genetic diversity in the world exists in sub-Saharan Africa . . . [and] vary the most because most of the human genetic diversity evolved in Africa" (51–52) and, finally, quoting Deborah Bolnick, making "non-Africans . . . essentially a subset of Africans" (Roberts 52). Though science disproves the facticity of "race" and the centrality of Africanity in understanding the human as species, scientists appear to continue to pursue a socially prescribed need to find some scientific basis for racial differentiation (Roberts 26). In *Race Decoded*, a study not of the findings of genomics but of the scientists behind the studies on both sides of the Atlantic, Catherine Bliss shows that the dilemma plaguing what she terms "race-averse" scientists, or those sensitive not to reproduce racial categories or stereotypes, is how to navigate a definition of race by which "race is both a negative symbol of legacies of injustice and a positive marker of community struggle and personal growth" (7). Bliss, herself, opines that "'race' is a cipher for a set of relational meanings—meanings of difference that are always undermined, pliant, manifold" and that genomics and haplotype scientists are hampered, especially in the United States, by "[a] long-standing system of government classification [that] requires scientists to design all their research with official racial categories" (20). The obvious problem with this, of course, is that while scientific discoveries seem to eliminate racial categorization, scientists are then forced to make the science fit national discourses of race. "These policies," writes Bliss, "mandate genomicists to consider human variation in light of Census race," while census race is an invention of the state with no scientific basis. While the field sought to eliminate race-based categories, the area of "racial health disparities" or the inclusion of neglected minority population in health management, re-activated the pursuit of genetic variations even though health management shortfalls for minority populations often hinge more upon the institutionalization of their exclusion (from access to treatment and health benefits such as access to fresh foods), than they do upon actual biological variation.

14. Gray. "black, White and Colored."

15. In the performance with the playwright, a subsequent Q&A revealed that there were South Africans in the audience, adding another layer to responses that cannot be effectively measured without direct interviews with such audience members, given that often displacement to North America was a movement away from one settler society to another, one less inclined to see itself in these ways; some moved because they disagreed with apartheid and wanted to distance themselves from its volatility while others fled because of impending losses of privilege. In either case, emigration remains a marker of privilege; those who did speak during the Q&A and self-identified as South African overwhelmingly voiced their empathy for black South Africans or their shared sense of having been "witnesses," like the play's protagonist, to the disabling violence of South African apartheid politics.

16. This recalls Spillers invocation of "the flesh [as] a concentration of 'ethnicity' that contemporary critical discourses neither acknowledge nor discourse away," an elemental materiality upon which new inscriptions can be made or new histories of identity developed to explain what Spillers describes as the residue of state violence (via the work of Elaine Scarry), "lacerations, woundings, fissures, tears, scars, openings, ruptures, lesions, rendings, punctures of the flesh" (67), that serve as initiations to the disciplinary apparatus of the State.

Chapter 2. Autochthonomous Transfigurations of Race and Gender in Twenty-First-Century Transnational Genocide Testimonial Narratives

1. For more on this topic, also see Sybille Fischer's *Modernity Disavowed*.

2. Appolonia is fathered by the local, white clergyman, Brother Philip.

3. I am not suggesting that the harms enacted against sex workers should be dismissed but that the conflation of Mukandori with an acknowledged trope of single African women as sex workers only renders her less a victim and more a complicit actor in her own, postcolonial tragedy.

4. Though MacLeod cites Stassen's *Deogratias* as "having broken new ground for the adult-directed art form [bande dessinée], entering it into the long-existing dialogue between art and eugenics," she herself does not seem predisposed to explain how Stassen's text enters into this dialogue; she provides the context but not the analysis, so it is unclear whether she believes that Stassen's text has sidestepped or reinscribed eugenics.

5. Rwandan genocide survivor, Rupert Bazambanza, utilizes the figure of the silverbacked gorilla as a symbol of silent witness in his graphic novel, published in Canada, *Smile through the Tears* (2007). The gorillas, as symbols of Rwanda's unspoiled beauty and resources, open the text, disappear, then re-appear later on as silent, impotent bystanders. Never, however, are they conflated with Rwandans themselves. Bazambanza's discourse around animals is restricted either to unspoiled nature or inhumane acts, as when one character, Albert, in attempting to organize a congregation of frightened Tutsi states: "The smell of fear is what makes any wild animal attack a man. Let's stick together and defend ourselves against these beasts" (Bazambanza 44), referencing the Interahamwe; still, the perpetrators are not themselves depicted as animals. The difference in representation here is instructive as it speaks to insider/outsider perspectives. Bazambanza, however, as a survivor himself is unable to depict Rwandan characters without resorting to colonial "types," showing the pervasiveness of the colonial apparatus even for those attempting to decolonize themselves from it.

6. Parts of the following analysis were previously published in my essay "Desecrated Bodies/Phantom Limbs: Post-Traumatic Reconstructions of Corporeality in Haiti/Rwanda," *Atlantic Studies* 8:1 (Routledge), (March 2011): 109–123.

7. Azoulay does not stop to consider the presence of rape *within* the production of pornography itself via, for example, illegal "snuff" films; it would be interesting to see how an acknowledgment of rape within "hard core" pornography might alter her arguments.

8. Azoulay provides as a case study a 1996 film by a Dutch woman director, *Antonia's Line*—in which the director first chooses to show a rape on screen from the perspective of the victim in order to show the rape as one made permissible by the community but subsequently withholds showing the rape of the film's protagonist, by the same rapist, as a means to show how the perpetrator has insinuated himself back into the community, which now refuses to be complicit with the act of rape; in the second case, the film not only refuses to show the rape but instead focuses on the rapist being run off and injured by the women of the second victim's family.

9. In an email exchange with the filmmaker in the fall of 2013, Peck did, however, affirm that he was conscious of the similarities and informed by them even if they were not consciously worked into the film itself.

10. Gourevitch, *We Wish to Inform You*, 54.

11. Ibid., 55.

12. Ibid., 54.

13. Ibid., 23.

14. See my *From Sugar to Revolution* (2014) in which I give a detailed account of the massacre, as understood from both Haitian and Dominican historical sources.

15. In the postproduction interview with Mitchel, included with the DVD of the film, Peck cites militant film of the 1970s as an influence; Third cinema might be understood as belonging to this wider tradition of resistance cinema.

Chapter 3. Subjectivity in Motion

1. Lacan's "j/e" is a conceit more easily understood in the French where the pronoun "I" is "je"; in the reflexive address, to speak of what one does or the impact of an action upon the self, one inserts "me" to speak of oneself. This is the equivalent, in English, of the pronominal "myself." So, one is both "je" and "me"—"j/e" or "I/self."

2. Indeed, historically, Fanon's reading has taken the place of the original work itself, until recent critical re-editions of Capécia's texts mentioned here.

3. Please note that whenever the term "Black" is capitalized in the following, it is to follow Fanon's usage in historical context, usually in reference to Black men, as a sociocultural class.

4. In fact, what continues to be surprising is the degree to which Fanon's adherents are unwilling to revisit Capécia's work, in the original, and base their own findings *through* Fanon's completely and deliberately flawed presentation; in this respect, Fanon understood (part of) his audience well: those more than willing to dismiss black women's intellectual and literary works in the struggle for decolonization. One question that such critics fail to answer is the following: if Capécia's work was unimportant and not worth revisiting, then why did Fanon spend so much time on the text in one of his most important works? By demonstrating how Fanon distorted the text to serve his own purposes, and by returning to the original text, I answer this question, which reveals the importance of Capécia's novel both to Fanon's thought (not for what he says of it but what the text itself suggests) and, more largely, then, to decolonial thought.

5. A blind reviewer for this manuscript suggests that the phrase, "Nous n'en savons rien," in the original "Nous n'en savons rien" refers to the conclusions ('en'), not to the woman, and that if he meant to refer to the woman, that Fanon would have written "Nous ne savons rien d'elle." Out of context, this might be plausible; the "n'en" could be translated to mean "Des conclusions que nous proposerions . . . nous n'en savons rien" but this would be extremely stilted language; the reason that the referent "n'en" is commonly translated by Philcox, and previous translators, as "of her" in English translations, is because, were the reference clearly "our findings"—Fanon would have written "nous n'en n'avons aucunes" or "nous n'en n'avons pas"—"we have none." "Nous n'en savons rien" is otherwise a common response to refer to persons of whom one knows nothing, or with whom one is not acquainted. Even if the referent could be interpreted as "findings" only, the response Fanon imagines about women of color's plight would still mean that he can come to *no conclusions* on the matter *of what it is that women of color or black women think* (the referent would, in other words, be a mode of thinking of a group of people, not to abstract findings), because (one can extrapolate) he knows nothing or little about the black woman or woman of color. As such, despite the multiple readings possible, my findings remain unchanged. The phrase in question here may be ambiguous, but the analysis of Capécia's work that Fanon advances in one of his most widely read and influential works is not.

6. Omise'eke N. Tinsley has suggested: "Capécia's prismatically colorful novel can be read not only as authored by a Mayotte but itself as a *lamayòt*." She elaborates: "While superficially submitting to norms of French grammar and French images of Caribbean women, this scribal labor allows her to simultaneously reveal the hidden realities—the inside of the box, the dirty laundry—of race, gender, and sexuality in colonial Martinique" (145). Tinsley similarly observes that Fanon "remained oblivious to this *lamayòtaj*" in his criticism of Capécia, but her analysis, different than mine, abandons the reasons for Fanon's dismissal and proceeds to focus on Capécia's rendering of psychosexual relations between women and her specific representation of the laundress, which is her main interest. Tinsley's reading of Capécia's choice of pseudonym is based on its seeming reference to a traditional Haitian carnival practice called "lamayòt," in which a masked individual offers participants the opportunity to open a box for a minimal cost; the box may have in it a surprise or nothing. As Tinsley observes, via a reference to Edwidge Danticat's writing on the practice, to "lamayòt" has become ubiquitous in Kreyol for someone who dissimulates or tricks. There is, however, little to no evidence that this linguistic slip or practice exists in the French Departments; it is, however, possible that it was a shared historical practice for which there remains little present-day evidence.

7. In the same chapter, Fanon later writes, from the perspective of the white man: "Je suis Blanc, c'est à dire que j'ai pour moi la beauté et la vertu, qui n'ont jamais été noires. Je suis de la couleur du jour . . . [I am White, which means that I hold beauty and virtue, which were never black. I am the color of day. . . .]" (Fanon 1952; my translation, 36).

8. Portions of this chapter, including the passages to follow on Seacole's text, appeared in shorter form in *Hypatia* Vol. 03, No. 02 (Spring 2015) under the title, "Subjectivity in Motion: Caribbean Women's (Dis)Articulations of Being from Fanon/Capécia to the Wonderful Adventures of Mrs. Seacole in Many Lands."

9. These images are collected in Robinson's 2004 biography; Gittings writes her appraisal in 2010.

10. Seacole, as it has been noted, makes disparaging comments with regard to other racial minorities she encounters (Gunning references her prejudiced comments targeting others of African descent and Native Americans, 965–966), yet few critics note that she disparages all deemed "others" referring often to her subalterns by nicknames derived from their ethnicity, "race" or infirmities. For example, she refers to two English sailors in the Crimea as "Big and Little Chips" (96) and refers to a Jewish servant as "Jew Johnny" (100); her comments on those of African descent are rarely as laced with overt prejudice. On the one hand, these nicknames reflect Seacole's own prejudices within the sphere of her Englishness; on the other, they can be read as her desire to ascribe to her reader's views; the truth of the matter is likely situated between these two extremes. Biographer Jane Robinson writes that Seacole "made it clear that she was a Creole, and Creoles, like whites did not approve of recalcitrant negroes." She elaborates: "Far from identifying with the plight of slaves, those removed from bondage by a mere generation or two, like Mary, were apt to be frightened and therefore angered by them" (29). Though Robinson assumes that this fear/anger would have been an effect of class ("All her life Mary looked upward, and ahead, but never down" (ibid.), it seems more accurate to say that the fear of downward mobility (a class effect) and what it entailed for those enslaved—loss of freedom and social death—would have been the product of racial *identification*. Distancing oneself, via class, from the slave class, was a means of distancing oneself from a dangerous similitude.

11. Scholars are in agreement that Seacole assumes a white, male, English, upper-class, identity in the tone of her text and that, in so doing, she challenges gender norms (Frederick 489; Alexander and Dewjee 39). Gunning concludes from these competing subject positions that Seacole seeks to validate "Jamaican Creole medical practices she learned from her mother" (965).

Chapter 4. Autochthonomous Ambiguities

1. See my essay on Edwidge Danticat and Edgar Wideman in this respect: "Floating Islands: Spectatorship and the Body Politic in the Traveling Subjectivities of John Edgar Wideman and Edwidge Danticat," *Small Axe* 36 (November 2011).

2. This was somewhat different for writers of African descent in other spaces, especially in the Caribbean, as we have seen, since mobility between former colonies and colonial powers, through linguistic ties, made travel for the educated accessible; so, for example, someone like Seacole produces a memoir cum travelogue; still, even Seacole's text, as we have seen, is not a standard travel narrative.

3. One still compelling such revision can be gleaned from Anne McClintock's *Imperial Leather* (1995), in which McClintock elaborated her theories of "commodity racism" and "contagion," contributing to a growing apparatus by which to identify

and analyze the constructions of racialized cultural identities, with attention, in particular, to African heritage.

4. "What our performances verify—be it a matter of teaching or playing, speaking, writing, making art, or viewing art—is not our participation in a power incarnated in the community. It is the capacity of anonymous individuals, the capacity which renders each equal to the other. This capacity asserts itself across irreducible distances; it exercises itself through a play of unpredictable associations and disassociations. . . . To be a spectator is not a passive condition that we ought to strive to turn into activity. It is our normal condition."

5. Rancière emphasizes: "L'effet de l'idiome ne peut être anticipé. Il demande des spectateurs qui jouent le rôle d'interprètes actifs, qui élaborent leur propre traduction pour s'approprier 'l'histoire' et en faire leur propre histoire" (28–29).

6. See Moira Ferguson's preface to *The History of Mary Prince* for further information on the difference between the genre of slave narrative emerging in the United States as opposed to British contexts.

7. See here the work of Jennifer Wenzel.

8. This recalls Raymond Carver's short story "Cathedral," in which a bigoted white male protagonist comes to connect with a blind man and begins to overcome his prejudice by drawing, hand in hand, the naves of cathedrals so that the blind man can "see" the cathedral; in the silence of drawing begins the breakthrough of communion . . . one wonders if Carver would have been familiar with McKay's discussion of Shaw's speech on cathedrals.

9. Photographs of the "wayside exhibitry" were provided for examination via email May 14, 2012, by Barry Moreno of the Museum Services Division, The Bob Hope Memorial Library, Ellis Island Immigration Museum, Statue of Liberty National Monument.

10. See Sybylle Fischer and Susan Buck-Morss for more on these topics.

11. Langston Hughes also visited Haiti and wrote poems emanating from that encounter as well as cowrote a play with Hurston based in Haiti (which ultimately resulted in the breakdown of their relationship and which most Haitians found insulting).

12. *Encyclopedia of World Biography*, "Henry Sylvester Williams," http://www. encyclopedia.com/history/historians-and-chronicles/historians-miscellaneous-biographies/henry-sylvester-williams (accessed July 5, 2017).

13. This is not to say that color prejudice did not exist in Haiti before this time, but that the U.S. occupation legalized such prejudice and installed a racialized social and political hierarchy reflecting the U.S. white supremacist organization.

14. Only one additional recent scholarly effort makes a concerted effort to examine the role of Haiti in the novel: John Lowney. "Haiti and Black Transnationalism: Remapping the Migrant Geography of Home to Harlem," *African American Review* 34, no. 3 (2000): 413–429.

15. Ifeoma Nwankwo, in her 2003 essay, "Insider and Outsider, Black and American: Rethinking Zora Neale Hurston's Caribbean Ethnography" (*Radical History Review*, 87 [2003]: 49–77) is one of the few scholars who has endeavored to reveal Hurston's

intradiasporic affiliations; in this essay, she argues that Hurston's work participates in "transnational engagements . . . born of the juggling of multiple affinities, multiple ideologies, and multiple modes of defining the self and engaging the other" (abstract) and investigates how Hurston does so through an analysis of Hurston's short story collection, *Mules and Men* (1935) grounded by recourse to her anthropological text, *Tell My Horse* of 1938. Similarly here, I utilize *Tell My Horse* as a means of investigating Hurston's motivations and affiliations but conclude, differently, that the text reveals less than does an investigation of the intradiasporic transnationalism embedded in her novel, *Their Eyes Were Watching God*.

16. What I earlier termed a "culture lacune" in *Framing Silence* (New Brunswick, N.J.: Rutgers University Press, 1997).

17. By this, I mean that if we do not read Hurston's phrase here as being indicative of a state of mind or a propensity to misinform but as reflection of what Xu refers to as a "folklorization strategy," one by which communal and personal self-repre-sentation is improvisational, romanticized, lyricized (134) against various forms of political and cultural suppression, then we can understand Hurston as placing Haitian self-representation as undergoing similar processes of revision, improvisation, and self-fashioning against State control. As Françoise Lionnet asserts, with reference to Hurston's *Dust Tracks on a Road*, in this latter text, Hurston advances her "own implicit theory of reading" by which "the flow of creative energy is an imaginative transfiguration of literal truth/content through rhetorical procedures" (102); in other words, one has to understand that folk songs and stories are dynamic and not static, changing contextually and referentially depending on the speaker and her/his audi-ence. "Truth," in such contexts, then, cannot be static but also shifts dynamically, allowing for an elasticity of cultural expression without, however, meaning that the substance of the utterance itself has been altered.

18. This first phrase can also be found in current black English as "putting me down," to mean ending a connection or relationship; it's meaning here, however, resonates with meaning(s) of the standard Kreyol saying.

19. I am indebted to native speaker, Adeline L. Chancy, for discussions of the Kreyol phrases discussed in this paper, of their literal as well as culturally contextual meanings.

20. Interestingly, as I have presented this material at various venues, African Ameri-can scholars have pointed out to me that this particular phrase has some resonance in Southern black English; one scholar remembered hearing this phrase spoken by relatives in rural Georgia who have roots in some part of the Caribbean though she could not localize their origins. This suggests to me that Hurston's writing locale may have both generated and recalled to her memory phrases used interchangeably in this time period in areas of the Americas between which there was a great deal of exchange during and post-enslavement. Also, though some interpretations of this phrase link the image to the sayings analyzed in the previous section, i.e., to provide images of Jody's hypermasculinity, the phrase here is used to mean, simply, "hunger." It is this rendering of the phrase's meaning in Hurston's texts that ties it explicitly

to a *Kreyolism* even if it may have a coterminous existence in the commonspeak of Southern African Americans.

21. Haitian practice of common-law marriage; this term is also commonly used in Louisiana, a former French possession to which many enslaved Hispaniola Africans were brought during the years of the Haitian Revolution and to which many free Haitians traveled post-Revolution.

22. Source: Jeanty-Brown (eds.), *999 Paròl Granmoun: Haitian Popular Wisdom*. Port-au-Prince: Editions Learning Center, 1976.

23. Interestingly, this trope can be found in Haitian writer Jan J. Dominique's 1984 novel, *Mémoire d'une amnésique* in which, without using the kreyol phrase, Dominique has her main character tell the story of a lesbian affair by telling her husband that she places the story in his mouth; in this case, transmuting the story negates its lesbianism. In both Dominique and Hurston's case, the idea of telling the story through a ventriloquist or amanuensis (depending on whether we read the stories as oral or textual), emerges from the Haitian phrase and its sentiment. There is no evidence that Dominique had any knowledge of Hurston's novel at the time of the writing of her own text.

24. I would agree here with Lionnet's assertion that Hurston's purpose was, as such, "to destroy the white stereotype of black *inculture* not by privileging "blackness" as an oppositional category to "whiteness" in culture but by unequivocally showing the vitality and diversity of nonwhite cultures around the Caribbean and the coastal areas of the South, thereby dispensing completely with "white" as a concept and a point of reference" (105).

Conclusion

1. I have found students struggling similarly with texts like Chimananda Adichie's *Half of a Yellow Sun*, with students focusing on the one white character in the text who is minor compared to the rest of the Nigerian/Biafran characters.

2. *Kinyarwanda*, a 2011 film by Jamaican filmmaker Alrick Brown, exemplifies similar intradiasporic concerns and goes further than Peck's film in exploring the interethnic exchanges that took place between Rwandans attempting to survive the violence during the genocide; it does less work at the level of gender and displacing male authority in producing collective narratives; otherwise, it would have fit in well in the current study.

Works Cited

Primary Sources

Butler, Octavia. *Kindred*. New York: Beacon Press, 2004 (1971).

Capécia, Mayotte. "Je suis Martiniquaise. In *Relire Mayotte Capécia*. Eds. Myriam Cottias and Madeleine Dobie. Paris: Armand Colin, 2012.

Fanon, Frantz. *Black Skin, White Masks*. Translated by Richard Philcox. New York: Grove Press, 2008.

———. *Peau Noire, Masques Blancs*. Paris: Éditions du Seuil, 1952.

Gien, Pamela. *The Syringa Tree* (play). New York: Dramatists Play Service, Inc., 2001.

Hugo, Pieter, and Linda Melvern. *Rwanda 2004: Vestiges of a Genocide*. London: Oodee, 2011.

Hurston, Zora Neale. *Tell My Horse: Voodoo and Life in Haiti and Jamaica*. New York: Harper and Row, Publishers, 1990.

———. *Their Eyes Were Watching God*. New York: Harper Perennial, 2006 (1937).

Koons, Jeff. *Michael Jackson and Bubbles*, from the *Banalities* series, 1988. Porcelain, 42 x 70.5 x 32.5 in. Los Angeles, The Eli and Edythe Broad Foundation.

McKay, Claude. *A Long Way from Home*. New Brunswick, N.J.: Rutgers University Press, 2007 (1937).

———. *Home to Harlem*. Illinois: Northeastern University Press, 1987 (1928).

Peck, Raoul, dir. *Sometimes in April*. DVD. HBO Home Video, 2005 (2004).

Piper, Adrian. My Calling (Card) #1 (Reactive Guerrilla Performance for Dinners and Cocktail Parties), from the My Calling (Card) series. 1986–1990. Performance prop published by Angry Art Press: calling card with offset lithographed text, 1986 on card stock, 3.5 × 2 in. Wellesley, Massachusetts, Davis Museum and Cultural Center.

Seacole, Mary. *Wonderful Adventures of Mrs. Seacole in Many Lands (1857)*. New York: Penguins Books, 2005.

Stassen, J. P. *Deogratias, A Tale of Rwanda*. New York: First Second, 2006.

Secondary Sources

Achebe, Chinua. "Colonialist Criticism." *The Post-Colonial Studies Reader*. 2nd Edition. Eds. Bill Ashcroft, Gareth Griffiths, and Helen Tiffin. London: Routledge, 2006.

Alcoff, Linda Martín. *Visible Identities: Race, Gender, and the Self*. London: Oxford University Press, 2005.

Alexander, Jacqui. *Pedagogies of Crossing*. Durham: Duke University Press, 2005.

Alexander, Ziggi, and Audrey Dewjee. *Mary Seacole: Jamaican National Heroine and Doctress in the Crimean War*. London: Brent Library Service, 1982.

Aléxis, Jacques-Stephen. "Of the Marvellous Realism of the Haitians." The Post-Colonial Studies Reader. 2nd Edition. Eds. Bill Ashcroft, Gareth Griffiths, and Helen Tiffin. London: Routledge, 2007.

Anderson, Mark. *Black and Indigenous: Garifuna Activism and Consumer Culture in Honduras*. Minneapolis: University of Minnesota Press, 2009.

Ashcroft, Bill, et al. *The Empire Writes Back*. 2nd Edition. New York: Routledge, 2002.

Atwood, Margaret. *Survival/La Survivance*. Toronto: House of Anansi Press, 2013 (1971).

Azoulay, Arielle. *The Civil Contract of Photography*. Cambridge: Zone Books (MIT Press), 2012.

Bansel, Peter. "Assembling Oscar, Assembling South Africa, Assembling Affects." *Emotion, Space and Society*, vol. 13, (2014): 40–45.

Barthes, Roland. *Camera Lucida*. New York: Hill and Wang, 1980.

———. *Mythologies*. Translated by Annette Lavers. New York: Hill and Wang, 1972.

Bazambanza, Rupert. *Smile through the Tears*. Ontario, Canada: Soul Asylum Poetry, 2009.

Beaubrun, Mimerose. *Nan Dòmi: An Initiate's Journey into Haitian Vodou*. San Francisco: City Lights Publishers, 2013.

Bergner, Gwen. "Who Is that Masked Woman? Or, the Role of Gender in Fanon's Black Skin, White Masks." *PMLA* 110, no. 1 (January 1995): 75–88.

Bernasconi, Robert. "Who Invented the Concept of Race?" *Race*. Ed. Robert Bernasconi. London: Wiley-Blackwell, 2001.

Bhabha, Homi K. *Location of Culture*. London: Routledge, 1994.

———. "Postcolonial Authority and Postmodern Guilt." *Cultural Studies*. Eds. Lawrence Grossberg, Cary Nelson, and Paula A. Treichler. New York: Routledge, 1992.

———. "Signs Taken for Wonders." *The Post-Colonial Studies Reader*. 2nd Edition. Eds. Bill Ashcroft et al. London: Routledge, 2007.

Bliss, Catherine. *Race Decoded: The Genomic Fight for Justice*. Palo Alto: Stanford University Press, 2012.

Bonilla-Silva, Eduardo. *Racism without Racists*. New York: Rowman and Littlefield Publishers, 2013.

Bourdieu, Pierre. *Outline of a Theory of Practice*. Cambridge: Cambridge University Press, 1972.

Brustein, Robert. "Pamela Gien and the Syringa Tree." *Rants and Raves: Opinions, Tributes, and Elegies.* Hanover, N.H.: Smith and Kraus, 2011, 23–26.

Buck-Morss, Susan. *Hegel, Haiti and Universal History.* Pittsburgh: University of Pittsburgh Press, 2009.

Burns, Lorna. *Contemporary Caribbean Writing and Deleuze: Literature between Postcolonialism and Post-Continental Philosophy.* New York: Bloomsbury, 2014.

Butler, Judith. *Giving an Account of Oneself.* New York: Fordham University Press, 2005.

Capécia, Mayotte. *I Am a Martinican Woman and the White Negress: Two Novelettes by Mayotte Capécia.* Edited and translated by Beatrice Stith Clark. Pueblo, Colorado: Passeggiata Press, 1998.

Capers, Bennett. *Reading Back, Reading Black.* Legal Studies Research Paper Series, Research Paper No. 07-2. 35 *Hofstra Law Review* 8 (2007).

Caruth, Cathy. "Introduction." *Trauma: Explorations in Memory.* Ed. Cathy Caruth. Baltimore: Johns Hopkins University Press, 1995, 3–12.

Carver, Raymond. "Cathedral." *Cathedral.* New York: Vintage Books, 1989.

Cervenak, Sarah Jane. *Wandering: Philosophical Performances of Racial and Sexual Freedom.* Durham: Duke University Press, 2014.

Chancy, Myriam J. A. *From Sugar to Revolution: Women's Visions of Haiti, Cuba, and the Dominican Republic.* Waterloo: Wilfrid Laurier University Press, 2012.

Chong, Doryun. "Adrian Piper, American, b. 1948." *Walker Center Collections,* 2005, 461–462.

Chouliaraki, Lilie. "Post-Humanitarianism: Humanitarian Communication beyond a Politics of Pity." *International Journal of Cultural Studies,* 13, no. 107 (2010): 107–126.

Chow, Rey. "The Politics of Admittance: Female Sexual Agency, Miscegenation, and the Formation of Community in Frantz Fanon." *Frantz Fanon: Critical Perspectives.* Ed. Anthony C. Alessandrini. London: Routledge, 1999.

Clifford, James. *Returns: Becoming Indigenous in the Twenty-First Century.* Cambridge: Harvard University Press, 2013.

———. *Routes: Travel and Translation in the Twentieth Century.* Cambridge: Harvard University Press, 1997.

———. "Traveling Cultures." *Cultural Studies.* Eds. Grossberg et al. London: Routledge, 1992.

Coates, Te-Nehisi. *Between the World and Me.* New York: Spiegel and Grau, 2015.

Cottias, Myriam, and Madeline Dobie. *Relire Mayotte Capécia: Une femme des Antilles dans l'espace colonial français (1916–1955).* Paris: Armand Colin, 2012.

Coundouriotis, Elena. "'You Only Have Your Word': Rape and Testimony." *Human Rights Quarterly* 35, no. 2 (May 2013): 365–385.

Danticat, Edwidge. Foreword. *Their Eyes Were Watching God,* by Zora Neale Hurston. Ed. Henry Louis Gates Jr. New York: Harper Perennial, 2006.

Dayan, Colin. "Civilizing Haiti." *Boston Review* (January 20, 2010), http://boston review.net/BR35.1/dayan.php. Accessed March 6, 2012.

———. *The Law Is a White Dog.* Princeton, N.J.: Princeton University Press, 2013.

DeLanda, Manuel. *A New Philosophy of Society: Assemblage Theory and Social Complexity*. London: Continuum, 2006.

De Lauretis, Teresa. "Sexual Indifference and Lesbian Representation." 1990 *Identities: Race, Class, Gender and Nationality*, 1st Edition. Eds. Linda Martín Alcoff and Eduardo Mendieta. Hoboken: Wiley-Blackwell, 2007.

Deleuze, Gilles, and Felix Guattari. *A Thousand Plateaus: Capitalism and Schizophrenia*. Translated by Brian Massumi. Minnesota: University of Minnesota Press, 1987.

De Sousa Santos, Boaventura, João Arriscado Nunes, and Mara Paula Menesis. "Introduction: Opening Up the Canon of Knowledge and Recognition of Difference." *Another Knowledge Is Possible: Beyond Northern Epistemologies*. Edited by Boaventura de Sousa Santos. London: Verso, 2008.

Didi-Huberman, Georges. *Quelle émotion! Quelle émotion?* Montrouge, France: Bayard Editions, 2013.

Dixon, Melvin. *Ride Out the Wilderness: Geography and Identity in Afro-American Literature*. Urbana: University of Illinois Press, 1987.

Du Bois, W. E. B. "The Browsing Reader." The *Crisis*, 35, no. 202 (June 1928).

Edwards, Brent Hayes. *The Practice of Diaspora: Literature, Translation, and the Rise of Black Internationalism*. Cambridge: Harvard University Press, 2003.

Eze, Emmanuel Chukwudi. *On Reason: Rationality in a World of Cultural Conflict and Racism*. Durham: Duke University Press, 2008.

Fabre, Michel. *Black American Writers in France, 1840–1980: From Harlem to Paris*. Urbana: University of Illinois Press, 1993.

Fanon, Frantz. *Black Skin, White Masks*. Translated by Richard Philcox. New York: Grove Press, 2008.

Ferguson, Moira. Preface. The History of Mary Prince, A West Indian Slave, Related by Herself. Michigan: University of Michigan, 1993.

Fischer, Sibylle. "Haiti: Fantasies of Bare Life." *Small Axe* 12, no. 1 (2007): 1–15.

———. *Modernity Disavowed: Haiti and the Cultures of Slavery in the Age of Revolution*. Durham: Duke University Press, 2004.

Fish, Cheryl J. *Black and White Women's Travel Narratives: Antebellum Explorations*. Gainesville: University Press of Florida, 2004.

Fish, Stanley. *Is There a Text in This Class? The Authority of Interpretive Communities*. Cambridge: Harvard University Press, 1982.

Fraser, Benjamin R. "Problems of Photographic Criticism and the Question of a Truly Revolutionary Image." *Chasqui* 33, no. 2 (2004): 104–122.

Frederick, Rhonda. "Creole Performance in *Wonderful Adventures of Mrs. Seacole in Many Lands*." *Gender and History* 15, no. 3 (2003).

Freire, Paulo. *Pedagogy of the Oppressed*. London: Bloomsbury Academic, 2000.

Fuss, Diana. *Identification Papers: Readings on Psychoanalysis, Sexuality and Culture*. London: Routledge, 1995.

———. "Interior Colonies: Frantz Fanon and the Politics of Identification." *Rethinking Fanon: The Continuing Dialogue*. Ed. Nigel C. Gibson. New York: Humanity Books, 1999.

Gabriele, Teshome H. "Towards a Critical Theory of Third World Films" and "Third

Cinema as Guardian of Popular Memory: Towards a Third Aesthetics." *Questions of Third Cinema*. Eds. Jim Pines and Paul Willemen. Norfolk: British Film Institute, 1989.

Gallagher, Mary. *Poetics, Ethics, Globalization*. Toronto: University of Toronto Press, 2008.

Gates, Henry Louis Jr. "Writing, 'Race', and the Difference It Makes." *Cultural Studies*. Eds. Grossberg et al. London: Routledge, 1992.

Gehl, Lynn. *Claiming Anishinaabe: Decolonizing the Human Spirit*. Regina: University of Saskatchewan Press, 2017.

Gikandi, Simon. *Maps of Englishness: Writing Identity in the Culture of Colonialism*. New York: Columbia University Press, 1996.

Gilroy, Paul. *Against Race*. Cambridge: Harvard University Press, 2002.

———. *The Black Atlantic*. Cambridge: Harvard University Press, 2000.

Gittings, Clare. "Mary Seacole in Focus." (Teacher's Guide) *National Portrait Gallery*. London, 2010.

Gladwell, Malcolm. *Blink: The Power of Thinking without Thinking*. New York: Black Bay Books, 2007.

Glissant, Edouard. *Poetics of Relation*. Ann Arbor: University of Michigan Press, 1997.

Godlin Roemer, Marjorie. "Which Reader's Response?" *College English* 49, no. 8 (1987): 911–921.

Goldberg, Elizabeth Swanson, and Alexandra Schultheis Moore. "Old Questions in New Boxes: Mia Kirshner's *I Live Here* and the Problematics of Transnational Witnessing." *Humanity: An International Journal of Human Rights, Humanitarianism, and Development* 2, no. 2 (Summer 2011): 233–253.

Goliath, Gabrielle. "Vestiges of a Genocide: Terror and the Sublime in the Work of Pieter Hugo." Dissertation (2011): 1–87.

Gordon, Leah. *Kanaval: Vodou, Politics and Revolution on the Streets of Haiti*. London: Soul Jazz Records Publishing, 2010.

Gordon, Lewis K. *Bad Faith and Antiblack Racism*. Atlantic Highlands, N.J.: Humanities Press, 1995.

Gourevitch, Philip. *We Wish to Inform You that Tomorrow We Will Be Killed with Our Families: Stories from Rwanda*. New York: Picador, 1998.

Gray, Paul. "Black, White and Colored." *New York Times*, August 6, 2006. http://www.nytimes.com/2006/08/06/books/review/06Gray.html?_r=0. Accessed September 12, 2015.

Groensteen, Thierry. *The System of Comics*. Jackson: University Press of Mississippi, 2009.

Grosz, Elizabeth. *Volatile Bodies*. Bloomington: Indiana University Press, 1994.

Gunning, Sandra. "Traveling with Her Mother's Tastes: The Negotiation of Gender, Race, and Location in *Wonderful Adventures of Mrs. Seacole in Many Lands*." *Signs* 26, no. 4 (2001).

Hall, Stuart. *The Fateful Triangle: Race, Ethnicity, Nation*. Cambridge: Harvard University Press, 2017.

Haraway, Donna. "A Cyborg Manifesto: Science, Technology, and Socialist-Feminism in the Late Twentieth Century." *Simians, Cyborgs and Women: The Reinvention of Nature.* New York: Routledge, 1984.

———. "Ecce Homo, Ain't (Ar'n't) I a Woman, and Inappropriate/d Others: The Human in a Posthumanist Landscape." *Feminists Theorize the Political.* Eds. Joan Scott and Judith Butler. New York: Routledge, 1992, 86–100.

Hardt, Guy, and Antonio Negri. "Imperial Sovereignty." In *The Post-Colonial Studies Reader.* 2nd Edition. Eds. Bill Ashcroft et al. London: Routledge, 2007.

Harlow, Barbara. *Resistance Literature.* London: Routledge, 1987.

Harney, Stefano, and Fred Moten. *The Undercommons: Fugitive Planning & Black Study.* Brooklyn: Minor Compositions, 2013.

Hartman, Saidiya V. *Scenes of Subjection: Terror, Slavery, and Self-Making in Nineteenth-Century America.* Oxford: Oxford University Press, 1999.

Hatfield, Charles. *Alternative Comics: An Emerging Literature.* Jackson: University Press of Mississippi, 2005.

Hatzfeld, Jean. *Into the Quick of Life: The Rwandan Genocide—The Survivors.* Philadelphia: Trans-Atlantic Publications, 2005.

Hawthorne, Evelyn J. "Self-writing, Literary Traditions, and Post-Emancipation Identity: The Case of Mary Seacole." *Biography* 23, no. 2 (2000).

Hayes, Chris. "How America Became a Colonial Leader in Its Own Cities." *Vanity Fair* (March 2017): 128–130.

Herschdorfer, Nathalie. *Afterwards: Contemporary Photography Confronting the Past.* Lausanne: Thames and Hudson, 2011, 42–45.

Holcomb, Gary Edward. *Claude McKay, Code Name Sasha: Queer Black Marxism and the Harlem Renaissance.* Gainesville: University Press of Florida, 2007.

Holland, Patrick, and Graham Huggan. *Tourists with Typewriters: Critical Reflections on Contemporary Travel Writing.* Ann Arbor: University of Michigan Press, 1998.

hooks, bell. "Homeplace." *Yearning: Race, Gender, and Politics.* Boston: South End Press, 1999.

Hron, Madelaine. "Itsembabwoko 'A La Française'?—Rwanda, Fiction, and the Franco-African Imaginary." *Forum for Modern Language Studies* 45, no. 2 (2009): 162–175.

Huhndorf, Shari M. *Mapping the Americas: The Transnational Politics of Contemporary Native Culture.* Ithaca: Cornell University Press, 2009.

Iragaray, Luce. *This Sex Which Is Not One.* Ithaca: Cornell University Press, 1985.

Jackson, Shona N. *Creole Indigeneity: Between Myth and Nation in the Caribbean.* Minneapolis: Minneapolis University Press, 2012.

Jacobus, Mary. "Is There a Woman in This Text?" *Reading Woman: Essays in Feminist Criticism.* New York: Columbia University Press, 1986, 83–109.

JanMohamed, Abdul. *Manichean Aesthetics: The Politics of Literature in Colonial Africa.* Amherst: University of Massachusetts Press, 1988.

Kafer, Alison. "The Cyborg and the Crip: Critical Encounters." *Feminist, Queer, Crip.* Bloomington: Indiana University Press, 2013.

Kaplan, Carla. "The Erotics of Talk: 'That Oldest Human Longing' in *Their Eyes Were Watching God.*" *American Literature* 67, no. 1 (March 1995).

Karem, Jeff. "Haiti, Pan-Africanism, and Black Atlantic Resistance Writing." *Haiti and the Americas*. Eds. Carla Calargé et al. Jackson: University of Mississippi, 2013.

Kilby, Jane. "The Visual Fix: The Seductive Beauty of Images of Violence." *European Journal of Social Theory* 16, no. 3 (2013): 326–341.

Kincaid, Jamaica. *A Small Place*. New York: Farrar, Straus, and Giroux, 2000.

Kubowitz, Hanna. "The Default Reader and a Model of Queer Reading and Writing Strategies or: Obituary for the Implied Reader." *Style* 46, no. 2 (Summer 2012): 201–228, 272, 275.

Laclau, Ernesto. *Emancipation(s)*. London: Verso, 1996.

Lao-Montes, Agustin. "Decolonial Moves," *Cultural Studies* 21, no. 2 (2007): 309.

Levine, Michael G. "Necessary Stains: Spiegelman's MAUS and the Bleeding of History." *American Imago* 59, no. 3 (2002): 317–341.

Liddiard, Kirsty. "(Re)Producing Pistorius: Patriarchy, Prosecution and the Problematics of Disability." *Sociological Imagination*. http://sociologicalimagination.org/archives/15144. Accessed March 13, 2015.

Lionnet, Françoise. "Autoethnography: The An-Archic Style of Dust Tracks on the Road," In her *Autobiographical Voices: Race, Gender, Self-Portraiture*. Ithaca: Cornell University Press, 1989.

Lionnet, Françoise, and Shu-mei Shih, Eds. *Minor Transnationalism*. Durham: Duke University Press, 2005.

Lowney, John. "Haiti and Black Transnationalism: Remapping the Migrant Geography of Home to Harlem." *African American Review* 34, no. 3 (2000): 413–429.

MacLeod, Catriona. "L'Eugénisme pour les enfants: Heroes, Villains and Racial Purity in *Le Téméraire*." *L'Esprit Créateur* 52, no. 2 (2012): 59–74.

Mbembe, Achille. *Critique of Black Reason*. Durham: Duke University Press, 2017.

———. *On the Postcolony*. Berkeley: University of California Press, 2001.

McClintock, Anne. *Imperial Leather*. London: Routledge, 1995.

McCloud, Scott. *Understanding Comics*. New York: William Morrow, 1994.

Mercer, Kobena. "'1968': Periodizing Politics and Identity." *Cultural Studies*. Eds. Lawrence Grossberg et al. London: Routledge, 1992.

Mignolo, Walter. *The Darker Side of Western Modernity: Global Futures, Decolonial Options (Latin America Otherwise)*. Durham: Duke University Press, 2011.

Mignolo, Walter, and Catherine Walsh. *On Decoloniality: Concepts, Analytics, Praxis*. Durham: Duke University Press, 2018.

Möller, Frank. "Rwanda Revisualized: Genocide, Photography, and the Era of the Witness." *Alternatives* 35 (2010): 113–136.

Montgomery, Hugh. "Who Do You Think You're Looking At?" *The Independent on Sunday* (April 10, 2011): 2–3.

Mudimbe, V. Y. *The Invention of Africa: Gnosis, Philosophy, and the Order of Knowledge*. Bloomington: Indiana University Press, 1988.

Muñoz, José Esteban. *Disidentifications: Queers of Color and the Performance of Politics*. New York: New York University Press, 1999.

Mykell, Gwendolyn. "When Horses Talk: Reflections on Zora Neale Hurston's Haitian

Anthropology." *Phylon (1960-)* 43, no. 3 (1982): 218–230. *JSTOR.* http://www.jstor.org/stable/274819. Accessed March 6, 2012.

Nwankwo, Ifeoma. "Insider and Outsider, Black and American: Rethinking Zora Neale Hurston's Caribbean Ethnography." *Radical History Review* 87 (2003): 49–77.

Oliver, Kelly. *Witnessing: Beyond Recognition.* Minnesota: University of Minnesota Press, 2001.

Ollman, Leah. "Around the Galleries: Photography that Goes Only Skin Deep." *Los Angeles Times* (February 9, 2007): E30.

———. "Pieter Hugo: Seeing South Africa Anew." *The Guardian* (2013).

Peck, Raoul, dir. *Lumumba: Death of a Prophet (Documentary).* Paris: Velvet Film, 1990.

Pelican, Michaela. "Complexities of Indigeneity and Autochthony: An African Example." *American Ethnologist* 36, no. 1 (February 2009): 52–65.

Perry, Adam. "Pistorius and South Africa's Culture of Violence." *Time Magazine* (March 10, 2013).

Phillipson, Robert. "The Harlem Renaissance as Postcolonial Phenomenon." *African American Review* 40, no. 1 (Spring 2006): 145–160.

Pickens, Therí. "'You're Supposed to Be a Tall, Handsome, Fully Grown White Man': Theorizing Race, Gender, and Disability in Octavia Butler's Fledgling." *Journal of Literary and Cultural Disability Studies* 8, no. 1 (2014): 33.

Poon, Angelia. "Comic Acts of (Be)Longing: Performing Englishness in *Wonderful Adventures of Mrs. Seacole in Many Lands.*" *Victorian Literature and Culture* 37 (2007).

Prabhu, Anjali. "Narration in Frantz Fanon's Peau noir, masques blancs: Some Reconsiderations." *Research in African Literatures* 37, no. 4 (Winter 2006): 189–210.

Price-Mars, Jean. *So Spoke the Uncle.* Translated by Magdaline W. Shannon. Washington, D.C.: Three Continents Press, 1983.

Ramesh, Kotti Sree, and Kandula Nirupa Rani. *Claude McKay: Literary Identity from Jamaica to Harlem.* London: McFarland and Co., 2006.

Rancière, Jacques. *Le spectateur engagé.* Paris: La fabrique, 2008.

———. *The Ignorant Schoolmaster: Five Lessons in Intellectual Emancipation.* Palo Alto: Stanford University Press, 1991.

Roberts, Dorothy. *Fatal Invention: How Science, Politics, and Big Business Re-create Race in the Twenty-first Century.* New York: The New Press, 2011.

Robinson, Jane. *Mary Seacole: The Most Famous Black Woman of the Victorian Age.* New York: Basic Books, 2004.

Rÿser, Rudolph C. *Indigenous Nations and Modern States: The Political Emergence of Nations Challenging State Power.* Abingdon, N.Y.: Routledge, 2012.

Sandiford, Keith. *The Cultural Politics of Sugar: Caribbean Slavery and Narratives of Colonialism.* Cambridge, U.K.: Cambridge University Press, 2010.

Sandoval, Chele. *Methodology of the Oppressed.* Minnesota: University of Minnesota Press, 2000.

Scheper-Hughes, Nancy, and Philippe I. Bourgois, Eds. *Violence in War and Peace: An Anthology*. Oxford, U.K.: Blackwell Publishing, 2004, 207–217.

Sheller, Mimi. *Citizenship from Below: Erotic Agency and Caribbean Freedom*. Durham: Duke University Press, 2012.

Simpson, Audra. *Mohawk Interruptus: Political Life across the Borders of Settler States*. Durham: Duke University Press, 2014.

Smith, Sidonie. "Construing Truth in Lying Mouths: Truthtelling in Women's Autobiography." *Women and Autobiography*. Lanham: Rowman and Littlefield, 1999.

———. "Performativity, Autobiographical Practice, Resistance." *Women, Autobiography, Theory: A Reader*. Eds. Sidonie Smith and Julia Watson. Madison: University of Wisconsin Press, 1998.

Sontag, Susan. *On Photography*. New York: Picador, 1973.

———. *Regarding the Pain of Others*. New York: Picador, 2003.

Spiegelman, Art. "Comix: An Idiosyncratic Historical and Aesthetic Overview." *Comix, Essays, Graphics and Scraps*. New York: Raw Books and Graphics, 1999.

Spillers, Hortense. "All the Things You Could Be by Now, if Sigmund Freud's Wife Was Your Mother." *Female Subjects in Black and White*. Eds. Elizabeth Abel, Barbara Christian, and Helene Moglen. Berkeley: University of California Press, 1997, 135–158.

———. "Mama's Baby, Papa's Maybe: An American Grammar Book." *Black, White and in Color: Essays on American Literature and Culture*. Chicago: University of Chicago Press, 2003.

Spivak, Gayatri C. "Can the Subaltern Speak?" *The Post-Colonial Studies Reader*. 2nd Edition. Eds. Bill Ashcroft et al. London: Routledge, 2007.

Sree-Ramesh, Koppi, and Kanudula Nirupa Rani. *Literary Identity from Jamaica to Harlem and Beyond*. North Carolina: McFarland Press, 2006.

Stith Clark, Beatrice, Ed. *I Am a Martinican Woman and the White Negress: Two Novelettes*. Pueblo, Colo.: Passeggiata Press, 1998.

Sutton, Kate. "Jeff Koons' Controversial Michael Jackson Sculpture and the Story behind It." *Billboard*. http://www.billboard.com/articles/news/6150392/jeff-koons-controversial-michael-jackson-sculpture-the-story-behind-it. Accessed July 25, 2017.

Swartz, Leslie. "Oscar Pistorius and the Melancholy of Intersectionality." *Disability and Society* 28, no. 8 (2013).

Thorsten, Marie. "Graphic 'Heart of Darkness': Two Visions of Current Affairs Comics." *International Political Sociology* 6 (2012): 221–240.

Tinsley, Omise'eke Natasha. *Thiefing Sugar: Eroticism between Women in Caribbean Literature*. Chapel Hill: Duke University Press University Press, 2010.

Trouillot, Michel-Rolph. *Silencing the Past: Power and the Production of History*. Boston: Beacon Press, 1995.

van Alphen, Ernst. "Symptoms of Discursivity: Experience, Memory and Trauma."

Acts of Memory: Cultural Recall in the Present. Eds. Bal, Crewe, and Spitzer. Hanover, N.H.: Dartmouth College Press/UPNE, 1999, 24–38.

Vanderbeke, Dirk. "In the Eye of the Beholder." *Comics as a Nexus of Cultures: Essays on the Interplay of Media, Disciplines and International Perspectives (Critical Explorations in Science Fiction and Fantasy).* Eds. Mark Berninger et al. Jefferson, North Carolina: McFarland, 2010.

Walcott, Derek. "The Muse of History." In *The Post-Colonial Studies Reader.* 2nd Edition. Eds. Bill Ashcroft et al. London: Routledge, 2007.

Watkins, Ross. "Disaster Dialogues: Word, Image and the Effective/Ethical Spaces of Illustrated Books." *Social Alternatives* 31, no. 2 (2012): 11–14.

Weheliye, Alexander G. *Habeas Viscus: Racializing Assemblages, Biopolitics, and Black Feminist Theories of the Human.* Durham: Duke University Press, 2014.

Wenzel, Jennifer. "Remembering the Past's Future: Anti-Imperialist Nostalgia and Some Versions of The Third World." *Cultural Critique* 62 (Winter 2006).

Wexler, Laura. "Seeing Sentiment: Photography, Race, and the Innocent Eye." *Female Subjects in Black and White.* Eds. Elizabeth Abel, Barbara Christian, and Helene Moglen. Berkeley: University of California Press, 1997, 159–186.

Wordsworth, William, and Matthew Arnold. *Poems of Wordsworth.* New York: Macmillan, 1880. https://hdl.handle.net/2027//hvd.hwpk8t.

Wynter, Sylvia. "No Humans Involved: An Open Letter to My Colleagues." *Forum NHI: Knowledge for the 21st Century* 1, no. 1 (1994).

Xu, Dejin. *Race and Form: Towards a Contextualized Narratology of African American Autobiography.* Berlin: Peter Lang Publishers, 2007.

Young, Harvey. *Theatre and Race.* London: Palgrave, 2013.

Zeleza, Paul Tiyambe. "Pan-Africanism in the Age of Obama: Challenges and Prospects." *Black Scholar* 41, no. 2 (2011; 2014): 34–44. Sociological Collection. Web. 17.

Zeleza, Paul Tiyambe, and Kamari Clarke. "Reconceptualizing African Diasporas: Notes from a Historian." *Transforming Anthropology* 18, no. 1 (2010): 74–79. *ProQuest.* Web. December 24, 2014.

Index

MYRIAM J. A. CHANCY is a Guggenheim fellow and the Hartley Burr Alexander Chair of the Humanities at Scripps College. Her academic books include *From Sugar to Revolution: Women's Visions of Haiti, Cuba, and the Dominican Republic*, *Framing Silence: Revolutionary Novels by Haitian Women*, and *Searching for Safe Spaces: Afro-Caribbean Women in Exile*..

The New Black Studies Series

The University of Illinois Press
is a founding member of the
Association of University Presses.

Composed in 10.5/13 Minion Pro
by Lisa Connery
at the University of Illinois Press
Cover designed by Jennifer S. Fisher
Cover illustration: *Migrant Boat, #Noplace* (Artist Unknown), Street Art/
Le Marais, Photographed by MJA Chancy, February 2019, Paris.

University of Illinois Press
1325 South Oak Street
Champaign, IL 61820-6903
www.press.uillinois.edu